Infrastructure Investing

Infrastructure Investing

Managing Risks & Rewards for Pensions,
Insurance Companies & Endowments

RAJEEV J. SAWANT

WILEY

John Wiley & Sons, Inc.

Published by John Wiley & Sons, Inc., Hoboken, New Jersey.

Published simultaneously in Canada.

For general information on our other products and services or for technical support, please contact our Customer Care Department within the United States at (800) 762-2974, outside the United States at (317) 572-3993 or fax (317) 572-4002.

Wiley also publishes its books in a variety of electronic formats. Some content that appears in print may not be available in electronic books. For more information about Wiley products, visit our web site at www.wiley.com.

Library of Congress Cataloging-in-Publication Data:

Sawant, Rajeev J.
  Infrastructure investing : managing risks & rewards for pensions, insurance companies & endowments / Rajeev J. Sawant.
     p. cm. – (Wiley finance series)
  Includes bibliographical references and indexes.
  ISBN 978-0-470-53731-2 (cloth)
1. Infrastructure (Economics)–Finance.   2. Public works–Finance.   3. Investments.
4. Financial risk management.   I. Title.
  HC79.C3S36 2010
  332.6–dc22

                                                                    2009038770

10 9 8 7 6 5 4 3 2 1

I dedicate this book to my parents, Janardan and Charulata Sawant, whose encouragement, passion, and personal example made all this possible; to Manisha for her patience, unwavering support, and understanding; to Rahul for constant and loyal support; and to Mehr and Manav, who are my personal attachment to the future.

Contents

Preface   xi

Acknowledgments   xvii

CHAPTER 1
Infrastructure Demand and Investment Funds   1
    An Overview of Infrastructure Demand   2
    Availability of Funds   19
    Conclusion   26

CHAPTER 2
Infrastructure Asset Characteristics   27
    Defining Asset Classes   28
    Portfolio Perspective on Asset Classification   29
    Large Up-front Investments   32
    Strong Cash Flows   34
    Stable Cash Flows   36
    Long Life   38
    Irreversible Investments   38
    Location Specificity   39
    Growth Options   39
    Value under Default   44
    Conclusion   47

CHAPTER 3
Equity Infrastructure Indexes   49
    Infrastructure Investment Options   49
    Equity Infrastructure Indexes   51
    Macquarie Global Infrastructure Index   54
    S&P Global Infrastructure Index   58
    CSFB Emerging Markets Infrastructure Index   59
    Infrastructure Equity Indexes Correlations   63
    Efficient Frontier   65
    Conclusion   69

CHAPTER 4
Debt versus Equity Mode of Investment   **71**
Theories of Capital Structure   71
Pecking Order Theory   74
Free Cash Flow Theory   76
Trade-off Theory of Capital Structure   78
Governance and Capital Structure   81
Options Approach   82
Private Equity Model of Investing   86
Conclusion   94

CHAPTER 5
Infrastructure and the Threat of Holdup   **95**
Transaction Cost Economics   95
Solutions for the Holdup Problem   102
Conclusion   113

CHAPTER 6
Infrastructure Assets and Political Risk   **115**
Political Risk Typology   115
Sovereign Holdup   120
Types of Risk   124
Hedging Sovereign Holdup   130
Risk Mitigation Strategies   134
Conclusion   142

CHAPTER 7
Project Finance and Infrastructure   **145**
Project Finance Structure   146
Project Finance versus Corporate Finance   147
Ras Laffan Revisited   156
Project Risk Analysis   161
Credit Rating Agencies   165
Using the Project Finance Structure   169
Role of Government   172
Conclusion   175

CHAPTER 8
Infrastructure Asset Valuation and Bond Returns   **177**
An Overview of Infrastructure Valuation Theory   178
Basel II and Infrastructure Lending   187
Infrastructure Bond Returns   199
Conclusion   208

CHAPTER 9
  Case Studies **211**
    Case Study 1: Aguas Argentinas S.A. 211
    Case Study 2: Dabhol Power Company 223
    Conclusion 230

Conclusion **233**

Notes **237**

About the Author **253**

Index **255**

Preface

Good roads, canals, and navigable rivers, by diminishing the
expense of carriage, put the remote parts of the country more
nearly upon a level with those in the neighbourhood of the town.
They are upon that account the greatest of all improvements.
                                          —Adam Smith, *Wealth of Nations*

Future investment trends will be shaped by, among other things, infrastructure demand and spending. On the demand side of the market, the
future looks rosy. As the BRIC economies (Brazil, Russia, India, and China)
bring millions of people into the middle class, demand for better roads,
electricity, telecommunications, airports, and clean water is expected to rise.
Asia alone needs $1 trillion over the next five years to meet its infrastructure
needs.[1] Infrastructure also enables economic growth. BRIC countries as well
as vast tracts of Africa, Asia, Central Europe, and South America need
investments in development infrastructure. The developed economies of
North America and Europe also need investments as they repair and replace
their aging infrastructure assets. The 2007 rush hour collapse of the I-35W
bridge in Minneapolis, Minnesota, was a stark reminder that infrastructure
cannot be taken for granted.

   What about the supply side? Governments have traditionally provided
most infrastructure funds. The increasing demand on government resources
and the sheer magnitude of the funding required to develop infrastructure
ensures that private capital has a very important role to play in the future.
This book focuses on private funds for infrastructure, invested with the aim
of generating a return over investment for capital providers. As such, I do
not examine flows of capital through developmental aid activities or any
other form of investing that does not explicitly require a return on
investment.

Although governments encourage private capital in infrastructure, governments regulate these assets severely and are liable to constrain returns because of infrastructure's characteristics. Infrastructure asset characteristics also expose investors to other unique risks. The book examines these risks through a Transaction Cost Economics framework for which Oliver Williamson was awarded the Nobel Prize in Economics in 2009. The book suggests options for hedging and mitigating these risks. The book's analysis shows that the private equity model of infrastructure investing that is followed by a vast majority of investment vehicles suffers from drawbacks that are likely to jeopardize infrastructure's promise of long-duration, stable returns. While the private equity model possesses governance advantages, traditional private equity skills must be supplemented by political management skills to exploit these advantages. The book makes the case that investors pursuing high private equity type returns to compensate for political risk end up exacerbating those very risks due to a *feedback* effect in infrastructure investing. It is perhaps not surprising that infrastructure investing has been prone to boom and bust cycles.

INFRASTRUCTURE INVESTMENT PATTERNS

Investments flowing into emerging market infrastructure in the 1990s were an average of $185 billion per year.[2] The investment boom of the 1990s collapsed as the multibillion-dollar Dabhol and Paiton projects in India and Indonesia went into default. New lending to emerging markets was close to zero from 1998 to 2002, and in 2001 the private lending total to emerging markets was negative $32 billion.[3] The cycle reversed itself in 2004–2005 and in 2006 reached $212 billion, which was an increase of 35 percent over 2005.[4] Investors flocked to infrastructure funds, and the number of infrastructure funds and the amounts raised increased astonishingly. Seventy-two funds (not including funds focused on oil and gas) raised an amazing $160 billion in an 18-month period before June 2007.[5] A large portion of these funds—approximately 60 percent of the number of funds and approximately 75 percent of dollars raised—remain focused on investing in U.S. and European infrastructure assets.

As more and more money chases fewer assets in these markets, rising asset prices puts pressure on returns.[6] So far, emerging markets are some way off from these pressures and ought to play a role in investor portfolios, provided the returns are commensurate with the risks.

The growing appetite for infrastructure assets from pension funds, endowments, family offices, and high net worth individuals reflects a growing belief that infrastructure is a separate asset class, among other alternative asset classes like hedge funds, venture funds, private equity, commodities, credit derivatives, and corporate governance.[7] Traditionally insurance companies provided over 70 percent of the funding for infrastructure.[8] The development of capital market instruments in the form of widely held bonds is also a relatively recent phenomenon, with about 10 percent of infrastructure funding coming through bonds.[9] An analysis of these different forms of investment in infrastructure remains incomplete.

What differentiates infrastructure investing from other asset classes? Does infrastructure change the efficient investment frontier of a portfolio? How do investors break out of the boom-bust cycles and realize the promise of long-term stable returns that infrastructure promises? This book utilizes infrastructure asset characteristics as a focal point of analysis. These characteristics create distinctive risks, returns, and correlations with other asset classes. The book then analyzes the mitigation of these risks, particularly through the use of the governance and financing structure of *project finance*.

OVERVIEW OF THE CONTENTS

Chapter 1 breaks down the demand side of the infrastructure market, looking at sectoral and geographical demand. Chapter 1 analyzes pension fund liabilities and their traditional asset holdings, and makes the case that the long duration of pension fund liabilities matches the long duration of infrastructure returns.

Chapter 2 begins with an analysis of asset classes, but its main focus is on infrastructure asset characteristics. Infrastructure assets are lumpy (e.g., a half-bridge is useless), capital-intensive assets with large sunk costs, low variable costs, long lives, and in relative monopolistic positions. They generate cash flows without relying on growth options, unlike say biotechnology or high technology, and are relatively easy to manage. In short, they are boring and predictable from a business perspective. But they are also fixed to the ground and subject to holdup and political risks which assume far more importance than other types of risk.

Chapter 3 compares existing equity-based infrastructure indexes to broad indexes for equities, bonds, commodities, and real estate in terms of risk, return, and correlations. The aim is to ascertain whether equity-based infrastructure indexes provide the desired exposure to this sector.

Chapter 4 examines the characteristics of debt versus equity funding by applying the latest theoretical capital structure research to infrastructure funding. The chapter examines the advantages and disadvantages of the private equity model of infrastructure investing, utilized by over half the infrastructure funds formed in 2006–2007.[10]

Chapter 5 focuses on infrastructure risk factors, in particular the threat of counterparty holdup and the incentives this threat engenders. Chapter 5 uses a transaction cost economics lens to tease out those risk factors that most impact returns. The risk of post-investment holdup and political risk are among the most difficult to manage. Chapter 5 examines the transaction cost economics literature to lay out the governance structures designed to minimize threats of holdup.

Chapter 6 examines the literature on political risk and the mechanisms by which political risk is mitigated.

Chapter 7 examines project finance. Given the nature of risks facing infrastructure, this chapter examines the strategic use of capital structure as a risk mitigation tool. The chapter looks at how and why project finance incorporates mechanisms to deal with holdup and political risk. Chapter 7 lays out the implications for the various actors participating in the infrastructure market: institutional investors, commercial lending banks, rating agencies, multilateral funding agencies, infrastructure firms, and governments.

Chapter 8 examines infrastructure asset valuation issues and the return characteristics of a project finance infrastructure bond portfolio. The chapter also examines the Basel II rules for commercial bank project finance lending. Finally, the chapter examines the advantages and disadvantages of using a syndicate structure of debt versus capital market securities like bonds.

Chapter 9 looks at two case studies that did not live up to the promise of infrastructure and applies the frameworks developed throughout the book: the Aguas Argentinas concession in Argentina and the Dabhol electricity project in India. Aguas Argentinas examines the perils of increasing tariffs for users and the political sustainability of indexing tariffs to a rapidly devaluing currency. The Dabhol electricity project in India draws lessons about the management of risk from a single buyer, especially when the buyer is a government entity.

IN CLOSING

In closing, the book analyzes the options available to investors seeking exposure to infrastructure. The book examines for the first time the return characteristics of equity infrastructure indexes and infrastructure bonds and their suitability as part of investor portfolios. By pointing out the areas of concern in the private equity model of investing and the rating methodology followed by the rating agencies, the book hopes to contribute to improving the returns that investors can expect from infrastructure assets. Ultimately, by illuminating the precise nature of infrastructure risks and focusing on their mitigation, the book hopes to improve the returns that investors are able to obtain from their infrastructure investments while increasing the physical stock of infrastructure in the world and thereby improving the quality of millions of people's lives.

Acknowledgments

This book would not have been possible without the dedication, advice, encouragement, and passion of my teachers. In particular, my Ph.D. committee at the Fletcher School at Tufts University supported the research from which this book grew. Professor Laurent Jacque has been unstintingly generous with his time, knowledge, insights, and support. I have learned immensely from Professors Paul Vaaler, Patrick Schena, Bruce Everett, Jeswald Salacuse, Richard Shultz, Carsten Kowalczyk, Joel Trachtman, Ravi Sarathy, Sanjiv Das, and Julie Schaffner. I am indebted to the Hitachi Center for Technology and International Affairs at the Fletcher School for providing me with a writing infrastructure, and to the Edwin Ginn Library for a research infrastructure. I am also grateful to Alok Srivastava, Felton "Mac" Johnston at Robert Wray PLLC, Swaminathan Venkataraman at Standard and Poor's, and Burkhard Schrage at Singapore Management University for sharing their experience and insights and for giving their time so generously. The book also benefited immensely from the dedication, support, and painstaking review from my editors, Pamela Van Giessen and Emilie Herman. All errors, of course, remain entirely my responsibility.

Rajeev Janardan Sawant
Medfield, Massachusetts

CHAPTER 1

Infrastructure Demand and Investment Funds

Bijli, sadak aur paani (Hindi for "Electricity, roads and water")
—Election slogan in India, 2004

Roads probably constitute the earliest human demand for infrastructure, and the earliest known constructed roads have existed in Ur in modern-day Iraq since 4000 BC.[1] Indeed, the pyramids couldn't have been built without the roads on which the giant limestone blocks were dragged around between 2600 and 2200 BC. Civilizations advanced or declined around the quality of their road networks. The ancient Roman, Persian, Indian, and Chinese civilizations all built road networks that allowed them to rapidly transport military units while simultaneously encouraging commerce and trade. Trade routes joined the empires of China, India, Asia Minor, North Africa, and Rome. The next major infrastructure development came from the great discoveries of electricity and its applications by Benjamin Franklin, Nikola Tesla, André-Marie Ampère, Michael Faraday, Thomas Edison, and many others in the eighteenth and nineteenth centuries.

In the modern era, the term *infrastructure* refers to a wide array of industries with different characteristics. Traditionally, *infrastructure* refers to the following sectors of the economy: transportation, energy, telecommunications, water, and sanitation. *Transportation* refers to road, rail, airports, and ports. *Energy* refers to oil, gas, petrochemicals, and electricity generation, transmission, and distribution. *Telecommunications* refers to fixed lines and mobile telephony. Recently, information technology

1

infrastructure that refers to the physical hardware used to connect computers and users is sometimes grouped with traditional infrastructure.*

Commentators have also grouped social infrastructure like schools, prisons, hospitals, and courts under the rubric of infrastructure.[2] Grouping fundamentally different industries like mobile telephony with schools and prisons obscures the fact that the risk and return profile of these assets is very different. Consequently these assets demand different investment strategies. We therefore need consistent criteria for classifying infrastructure industries.

In this book, I use asset characteristics as classifying criteria. Using asset characteristics as an analytical scalpel yields insights into infrastructure asset risks that help us design optimal investment strategies. For example, electricity generation using coal, oil, and nuclear fuel differs in fundamental and important ways from alternative energy sources like solar, wind, and so on. Chapter 2 is entirely devoted to this topic. In this chapter I choose the traditional infrastructure industries which Chapter 2 shows possess distinct characteristics—electricity, transportation (road and rail), water and sanitation, fixed-line telecommunication, and pipelines—for analyzing demand across different countries.

Using two distinct methodologies for analyzing infrastructure demand, I make the case that demand is growing and requires large investments that private investors can provide. Demand analysis shows which sectors and geographical areas are likely to be attractive to investors. Furthermore, the returns from these investments match the needs of pension funds and insurance companies in particular and therefore offer attractive investment opportunities.

AN OVERVIEW OF INFRASTRUCTURE DEMAND

Infrastructure demand refers to the investment necessary to satisfy retail consumer demands as well as producer or industry demands based on projected GDP growth. This makes sense because it's reasonable to assume that as disposable income rises, demand for a better quality of life in terms of electricity, water, sanitation, telecommunications, and transportation (air, sea, road, and rail) should increase. Industry, too, demands increased electricity, transportation, telecommunication, energy, commodities, and

---

* In some definitions, *information technology infrastructure* refers to everything that supports the flow and processing of information. Therefore, phone lines, data lines, computer hardware, software, and devices that control transmission paths would all qualify as information technology infrastructure.

EXHIBIT 1.1 Historical Change in Composition of Infrastructure Stocks

	1960	1970	1980	1990	2000	2010
Electricity	22%	32%	40%	43%	44%	42%
Roads	47%	46%	45%	44%	44%	43%
Rail	29%	19%	13%	9%	6%	5%
Telecom	2%	3%	3%	4%	6%	10%
Total	100%	100%	100%	100%	100%	100%

Source: M. Fay and T. Yepes, "Investing in Infrastructure: What Is Needed from 2000 to 2010?" *World Bank Policy Research Working Paper 3102, 2003.*

other inputs to keep pace with growth in its output. Demand, however, is unlikely to be uniform across industries and countries. This has been true historically and is likely to persist in the future. An analysis of sectoral and geographical demand is helpful to investors for targeting the appropriate industry and country. Exhibit 1.1 shows the change in worldwide composition of infrastructure stocks from 1960 to 2010. Water and sanitation is excluded because of lack of data.

Exhibit 1.1 shows that the share of rail dropped from a third to a mere 5 percent and the share of electricity doubled while telecommunications quintupled, albeit from a low 2 percent to 10 percent, over the 50-year period. Therefore, any linear extrapolation into the future based on past trends even in mundane infrastructure must be interpreted with caution.

A complex interplay of factors influences demand in different infrastructure sectors. Some of these include technology, substitutability (mobile for fixed line, road for rail), complementarities (electricity generation to electric trains), sectoral structure (number and strength of established firms resistant to change), macroeconomic factors (GDP per capita), and so on. Technology has affected demand for fixed-line telecommunications with mobile telephony replacing fixed lines in high income countries and leap-frogging investments in fixed lines in low- and middle income countries. Technology also influences oil, gas, and electricity generation with the development of alternative energy sources, although these are not likely to catch up with traditional oil, gas, and coal even by 2030.[3] Exhibit 1.2 displays the factors affecting demand for each sector and the interaction of the sectors.

In addition to the factors and interactions shown in Exhibit 1.2, investors must take into account cultural attitudes and government policy encouraging or discouraging particular infrastructure industries in order to forecast infrastructure demand with any degree of precision. The next section develops broad estimates of infrastructure investments up to 2030.

EXHIBIT 1.2 Infrastructure Demand Drivers and Interactions

Industry	Substitutes	Complements	Demand Interaction with Other Factors
Electricity generation using coal, oil, gas, hydro, and nuclear fuels only	Generation using wind, geothermal, solar, fuel cells Generation using waste recycling	Telecom, water services for metering, billing, and service provision High-speed rail network	Demand sensitive to GDP growth Nuclear, coal, and oil demand sensitive to environmental considerations such as reduction of pollution, disposal of nuclear waste
Road	Rail—transportation of basic commodities and intermediate goods Telecommuting substitutes for road and rail travel. Effect is ambiguous for long-distance travel; for example, off-shoring might increase or decrease local road/rail demand	Complements right of way for electricity transmission, fixed telecom lines	Demand unlikely to be sensitive to technological changes Demand sensitive to GDP growth, number of automobiles, cost of auto fuel, and disposable income
Rail	Road Telecommuting	Complements right of way for electricity transmission, fixed telecom lines, fiber optic cable	High-speed technology Demand sensitive to cost of fossil fuels Demand sensitive to environmental considerations for reduction in pollution and conservation of fossil fuels
Telecom—fixed lines	Mobile, IP telephone, WWAN		Demand extremely sensitive to technology
Water			Demand sensitive to environmental considerations—climate change, water conservation
Sanitation			Demand sensitive to environmental considerations—reducing pollution

Source: Author analysis.

Note that forecasts tend to lose accuracy as the forecasting period increases, and a forecasting period up to 2030 is still very long. The forecasts presented are therefore meant to be interpreted as providing broad estimates and are meant to provide insights into asset allocations across industries and geographies.

Forecasting Infrastructure Demand

In this chapter I explore the methodology followed by the World Bank and the Organisation for Economic Co-operation and Development (OECD) to forecast investments for new assets as well as maintenance of existing infrastructure assets, using historical investment patterns as a percentage of gross domestic product (GDP). In addition, I use gross national income (GNI) to compare infrastructure stocks across countries with different levels of GNI. In the GNI method I extrapolate the future demand in low and middle income countries to match infrastructure in the high income countries.

In the percentage of GDP methodology, total spending on new infrastructure and maintenance varies with the GDP of countries. Developing countries need to spend a higher proportion of their GDP on infrastructure because of their lower infrastructure stocks and their greater growth rates. Estimates for new investments in developing countries range from 4 percent of GDP in the World Development Report[4] to 3.2 percent in Fey and Yepes (2003). Middle income countries spend about 2.6 percent of GDP while high income economies spend about 0.4 percent of GDP on new infrastructure investment. The estimates for maintenance follow a similar pattern, with low income countries estimated to spend about 3.73 percent, middle income countries about 2.5 percent, and high income countries about 0.42 percent.

Apart from the demand for new infrastructure stocks, investments are also required for maintenance and replacement of existing stocks. Although total investments required in infrastructure should include funds for maintenance, maintenance funds essentially comprise costs required to keep the assets functioning smoothly. For the purposes of analyzing investment strategies, these costs determine working capital requirements and available free cash flows which in turn determine the return over investment. High maintenance costs naturally reduce free cash flow and returns. I do not consider maintenance funds further here since maintenance funds are not investments and do not translate into claims on assets. Suffice it to say that maintenance funds for electricity, road, and rail make up about 2 percent of the replacement cost of the capital stock, 3 percent for water and sanitation, and up to 8 percent for telecom fixed lines.[5]

Should we consider funds for replacement of existing infrastructure stocks? The amount of funds needed for the replacement of existing infrastructure depends on the level of existing infrastructure stock, the total life of the stock, and the rate of depreciation. For example, if we assume that the life of roads is 30 years and the rate of depreciation is spread out equally over the 30 years, then 1/30 of the road stock needs to be replaced every year. In the case of developing countries, since the level of stocks is low to begin with and the need to develop new infrastructure is high, funds needed for replacement as compared to new investments are likely to be low. In the case of developed countries, however, replacement funds are likely to constitute a large proportion of infrastructure spending. For investors, however, it is important to note that investment in replacement assets must translate into clearly defined claims over the assets.

Unfortunately, replacement investments do not readily translate into claims over the assets because of the lumpy nature of infrastructure assets, although there are certainly creative solutions. For example, it would be difficult to segregate revenues from replacing or adding an additional lane on a road, but a portion of the road could be replaced and converted into a toll road; or a portion of a transmission grid could be replaced—for example, from overhead lines to underground cables—and revenues generated from the replaced portion separated from revenues from the rest of the grid. This needs evaluation on a case-by-case basis and is akin to investing in existing assets.

I interpret the investment needs identified here as the demand for stocks of infrastructure, such as miles or kilometers of paved highways or pipelines or rails. I do not consider their intensity of use. In developing countries the intensity of use is typically higher than in high income countries. This lowers the overall demand for infrastructure stocks. It also increases revenues from subscribers for the same level of fees but at the same time increases maintenance costs. The net effect on operating profits and free cash flow available to investors as return on investment depends on relative rate of increases in revenues and costs, which in turn depends on the intensity of use. This raises the issue of the optimum intensity level that maximizes revenues while simultaneously limiting maintenance costs. The fees charged to subscribers are subject to market conditions and political constraints, especially in the case of infrastructure. The monopoly nature of infrastructure services implies that customer segmentation strategies (i.e., providing a higher level of service to higher paying customers or denying service to some users) are difficult for political reasons. Strategies for achieving optimum intensity levels through fees, user incentives, user segmentation, and so on, therefore require detailed analysis on a case-by-case basis. In the next sections I explore the percentage of GDP methodology, followed by the GNI methodology.

EXHIBIT 1.3   Estimated Annual Infrastructure Demand in US$ Billions (Percent of GDP Methodology)

	2000–2010	Percent of World GDP	2010–2020	Percent of World GDP	2020–2030	Percent of World GDP
Annual world GDP	$57,253.52		$76,184.74		$100,502.79	
Road	$220.00	0.38	$245.00	0.32	$292.00	0.29
Rail	$49.00	0.09	$54.00	0.07	$58.00	0.06
Telecom	$654.00	1.14	$646.00	0.85	$171.00	0.17
Water	$576.00	1.01	$772.00	1.01	$1,037.00	1.03
Electricity— transmission and distribution	$127.00	0.22	$180.00	0.24	$241.00	0.24
Electricity— generation	$377.87	0.66	$495.20	0.65	$653.27	0.65
Grand Total	$6,848.34	3.5	$1,897.00	3.14	$1,799.00	2.44

Source: Infrastructure to 2030: Telecom, Land Transport, Water and Electricity (OECD Publishing, 2006); author analysis.

Percentage of GDP Methodology

I begin by getting a sense of the magnitude of investments required using a simple percentage of GDP methodology. The methodology uses historical investment trends identifying infrastructure spending as a percentage of GDP and projecting these into the future over a GDP growth rate assumption. Exhibit 1.3 presents these worldwide estimates on an annual basis over the next two decades.[6]

The estimates range from annual expenditure of approximately 3.5 percent of GDP between 2000 and 2010 to 2.44 percent between 2020 and 2030. The total annual expected demand for new infrastructure is around $6.8 trillion, with investment requirement of 0.66 percent of world GDP for electricity generation using traditional oil, gas, and coal investments. By 2030 investments required will be of the magnitude of $65 trillion, rising to $71 trillion if other energy-related investments are included in the estimates.

These massive investments are similar in magnitude to estimates developed using more complex models that explicitly incorporate different factors impacting demand. The International Energy Agency (IEA) estimates electricity demand using different fuel types based on increased capacity additions.[7] Exhibit 1.4 displays IEA estimates for electricity generation, transmission, and distribution to 2030.

The IEA uses a methodology that includes four major factors to estimate investments in energy infrastructure: GDP growth, population growth, energy prices, and technology. The methodology is delineated as follows.

1. *GDP growth.* The primary driver of energy demand is GDP growth. The IEA uses the income elasticity of demand (percentage change in energy demand for a 1 percent change in GDP) to estimate energy demand. Between 1971 and 1990 it was 0.66 percent, dropping to 0.44 percent in 1990–2000 and recovering to 0.68 percent in 2000–2006. A drop in energy intensity is likely to prevail, however, due to conservation efforts arising from the challenges of global warming and rising energy prices. The IEA uses International Monetary Fund (IMF) assumptions of economic growth, predicting that the GDP growth will recover to 4.5 percent per year by 2010 and then slow to an average of 3.3 percent per year to 2030. GDP growth is expected to average 4.2 percent per year in 2006–2015 and 2.8 percent per year in 2015–2030.

2. *Population growth.* Population as a driver of energy demand affects demand not only through overall population growth but also through the location of growth. Urban population growth increases energy demand significantly since most energy is consumed within or close to cities. The rapid urbanization of most countries in the developing world along with their higher growth rates affects the geographical distribution of energy demand.

3. *Energy prices.* Energy prices are an exogenous input in the IEA model, and price determines demand and supply of electricity. The oil price is assumed to average $100 per barrel in 2007 dollars till 2015, rising to $122 per barrel by 2030. The IEA assumes coal prices will settle at $120 per ton in real terms and then fall back to about $110 per ton by 2030. The IEA further assumes that gas prices linked to oil prices through indexation in long-term supply contracts or competition between end-users will remain at 60 to 70 percent of oil prices. The IEA model also considers policies by governments that reduce subsidies for energy since a large portion of the demand for energy comes from countries that subsidize energy.

4. *Technology.* The demand for energy from fossil fuels is very sensitive to the assumptions made about technology. The IEA does not assume any radical technological change. On the demand side it assumes that the efficiency of cars and trucks, heating and cooling equipment, boilers,

EXHIBIT 1.4 Estimated Annual Investment Demand in Electricity Generation, Transmission, and Distribution from 2007 to 2030

	Investment, 2007–2015 (2007 $ Billion)				Investment, 2016–2030 (2007 $ Billion)			
	Capacity Additions—MWs	Power Generation	Transmission	Distribution	Capacity Additions—MWs	Power Generation	Transmission	Distribution
OECD	514	$982.00	$278.00	$656.00	1,107	$2,467.00	$403.00	$922.00
North America	215	$379.00	$121.00	$260.00	480	$1,136.00	$238.00	$512.00
Europe	221	$457.00	$93.00	$281.00	465	$1,048.00	$94.00	$286.00
Pacific	78	$146.00	$65.00	$115.00	163	$283.00	$71.00	$124.00
Non-OECD	1,177	$1,215.00	$589.00	$1,285.00	1,730	$2,177.00	$837.00	$1,793.00
Eastern Europe/Eurasia	137	$180.00	$55.00	$183.00	159	$274.00	$51.00	$173.00
Asia	781	$794.00	$433.00	$894.00	1,170	$1,379.00	$596.00	$1,231.00
China	574	$521.00	$296.00	$612.00	718	$753.00	$299.00	$618.00
Middle East	78	$59.00	$32.00	$67.00	160	$135.00	$71.00	$146.00
Africa	59	$59.00	$28.00	$58.00	91	$159.00	$47.00	$97.00
Latin America	121	$123.00	$41.00	$84.00	149	$230.00	$72.00	$148.00
World	1,691	$2,197.00	$867.00	$1,941.00	2,837	$4,644.00	$1,239.00	$2,716.00

Source: IEA, *World Energy Outlook* (OECD Publishing, 2008).

EXHIBIT 1.5   World Energy Demand by Fuel (Million Tonnes of Oil equivalent)

	1980	2000	2006	2015	2030	2006–2030*
Coal	1,788	2,295	3,053	4,023	4,908	2.00%
Oil	3,107	3,649	4,029	4,525	5,109	1.00%
Gas	1,235	2,088	2,407	2,903	3,670	1.80%
Nuclear	186	675	728	817	901	0.90%
Hydro	148	225	261	321	414	1.90%
Biomass and Waste	748	1,045	1,186	1,375	1,662	1.40%
Other Renewables	12	55	66	158	350.00	7.20%
Total	7,223	10,034	11,730	14,121	17,014	1.60%

Source: IEA, *World Energy Outlook* (OECD Publishing, 2008).
*Average annual rate of growth.

and so on, will improve. On the supply side the IEA assumes that efficiency of electricity generating plants, oil and gas exploration, and rates of recovery will increase with the availability of new technologies like carbon capture and storage, the conversion of coal to liquids, and the second generation of biofuels.

These projections are much higher than in the simple percentage of GDP method because they include the run-up in commodity prices and energy prices in 2007–2008. Higher prices of steel, copper, aluminum, cement, and other commodities significantly impact construction costs for electricity generation plants, fuel supply pipelines, transmission grids, distribution substations, transformers, metering equipment, and other costs. The estimates are also likely to vary with differing costs for land acquisition that are largely determined locally by country and in local regions within countries. Exhibit 1.5 summarizes demand for the different types of fuel.

Exhibit 1.5 reveals that although renewables are likely to record the fastest annual growth rate of 7.2 percent, they still make up only 2.05 percent of world energy demand by 2030. Coal grows fastest at 2 percent annually and constitutes 28.84 percent of world energy demand. Oil and gas make up 30.02 percent and 21.57 percent respectively by 2030. Should we consider investments in renewable energy as infrastructure investment? I visit this question in Chapter 2.

The next section deals with surface transportation infrastructure, primarily road and rail. These estimates are comparable to the percentage of

EXHIBIT 1.6   Estimated Annual Road and Rail Investment, 2000–2030
(US$ Billions)

	Road Construction Forecast			Rail Construction Forecast		
	2000–2010	2010–2020	2020–2030	2000–2010	2010–2020	2020–2030
OECD (Total)	159.5	167	178.2	31.1	34.2	33.5
North America	71.8	75.5	80.9	7.1	7.8	10.9
United States	62.4	65.6	69.3	5.2	6.3	8.8
Mexico	2	2.2	3.5	0.6	0.4	0.8
Europe	67.4	70.3	74.7	19.3	21.6	17.2
Germany	4.3	4.6	5.8	4	4.5	3.5
United Kingdom	5.8	6	6.1	1.8	2	1.6
France	13.2	13.7	14.3	2.6	2.9	2.3
Italy	7.1	7.4	7.8	2.7	3	2.6
All others	37	38.6	40.7	8.2	9.2	7.2
Pacific	20.3	21.2	22.6	4.7	4.8	5.4
Japan	13.5	14.2	15.1	3.2	3.4	3.7
All others	6.8	7	7.5	1.5	1.4	1.7
Non-OECD (Total)	52.3	68.6	101.1	15.7	16.7	21.3
Eastern Europe/Eurasia	12	15.9	20.5	3.4	3.7	4.2
Asia	15.8	18.6	25.4	2.6	2.9	5.4
China	15.2	23.8	37.8	7.3	8.1	7.7
Middle East	2.9	3.4	6.3	0.6	0.5	1.5
Africa	1.4	1.4	2.2	0.4	0.4	0.5
Latin America	4.8	5.6	8.9	1.4	1	2.1
World (Total)	211.8	235.6	279.3	46.8	50.9	54.8

Source: Infrastructure to 2030: Telecom, Land Transport, Water and Electricity
(OECD Publishing, 2006); author analysis.

GDP methodology. Exhibit 1.6 shows annual estimated road and rail
expenditure through 2030.

These estimates are derived from a model that the OECD developed,
as follows:

- Road and rail demand are functions of growth in population and GDP
  per capita.

▪ The link between GDP per capita growth and road and rail demand is expressed in elasticity. A key measure used is elasticity of paved road capital stock with respect to GDP per capita. This elasticity measure has a range of 0.12 to 0.90 with a mean estimate of 0.20—in other words, a 1 percent increase in GDP per capita increases the paved road capital stock by about 0.20 percent. Similar measures for rail infrastructure are used but are not wholly reliable due to lack of sufficient data.

The model uses additional road infrastructure inputs like measures of road use and vehicle ownership. Demand for roads is proportional to increased vehicle ownership and increased road use. The study uses an elasticity of vehicle stock (measured in vehicles per 100 people) with respect to GDP per capita of 0.75 to 1.25 with a mean of 1.0, implying that a 1 percent increase in GDP per capita raises vehicle ownership by 1 percent. Since this relationship is nonlinear—once GDP per capita crosses $5,000, vehicle ownership accelerates—the model uses a step function. The model incorporates road use with elasticity of annual per-vehicle driving distance in kilometers with respect to GDP per capita, which has a range of 0.05 to 1.60, with a mean of 0.2. This implies that a 1 percent increase in GDP per capita raises road use by 0.2 percent.

Now that we have obtained a sense of the sectoral distribution of investments, we aggregate the data in terms of regions and country. This allows us to get a better sense of which sectors are important in which regions.

Geographical Distribution of Infrastructure Demand   In order to compare the investment demand by geography we combine electricity, road, and rail investment forecasts. Exhibit 1.7 displays annual investment demand for electricity (generation, transmission, and distribution), road construction, and rail construction over the next two decades by geography. North America comprises the United States, Canada, and Mexico; Asia includes India and Indonesia; and Latin America includes Brazil.

Investments in electricity generation, transmission, and distribution dominate investments in road and rail. In terms of time periods, total annual electricity investments in 2010–2020 are shown as greater than investments in 2020–2030. However, annual investments in the North American electricity sector increase in the 2020–2030 period over the 2010–2020 periods, while Asian and Chinese electricity sectors slow down in 2020–2030. Total annual road transportation investments in 2020–2030 are higher than investments in 2010–2020. The geographical distribution of estimated

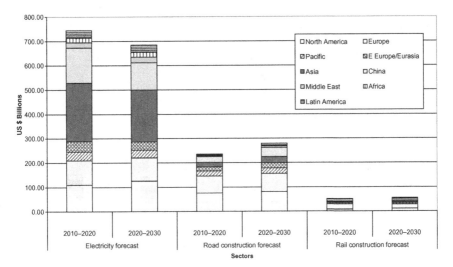

EXHIBIT 1.7 Annual Investment by Sector and Geography, 2010–2030
Source: Infrastructure to 2030: Telecom, land transport, water and electricity. 2006 (OECD Publishing, 2006); IEA, *World Energy Outlook 2008*; author analysis.

investments is also instructive. Estimated demand in the electricity sector in Asia and China is larger than their demand for road and rail transportation. Estimated demand for road transportation in Europe and North America is larger than demand in Asia and China.

The OECD does not consider pipeline networks in its estimates. However, pipeline networks constitute highly efficient means of gas, oil, and petrochemical delivery and possess characteristics that classify them as infrastructure. Total pipeline density (kilometers per million people) also follows income growth and road and rail network distributions. I consider pipelines along with the other sectors in the methodology developed in the next section.

GNI Methodology

The second methodology uses income to estimate infrastructure demand. The World Bank classifies countries into low, middle, and high income countries in terms of gross national income (GNI) per capita and estimates that a per capita income of $5,000 is necessary before demand for services translates into revenues for suppliers of services. The methodology therefore

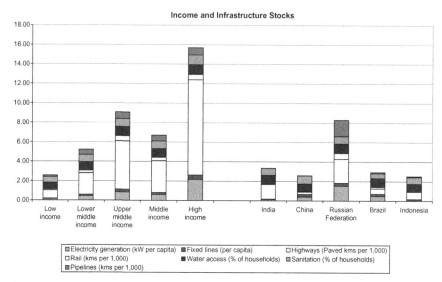

EXHIBIT 1.8   Gross National Income per Capita and Infrastructure Stocks

estimates demand in low- and middle income countries by extrapolating the present consumption of infrastructure services in the high income countries to middle and low income countries. Exhibit 1.8 presents the massive gap between infrastructure stocks in the high income countries and the middle income, low income, and the big five countries of Brazil, Russia, India, Indonesia, and China. Data sources are identified in the accompanying Exhibit 1.9.

Exhibit 1.8 immediately indicates the different relative rates at which infrastructure sectors are likely to grow in different countries. For example, a comparison between the big five countries shows that demand for electricity is likely to be higher in India, Indonesia, and China, while demand for roads is likely to be higher in China, Brazil, and Indonesia.

We can obtain a reasonable sense of the investment demand by comparing the level of infrastructure stocks present in the different income level countries. Comparing the upper middle income countries (GNI per capita between $3,035 and $9,386) and the high income countries shows that high income countries possess more than 2.5 times the electricity generating capability (in kilowatts per capita) and about twice the level of paved highways (in kilometers per 1,000 people) than upper middle income countries. Water and sanitation infrastructures are comparable. This suggests that the electricity and road sectors are likely to grow at a faster rate than water, sanitation, and railroads. In addition, the electricity sector is likely to grow

EXHIBIT 1.9 Income and Infrastructure Stocks

	GNI per capita	Population (Mils)	GDP per capita (PPP)	Electricity Generation (kW per capita)	Fixed lines (number per 1,000 people)	Highways (paved km per 1,000 people)	Rail (km per 1,000 people)	Water access (percent of households)	Sanitation (percent of households)	Pipelines (km per million people)
Low income countries	<$765	2,597.39	$1,840.16	0.16	36.71	0.85	0.12	0.66	0.59	148.45
Middle income countries	$765–$9,386	2,579.90	$8,543.77	0.60	188.66	3.28	0.36	0.88	0.78	597.94
a. Lower middle income	$765–$3,035	2,270.45	$5,911.06	0.46	130.20	2.22	0.27	0.86	0.76	524.65
b. Upper middle income	$3,035–$9,386	309.45	$12,736.60	0.85	288.66	4.95	0.54	0.92	0.84	666.92
High income countries	>$9,386	916.81	$29,745.71	2.18	448.24	9.77	0.55	0.99	1.00	769.43
Big Five										
India	$441.56	1,123.32	$3,113.10	0.13	45.45	1.52	0.06	0.86	0.72	16.93
China	$865.03	1,319.98	$5,453.31	0.39	268.63	0.25	0.06	0.77	0.83	25.61
Russian Federation	$1,764.05	141.64	$9,821.52	1.54	280.20	2.45	0.61	0.97	0.76	1,675.65
Brazil	$2,842.36	191.60	$7,967.52	0.49	230.45	0.55	0.16	0.90	0.50	113.20
Indonesia	$599.24	225.63	$3,222.33	0.11	57.91	0.78	0.03	0.77	0.70	74.76

Source: World Bank WDI indicators (GNI per capita, GDP per capita, population); NationMaster (www.nationmaster.com)—telecomm, road, rail, water, sanitation, and pipelines; U.S. Department of Energy—electricity generation capability; author analysis.

EXHIBIT 1.10   Unit Costs of Infrastructure Investments

Sector	Cost in US $	Unit
Electricity	$2,553	Per kilowatt of generating capacity, including associated network costs.
Roads	$551,006	Per kilometer of two-lane paved road.
Railway	$1,209,525	Per kilometer of rail, including rolling stock.
Sanitation	$941	Per connected household.
Water	$538	Per connected household.
Telecom fixed main lines	$538	Per line
Pipelines	$1,000,000	Per kilometer including right of way, labor, and materials

Source: Marianne Fay and Tito Lepes, "World Bank Policy Research Working Paper 3102 (July 2003), adjusted for inflation assumed at 3 percent per year from 2003.

faster than the road sector. We can use the differences in infrastructure stocks to generate individual countries' investment demand by combining a country's present infrastructure stock level, population, and unit costs for infrastructure. Exhibit 1.10 presents the unit costs for creating new infrastructure stock.[8]

Costs presented in Exhibit 1.10 will vary widely across countries because costs for building roads, rail, pipelines, and water and sanitation networks depend a great deal on terrain, weather, costs of obtaining licenses and permits, and labor and material costs. For example, electricity generation, transmission, and distribution costs have risen substantially with the rise in the prices of raw materials. These costs are therefore merely guides and we must interpret them with caution.

Exhibit 1.11 displays cumulative investment scenarios needed for electricity, paved highways, fixed telecomm lines, railways, water, sanitation, and pipelines for BRIC and Indonesia based on their present infrastructure stocks, and the difference between stocks in upper middle income countries and lower middle income countries.

The Russian Federation already possesses infrastructure stocks greater than upper middle income countries, and Exhibit 1.11 indicates investments needed to reach high income country levels. In order to calculate

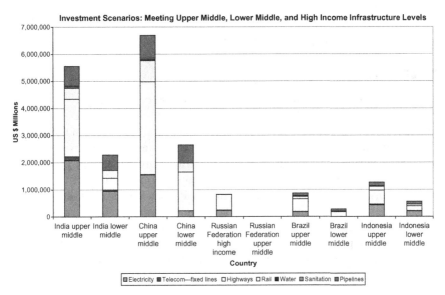

EXHIBIT 1.11 Cumulative Investments in Big Five Countries
Source: Author analysis.

water and sanitation investment data the unit of analysis is a household. The model therefore gathers data about the number of people per household. The average size of households in India is obtained from De Silva (2003).[9] The average size of households in Russia is obtained from the Russian Longitudinal Monitoring Study data at the University of North Carolina.[10] Data on average size of households in China, Brazil, and Indonesia comes from the *United Nations Demographic Yearbook*.[11] This provides the total number of households that need access to water and sanitation and the investments necessary. Exhibit 1.11 shows water and sanitation investments required to provide coverage for all households.

This methodology does not provide an indication of the time period over which these investments will be done. It assumes that the unit costs presented in Exhibit 1.10 and the size of households remain constant during this period. Costs, however, are likely to rise and the size of a household is dropping, which implies that these investments are underestimated.[12] Exhibit 1.11, however, shows which countries are likely to demand investments and which sector is likely to grow fastest in each country, assuming that government policies remain constant and are not altered to favor a particular sector (e.g., rail over road).

Conclusion

The discussion so far provides broad implications for targeting investments both geographically and in terms of infrastructural sectors. Developing countries with per capita GNI above $5,000, which places them in the lower middle income and upper middle income countries, are relatively more attractive destinations for investment. Electricity investments are likely to be more attractive, followed by road transportation, particularly in India and China, and to a lesser extent in Brazil, Russia, and Indonesia. OECD nations are likely to require relatively higher investments in road transportation than electricity. The discussion also highlights the fact that each country's individual policy environments are essential to developing an investment strategy, particularly with respect to favored mode of transportation, favored fuel for electricity generation, environmental policies, infrastructure tariffs, and so on.

Although Exhibit 1.11 shows investments for fixed telecom lines, an analysis of fixed telecom line demand is particularly difficult to predict. Although fixed telephone lines in high income countries are about 1.5 times those of upper middle income countries, predicting demand for fixed lines is difficult because of the adoption of mobile telephony as a substitute for fixed lines. The number of fixed lines in high income countries is actually declining (from 550.14 lines per 1,000 people in 2000 to 448.24 lines in 2007). Fixed-line networks might mimic the evolution of rail networks from 1960 to 2000 as mobile networks take their place.

What about the case for investing in mobile networks as a form of infrastructure? I do not consider mobile telephony to be an infrastructure sector because the impact of technology is difficult to predict. The development of a wireless wide area network (WWAN) utilizing WiMax or any of the numerous technologies in development now could disrupt an existing mobile network by providing users with Internet-based Voice over Internet Protocol (VoIP) telephony service that is virtually free.[13] WiMax is a wireless broadband technology standard that aims to provide fast wireless data connections over long distances, as opposed to Wi-Fi which provides fast wireless data connections over about 50 feet only. A consumer with a fast data connection can then transmit voice calls over the Internet using a slew of services available at almost no charge. As these technologies leapfrog over fixed lines and even mobile networks, investments in building fixed-line and mobile networks no longer possess infrastructure characteristics. I explore the topic further in Chapter 2.

AVAILABILITY OF FUNDS

Infrastructure has traditionally relied on public expenditure for financing. The enormous funding requirements we saw in the previous section imply that governments must consider the use of private capital to provide infrastructure services. Among private sources of capital, insurance companies traditionally provided the long-term funds needed for infrastructure.[14] Other private sources of capital include pension funds, mutual funds, petrodollars, hedge funds, private equity, endowments, and Asian central banks. Exhibit 1.12 displays the amount of capital these sources held in 2006.

Although the following discussion focuses on pension funds, insurance firms face similar asset allocation challenges and regulatory constraints. Infrastructure risks and their mitigation also apply equally well to all private capital, including insurance firms and private endowments. As Exhibit 1.12 shows, pension funds form the largest source of private capital that can meet the demand for investments at $21.6 trillion. Although pension funds

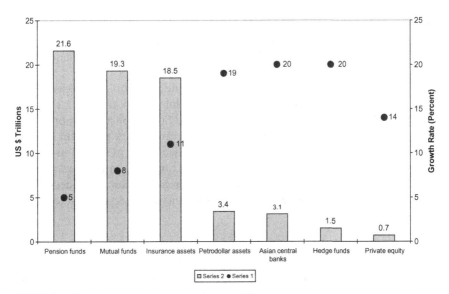

EXHIBIT 1.12   Assets under Management, 2006
Source: McKinsey Global Institute, *The New Power Brokers: How Oil, Asia, Hedge Funds, and Private Equity Are Shaping Global Capital Markets* (McKinsey Global Institute, October 2007).

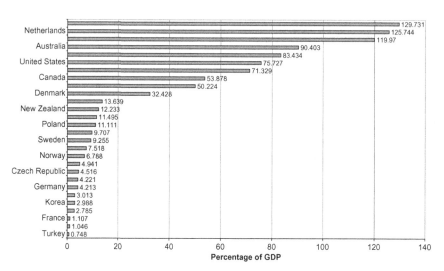

EXHIBIT 1.13   Pension Fund Assets: Percentage of GDP in 2006
Source: OECD Global Pension Statistics project; author analysis.

grew at 5 percent compound annual growth rate (CAGR) in 2000–2006 compared to 20 percent CAGR for hedge funds, pension funds possess a unique liability structure. I examine pension funds in greater detail in the following sections. Exhibit 1.13 shows details of pension fund assets for 2006 in different countries as a percentage of their GDP.

In Iceland, the Netherlands, and Switzerland, pension fund assets now exceed the total GDP of these countries while pension fund assets in Australia, the United Kingdom, and the United States constitute more than 75 percent of GDP. Pension funds therefore constitute a powerful source of capital that has altered asset markets worldwide. The next section examines present pension fund asset allocations and focuses on the duration of pension fund liabilities as one factor in their asset allocation decisions. Following that, I examine whether infrastructure meets pension fund objectives.

Pension Fund Asset Allocation

Private pension funds can be broadly categorized into *defined contribution* and *defined benefit* pension schemes along with many hybrid forms. A defined contribution fund pays its members their contribution with additional returns generated from their contributions, if any. A defined

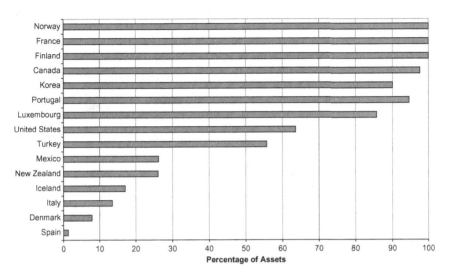

EXHIBIT 1.14 2007 Defined Benefit Pension Plans: Percentage of Total Pension
Fund Assets
Source: OECD Global Pension Statistics project; author analysis.

benefit fund promises to pay its members retirement benefits at a certain
level based on some formula that typically includes length of employment
and member salaries. The fund must therefore have sufficient assets to
meet its payment obligations. Typically, sponsoring employers establish a
legally separate fund or hold in reserves separate funds to meet their future
payment obligations. Worldwide, defined benefit funds form the vast majority of pension funds. Exhibit 1.14 shows percentage of defined benefit plan
assets as a percentage of total pension plan assets in selected countries. U.S.
pension plan assets dwarf other countries' pension plan assets at about
$17 trillion, and defined benefit plan assets make up about 64 percent of
all assets.

How have pension funds allocated their capital? Exhibit 1.15
provides details of assets under management in pension funds in 2005 for
countries with the six largest funds other than the United States, namely
the United Kingdom, Canada, the Netherlands, Australia, Switzerland, and
Denmark.

Exhibit 1.16 shows total U.S. pension fund assets from 2001 to 2007
along with the asset classes to which funds are allocated.

Comparing Exhibits 1.15 and 1.16, we see that total assets under management (AUM) in the United States dwarf those in the United Kingdom,

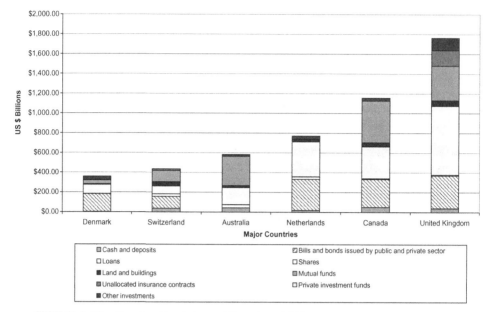

EXHIBIT 1.15 Pension Fund Asset Allocation, 2005
Source: OECD Global Pension Statistics project; author analysis.

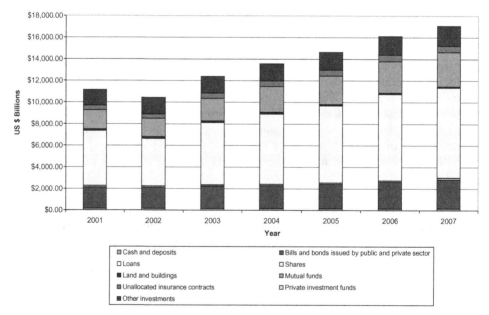

EXHIBIT 1.16 U.S. Pension Fund Asset Allocation, 2001–2007
Source: OECD Global Pension Statistics project; author analysis.

Canada, the Netherlands, Australia, Switzerland, and Denmark, with U.S. AUM in 2005 totaling almost three times the *combined* AUM for the largest six countries. Exhibits 1.15 and 1.16 also display asset allocation totals across asset classes. Except for Denmark, equities dominate the portfolios of pension funds invested either through mutual funds or direct holdings, with Australia at 80.4 percent, the United States at 66.63 percent, Canada at 64.47 percent, the United Kingdom at 59.2 percent, the Netherlands at 46.2 percent, and Switzerland at 44.41 percent. The drop in U.S. pension fund assets in 2002 likely reflects the dot-com bust and the decline in U.S. equity markets. We are likely to see a similar severe contraction in U.S. and other pension fund assets from the collapse in equity values in 2008–2009.

Fixed-income products through bills and bonds from both public and private issuers are the second largest holding. "Other investments" shown in the figures comprise investments in alternative asset classes like hedge funds, private equity, and commodities.

Pension funds have not been large participants in the infrastructure investment space. Funds allocated to infrastructure form a negligible portion of asset portfolios, although precise estimates are difficult without further granularity in the data. One problem relates to how infrastructure is classified. Infrastructure investments may be classified as equities if assets are allocated to firms engaged in infrastructure sectors, like AES or Fluor Corporation, or investments may be classified as bills and bonds, loans, or "other investments." For example, Australia and Canada have been pioneers in developing infrastructure investments. Australian pension funds allocated about 5.5 percent toward loans in 2005 that could be for infrastructure projects structured as project finance, where a large proportion of the capital is funded in the form of debt. Canadian pension funds allocated 24.43 percent to bills and bonds that may include bonds for infrastructure projects.

Pension Fund Asset Allocation Challenges

Pension funds are exposed to longevity risk, the risk of members living longer than benefits are planned for; and to financial risks, the risk that contributions from members and employers invested over long time horizons do not earn sufficient returns to meet fund obligations. If the estimated market value of a fund's assets falls below the value of its estimated liabilities, a funding gap exists. In 2002 and 2003, after the dot-com bubble burst, equity values fell while long-term interest rates also fell. A large proportion of pension fund assets invested in equities declined. Since long-term interest rates were used to calculate the value of liabilities, the value of liabilities rose, creating a funding gap.

A similar situation exists in 2008–2009. The enormous destruction of equity values has shrunk pension fund assets. The flight to safety of investments moving from equity markets to government securities, along with central banks lowering interest rates, resulted in historically low long-term interest rates. The resulting rise in the value of pension fund liabilities creates significant funding gaps in defined benefit pension plans. This funding gap has resulted in a sharper focus on risk management through closer asset-liability matching.[15]

The OECD's guidelines on pension fund asset allocation[16] require a fund's retirement income objectives to be taken into account before making asset allocation decisions. The guidelines recommend risk management processes for each fund's assets and liabilities and recommend a level of asset-liability matching that the pension fund's governing body can monitor. Interestingly, the guidelines do identify prudent quantitative limits for exposure to a single security or issuer but consider limitations on foreign investment and broad asset classes like equities and bonds as potentially constraining portfolio efficiency. The requirement of asset-liability matching increases with the dollar value of pensions in payment and in proportion to the number of pensioners. The looming retirement of U.S. baby boomers, along with changing demographics relating to the increase in expected life span after retirement, is almost certainly going to increase the proportion of pensioners in these countries' pension funds.[17] Although detailed data about pension fund liabilities is not available, most estimates put the duration of pension fund liabilities at around 15 years.[18]

The requirement of pension funds to match long-duration liabilities leads to a demand for long-duration assets with predictable cash flows. Defined benefit plans must particularly match cash flows from assets to meet promised payments to pensioners. Thompson (2003) points out there aren't sufficient assets for pension funds to implement a policy of asset-liability matching.[19] In fact, if pension funds shifted parts of their portfolio holdings to long-term bonds as a source of long-duration assets with predictable cash flows, there would be a scarcity of bonds.[20] Erwin and Schich (2007) compare future pension fund payment promises with the cash flows obtained from investing in government bonds in the G10 countries. Exhibit 1.17 shows the cash flow shortfall that pension funds would experience from 2012 onwards based on the level of funds allocated to government bonds.

An additional assumption underlying Exhibit 1.17 is that pension funds do not incur new liabilities and the payments are all made to *passive*

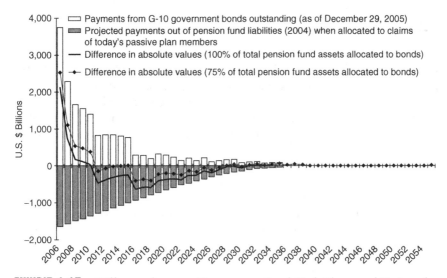

EXHIBIT 1.17   Difference between Government Bond Cash Flows and Projected Pension Payments in G 10 Countries
Source: C. Ervin and S. Schich, "Asset Allocation Challenges for Pension Funds," *Financial Market Trends* 1, no. 92 OECD, (2007): 129–147.

plan members. Passive plan members are members that do not contribute to the pension plan. It is likely that pension funds actually do incur new liabilities with the increase in retirees, which also leads to an increase in the number of passive members. Given the scarcity in long-term government bonds and other long-duration assets with predictable cash flows, can infrastructure fill this gap? Infrastructure investments till 2030 are estimated at $71 trillion. These investments will generate cash flows over the time horizon that pension fund obligations come due. Some experts have argued that pension fund liabilities are a better match for equities because of their longer tenor and because equities outperform bonds over the long term. Clearly, large portions of pension fund portfolios must be made up of equities.

In the following chapters I examine whether infrastructure investments provide the benefits of a separate asset class. and whether equities of firms in infrastructure sectors actually diversify an equity portfolio. Extending the analysis of investment form, I examine the risks from the private equity model of infrastructure investment, specifically whether it increases investors' exposure to political risk without commensurate returns.

CONCLUSION

Of the estimated $21 trillion in pension fund assets, almost $2 trillion would be immediately available for infrastructure investments if a mere 10 percent is allocated to infrastructure. Although these investments are insufficient to satisfy worldwide total infrastructure demand, they can meet a large portion of demand from upper middle income countries and the big five countries. These countries are most attractive from the perspective of revenues from subscriber fees. Countries differ in the investments needed in different sectors as shown. Countries also differ in infrastructure policies of regulation, pricing, and permits, and in the sectoral industry structures. Countrywide and sectoral analysis is therefore a necessary component of infrastructure investing, and it makes sense for investors to develop sectoral as well as geographical expertise before allocating capital.

Chapters 2 through 8 analyze infrastructure characteristics and develop the case for the precise form of investment.

CHAPTER 2

Infrastructure Asset Characteristics

Although gold dust is precious, when it gets in your eyes it obstructs your vision.

—Hsi-Tang Chih Tsang

In Chapter 1 I estimated the massive investments required to meet infrastructure demand in electricity, roads, railways, pipelines, water, and sanitation, while rather arbitrarily omitting cellular communications, information technology infrastructure, and alternative sources of electricity like solar, wind, and geothermal. Clearly alternative energy, cellular communications, and information technology infrastructure may also be attractive investments with huge demand. However, they differ from traditional infrastructure in vital ways, which I argue affects the investment strategy.

In this chapter I justify these omissions and anchor my analysis by focusing on infrastructure asset characteristics. In doing so, I hope to show that infrastructure constitutes a distinct asset class. Unfortunately the term *asset class* is used all too frequently without adequate precision. What exactly is an asset class? Intuitively, assets that have the same economic characteristics and are regulated together constitute one asset class. For example, equities and commodities have different economic characteristics and hence belong to different asset classes. However, investors rather care more about asset risk, return, and correlations in a portfolio. We should expect an asset's economic fundamentals to determine asset returns, risk, and correlations, and therefore I use both perspectives to determine asset classes, one utilizing economic fundamentals and the second utilizing a portfolio perspective with asset risk, returns, and correlations.

In subsequent sections of the chapter I examine the economic characteristics of infrastructure assets, including their large, up-front, irreversible capital investments; stable, long-duration cash flows; and high value under conditions of default. I examine infrastructure risk, return, and correlations in Chapters 3 and 8. I begin here with a taxonomy of asset classes utilizing economic fundamentals.

DEFINING ASSET CLASSES

Before we begin analyzing asset classes, we need to define an asset class. Robert Greer defines an asset class as a set of assets that bear some fundamental economic similarities to each other, and which have characteristics that make them distinct from other assets that are not part of that class.[1] This definition of an asset class focuses on the underlying economics of an asset that gives rise to its characteristics, as opposed to simply focusing on an asset's return correlation with other assets.

We can divide assets into the following three super asset classes:

1. *Capital assets.* Capital assets are assets that are an ongoing source of something of value.[2] Equities and bonds that provide a stream of expected future cash flows are capital assets. The value of these types of assets is therefore the present value of future cash flows, and investors value them through discounted cash flow (DCF) valuation. Real estate and infrastructure are also subclasses of this super asset class when they produce rents or subscriber fees. Valuation through DCF applies equally well to these assets.

2. *Consumable/transformable assets.* I define consumable or transformable assets as physical commodities that are consumed or transformed while making other products. These assets by themselves do not yield a stream of income although they may form part of a capital asset. The value of these assets is based on their price which itself is a result of supply and demand on a global basis. Oil, gas, and mined minerals are consumable/transformable assets that are classified under infrastructure since these assets possess infrastructural characteristics that we discuss in the later part of the chapter.

3. *Store of value assets.* Store of value assets are assets that do not generate a stream of income and are not consumed yet retain value. The classic example of this type of asset is art. A painting is a store of value since it neither generates a stream of income nor lends itself for consumption (except perhaps in a private utility form). Foreign currency is another example of a store of value asset. Although the assets are stores of value for different reasons—rarity, beauty for art, purchasing

power for currency—the value of this asset class is a result of its desirability to potential owners and is reflected in the prices at which the assets are bought and sold. Interestingly, real estate acts like a store of value asset (at least landowners for centuries have fondly hoped so) when it does not generate a stream of income. Infrastructure assets like transportation and electricity, however, do not act like store of value assets. Consumers use infrastructure and providers must maintain and replace them in return for user fees. Unused or neglected roads, electricity plants, and water supply and sewage networks simply crumble, rust, fall into disrepair, and waste away.[3] Clearly infrastructure does not belong to this class of assets and is basically a capital asset.

Although boundaries between these asset classes are sharply drawn for definitional purposes, in reality the boundaries are quite fuzzy. Some assets straddle boundaries; for example, gold is a store of value as well as an asset that is consumed. Financial engineering transforms consumable assets into capital assets by creating streams of income from underlying assets: Gold mining companies issue bonds with gold held as collateral, called gold bonds, which transforms gold into a capital asset with a stream of income. Apart from this conceptual framework that classifies assets based on underlying economic fundamentals, the next section analyzes asset characteristics from a portfolio perspective.

PORTFOLIO PERSPECTIVE ON ASSET CLASSIFICATION

From the investor's perspective, the definition of an asset class differs from the previous definition which relied on economic characteristics to classify asset classes. For an investor, an asset class is a group of assets that exhibit similar characteristics, behave similarly in different market environments, and are governed by the same laws and regulations.[4] What do we mean by *behave* and *characteristics*? Markowitz portfolio theory tells us that relevant asset characteristics are risk, return, and correlation of returns when assets are considered as part of a portfolio.[5] Therefore, the characteristics of an asset class are its returns, risk, and correlation of returns with other asset returns, while behavior means a change in these characteristics of the asset class in different market conditions. Assets belonging to one asset class display similar return distributions, risk or volatility of returns, and strong correlations among themselves. The following paragraphs lay out the equations for determining asset returns, risk, and correlations.

We measure the returns from a single asset as the percentage change in the price of the asset over one period:

$$r_i = \frac{p_t - p_{t-1}}{p_{t-1}} \qquad (2.1)$$

where

r_i = return of asset i
p_t = asset price at time t
p_{t-1} = asset price at time $(t-1)$

Equation 2.1 provides a historical measure of return, while investors care about future or expected returns. We define future expected returns in terms of future states of the world and the probability of occurrence of each state of the world. The expected return for an asset is the weighted average of asset returns in different states of the world, where the weights equal the probability of occurrence of each state of the world. In order to compute the expected return of an asset we use matrix algebra.[6]

Let p be a (s*1) vector of the probabilities of s states of the world where (s*1) means a vector of s rows and 1 column. Let r be a (1*s) vector (one row, s columns) of the asset's returns in each state of the world. The expected return of the asset is given by

$$\bar{r} = r * p \qquad (2.2)$$

where

$\bar{r}$ = expected return
* = matrix operation of multiplication

The expected return from a group of assets or portfolio of n assets is the weighted average of individual asset expected returns with weights equal to the value of each asset holding in the portfolio. Let x be a (n*1) vector of value of asset holdings in the portfolio. Let R be a (n*s) matrix of n asset returns in s states of the world. Then the return for portfolio P_r is given by

$$P_r = x' * R * p \qquad (2.3)$$

where

P_r = expected return of portfolio P
x' = transposition of the matrix x

We measure risk of an individual asset as the standard deviation of asset returns over s states of the world:

$$\sigma = \sqrt{\frac{1}{s}\sum_{i=1}^{s}(r_i - \bar{r})^2\, pr_i} \qquad (2.4)$$

where

σ = Standard deviation of asset returns

pr = probability of state s

The risk of a portfolio of assets is the variance of the portfolio expected returns, which depends on the possible asset returns (matrix R), probability distribution across states of the world (vector p), asset holdings in the portfolio (vector x), and the covariance between individual asset expected returns. The covariance of asset returns affects portfolio risk because negative covariance between two assets reduces portfolio variance.

For two assets i and j the covariance is defined as:

$$Cov_{i,j} = E\big[\big(r_i - \bar{r}_i\big)\big(r_j - \bar{r}_j\big)\big] \qquad (2.5)$$

where E(expression) = expected or mean value of the expression in the brackets.

Let C be a (n*n) covariance matrix for n assets. Then the (i, j) element of the matrix will be equation 2.5. With the covariance matrix C, the variance of a portfolio P_v is given by equation 2.6.[7]

$$P_v = x' * C * x \qquad (2.6)$$

We use equations 2.1 through 2.6 for historical analysis of infrastructure returns as well. Chapters 3 and 8 analyze returns from investing in infrastructure equity indexes and infrastructure bonds, respectively. For now, we note that we need to combine the two definitions of asset classes sketched here to gain a better picture of asset classes. An asset's risk, return, and correlations must derive from underlying economic fundamentals. If we simply examine risk, return, and correlations we run the risk of using spurious correlations that arise and vanish over different time periods. For example, a particular group of small cap stocks may show low or even negative correlation with the S&P 500 over a given time period. However, as the time period changes, this desirable diversification property does not remain stable and can vanish. Risk, return, and correlations are likely to remain stable over time or at least follow a mean-reverting pattern only if the underlying economics of the asset class are truly distinct. With this in mind, let us turn to the underlying economic exposure that investors can expect from infrastructure assets.

LARGE UP-FRONT INVESTMENTS

Infrastructure assets require the bulk of the investments up front. A two-lane highway requires a sizeable block of capital investment before users pay tolls. An electricity plant needs to generate its rated capacity before revenues roll in; generation does not begin before investors make a large chunk of capital investment. Quite simply, bootstrapping is difficult in infrastructure.

Investors do not plan on meeting capital expenditures from revenues since revenues are hard to come by without investment of the entire planned capital expenditure in the first place. These investments are lumpy in nature and revenues are not generated without plant, road, or bridge completion. In the gas industry, firms need to prospect for gas, locate and drill the gas wells, process the gas, and then transport it to the end users. Firms must complete each stage of the process before receiving revenues and each stage of the process is capital intensive. Firms planning to increase production in existing gas wells must also invest substantial amounts before receiving revenues. The sidebar "Australia's North West Shelf (NWS) Project" shows a representative sample of capital investments in Australia's northwest shelf in the global gas industry.

AUSTRALIA'S NORTH WEST SHELF (NWS) PROJECT

Gas was discovered off the northwestern shore of Australia in 1971 and production began in 1980 after contracts were signed for domestic gas consumption. Reserves in the NWS project are estimated at about 61 trillion cubic feet (tcf). To put that in perspective, all of Australia consumed less than 1 tcf and exported about 1 tcf in 2002. The NWS project comprises two distinct phases, phase 1 for domestic consumption and phase 2 for export of liquefied natural gas (LNG). The ownership structure for each phase is structured separately. The domestic phase shareholders are Woodside Petroleum with 50 percent, BP with 16.67 percent, Chevron with 16.67 percent, Shell with 8.33 percent, and BHP Petroleum, a subsidiary of the mining giant BHP Billiton, with 8.33 percent. The export phase shareholders are the five original domestic partners along with a joint venture of Mitsui and Mitsubishi called Japan Australia LNG (MiMi), with each partner getting a one-sixth share.

Gas is extracted through offshore platforms and brought to a LNG processing plant onshore at Dampier. LNG production technology is undertaken through LNG *trains*. Each train produces between 3 and 4 million tons per year and is estimated to cost A$1 billion. NWS had three trains in production and it commissioned its fourth train in 2004 at a cost of A$2.75 billion. A fifth train is under development, primarily aimed at serving the Chinese market, specifically shipping 3.3 million tonnes of LNG per year to the Guangdong Dapeng LNG Terminal in China for 25 years. CNOOC NWS Private Limited is taking an equity stake in this NWS project. The cost of the fifth train is estimated at US$2.4 billion.

For domestic consumption the processed gas is transported through four pipelines. The 1,500-km pipeline from Dampier to Bunbury serves the area of Perth and is one-third owned by its utility, Diversified Utility and Energy Trusts. Another third of the pipeline is owned by Alcoa and the last third by Alinta, which owns pipeline assets in Australia. The Dampier to Bunbury pipeline cost US$1.5 billion to build. A second pipeline serves the goldfields in Australia. The goldfield pipeline is owned by the customers for the gas as well as one of the producers: Western Mining Corp. 62.66 percent, Poseidon Gold 25.50 percent, and BHP Petroleum 12 percent. The goldfield pipeline cost US$320 million to build. The third line serves the alumina industry and is owned by CMS Energy and Alcoa.

The total costs of exploiting the gas reserves from the northwest shelf exceed A$10 billion and had to be invested before any revenues were realized from the assets.

Infrastructure also needs large investments because economies of scale are crucial to the financial success of a project. Economies of scale mean that as the level of production increases, the marginal cost of producing an extra unit of output drops. Decreasing marginal costs lead to lower average costs. For example, investors can distribute the costs of obtaining right of way permits for road building over four lanes instead of two lanes, lowering the marginal costs of building additional lanes and the average cost of each lane. From the 1930s to the 1980s, the average cost of electricity generation continuously decreased through economies of scale. Economies of scale were engendered by power plant size which increased from 50 megawatts in the 1930s to 1,000 megawatts in the 1980s.[8] In this example, even as the cost per megawatt decreased, the total investment needed increased. Large capital investments are required to build to scale.

STRONG CASH FLOWS

A good measure of an asset's operating margin and cash generating capacity is earnings before interest, taxes, depreciation, and amortization (EBITDA). EBITDA does not deduct depreciation and amortization expenses, which are non-cash-flow accounting expenses, while interest and taxes depend on the capital structure of the assets. Exhibit 2.1 shows EBITDA from different industries. The exhibit shows the striking difference between infrastructure and other industries. Electric, gas, water utilities, oil producers, and transportation industries produce high EBITDAs (measured in index points per share) as compared to the computer, software, and pharmaceutical industries.

Exhibit 2.1 also implies that infrastructure assets exhibit high operating margins. Consequently these projects generate large cash flows. What explains the high operating margins and free cash flows from infrastructure

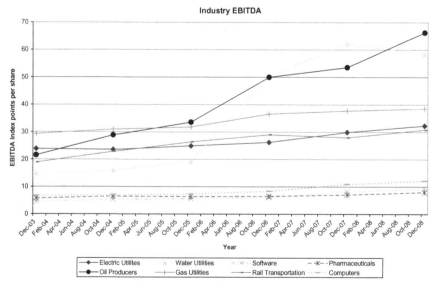

EXHIBIT 2.1 Industry EBITDAs
Source: Data from Bloomberg; author analysis.

assets? The following explanations are likely. First, infrastructure assets have very low variable costs. Sectors like transportation and pipelines use very few inputs to provide service to users and the marginal cost of providing service to additional customers is very low. Infrastructure assets are subject to economies of scale. The assets' monopolistic position allows them to take advantage of economies of scale. As a result, costs do not rise with the large number of users, which translates into strong cash flows.

Second, we have referred to the monopolistic nature of infrastructure assets. In a monopoly market it is difficult or even impossible for firms to profitably enter the market to expand supply. High fixed costs deter firms from profitably entering and competing. As noted, road, rail, electricity, and water supply demonstrate increasing economies of scale. Economies of scale imply that the market requires one large firm rather than numerous smaller firms. It is very costly and unnecessary for firms to replicate a water pipeline network or an electricity grid. Infrastructure assets command naturally dominant market positions that allow them to set prices higher than those resulting from a competitive marketplace or at least protect themselves from price erosion.

Third, demand for infrastructure is fairly inelastic. Although user demand for infrastructure services increases with income, it does not decrease as much with changes in user income. The income elasticity of demand is less than 1 since infrastructure is a necessity. In a modern economy, users require transportation (we can consider oil and gas services as part of transportation and electricity services), electricity, water, and sanitation services to maintain a basic minimum standard of living.

Fourth, infrastructure provides basic services for which substitutes are relatively unavailable. Electricity is generated from a small number of fuels (at least presently), but its use is irreplaceable for end users. The appliances, machines, and gadgets using electricity to perform the daily tasks of modern living are ubiquitous. We have also made enormous fixed investments in electricity transmission and distribution. It is therefore difficult to conceive of a technology that can substitute for electricity. Even in transportation infrastructure, where we might expect substitution among roads, rail, air, and sea, it is usually impractical to substitute road for air or sea. Over long distances, roads or rail can hardly substitute for passenger transport by air and for freight transport by sea. Over short distances, road and rail are more complementary with interlocking networks, making travel efficient and inexpensive. Customer demand for infrastructure therefore remains fairly steady. The combination of a monopolistic position with demand inelasticity permits infrastructure firms to manage revenues. On the cost side, as noted previously, variable costs remain low. This combination allows infrastructure providers to generate large cash flows.

We must, however, add a number of caveats to this analysis. First, the monopolistic position that infrastructure providers occupy leads governments to regulate them extensively. In addition, infrastructure services are socially important services. Infrastructure firms therefore labor under the yoke of government regulations that typically include pricing restrictions. Although this factor offsets infrastructure providers' pricing power, governments frequently permit cost-plus pricing. Second, some infrastructure sectors have greater exposure to demand variability than others. For example, toll roads experience far more demand variability than do oil and gas mines. Demand for these sectors is relatively elastic to the extent that substitute modes of transportation are available at low cost.

STABLE CASH FLOWS

Apart from high operating margins and large free cash flows, infrastructure assets produce relatively stable and predictable cash flows.[9] Stable cash flows result from an asset's monopoly position, inelasticity of demand, and the lack of substitutes for the service. Exhibit 2.2 shows the mean and the coefficient of variation (CV) of cash flows from 1979 to 1986 for infrastructure industries like electric and gas utilities and oil and gas extraction, and for noninfrastructure industries like industrial and computer equipment, electrical equipment, and investment offices.

The CV is a normalized measure of the dispersion of a distribution and is defined as the ratio of the standard deviation to the mean. Stable cash flows have low standard deviation and therefore low CV. Exhibit 2.2 displays the mean cash flows and the CV in the row below for each year and industry. Exhibit 2.2 shows that electricity and gas utilities had an average CV of approximately 0.60 during this period while investment offices had an average CV that was six times higher at 3.45. The CV for all firms was about four times greater at 2.15. Even after we account for the higher mean cash flows for investment offices, electric and gas utilities demonstrate very stable cash flows.

Stable cash flows create important implications for the governance of these assets. First, stable cash flows make infrastructure assets more akin to fixed income securities like bonds, rather than equity, which is far more volatile. Second, stable cash flows attract predatory attention from opportunistic governments and counterparties like major suppliers or buyers. I examine these facets in greater detail in Chapter 4.

EXHIBIT 2.2 Industry Cash Flow Mean and Coefficient of Variation

SIC[a] Code	Industry	1979	1980	1981	1982	1983	1984	1985	1986
1,300	Oil and gas extraction	.1103	.1198	.1019	.0904	.0755	.0759	.0414	-.0652
		.6662	.5843	.7655	.7977	.9176	1.090	2.9484	-4.6063
2,800	Chemical production	.0939	.0925	.0841	.0799	.0840	.0927	.0845	.0703
		.7064	.7006	.9512	.7916	.8829	.8425	1.1289	2.4720
3,500	Industrial and computer equipment	.0894	.0817	.0654	.0904	.0510	.0684	.0420	.0455
		.7420	.8026	1.9522	1.0017	1.4409	1.1877	2.6298	2.1422
3,600	Electric equipment	.0990	.0837	.0823	.0738	.0581	.0680	.0539	.0283
		.5803	.8860	.7490	.9771	2.4341	1.8190	1.7795	7.1375
4,900	Electric and gas	.0575	.0570	.0568	.0543	.0593	.0671	.0634	.0624
		.5500	.5548	.6099	.8027	.6080	.5373	.5902	.6207
6,700	Investment offices	.1476	.1684[a]	.2429	.2640	.2160	.2284	.3010	.1860
		4.1505	3.8088	3.4717	3.4359	3.1783	3.7058	2.6514	3.2150
All firms:	Mean	.0850	.0781	.0761	.0677	.0683	.0755	.0687	.0580
	Median	.0825	.0759	.0736	.0654	.0690	.0765	.0696	.0650
	CV	1.4118	1.6095	2.1432	2.5712	2.0912	2.2439	2.3290	2.8014

[a]Standard Industrial Classification.

Source: B. Ambrose and D. Winters, "Does an Industry Effect Exist for Leveraged Buyouts? *Financial Management* 21 (1992): 89–101.

LONG LIFE

Infrastructure assets generate cash flows over a long duration. Exhibit 2.3 shows the productive lives of infrastructure assets. From an investor perspective, a long productive asset life appears to balance the initial capital intensity and sunk costs. However, investments become more risky if investors must rely on cash flows that are 10 to 15 years into the future in order to recoup initial investments. The risk is compounded in environments with underdeveloped legal regimes where property rights are weakly enforced. The long productive lives of infrastructure assets means that they can match the long duration of pension fund liabilities we noted in Chapter 1. Any mechanism that protects the stable cash flows of these assets over their productive lives should therefore greatly enhance their attraction to pension funds.

IRREVERSIBLE INVESTMENTS

Infrastructure investments are irreversible because infrastructure assets are not store of value assets but capital assets that generate returns by producing and selling output. If the capacity of the assets to produce or sell output

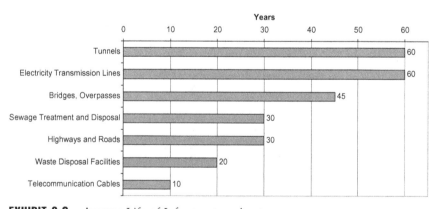

EXHIBIT 2.3 Average Life of Infrastructure Assets
Source: D. Rickards, "Global Infrastructure—A Growth Story": "Life of Infrastructure Assets before Major Maintenance Is Required," ed. Henry A. Davis, *Infrastructure Finance: Trends and Techniques* (London: Euromoney Books, 2008).

is impaired the investments cannot be recovered. The investments are sunk costs. The salvage value of electricity generating equipment, pipelines, or transportation infrastructure is very low compared to the investments needed to build them. The value of the investments lies primarily in the present value of cash flows from output sales. Additionally, costs incurred towards designing, prospecting, and feasibility studies are unrecoverable. Therefore, a combination of large capital outlays and irreversible investments makes greenfield infrastructure investment more risky than investing in existing assets. Sunk costs also give rise to the dynamic of opportunistic counterparties holding up investors. I examine this dynamic in detail in Chapter 4.

A related characteristic of these investments is that they are illiquid compared to equity and debt instruments. Since the assets need large sunk capital investments and are idiosyncratic in nature, it is difficult to bring together a large number of buyers and sellers. This may, however, change—first, because increased use of securitization allows infrastructure debt providers to transform illiquid loans into liquid tradable securities;[10] and second, because the rise of infrastructure funds looking to invest through equity participation increases the pool of buyers.[11]

LOCATION SPECIFICITY

Infrastructure assets are fixed to the ground. They remain tied locally in physical terms and, in a large proportion of cases, in terms of suppliers and customers. Roads and rail connect destinations. Electricity plants generate electricity mostly for local consumption. Oil, gas, and minerals are transported around the world but oil wells and mines are immobile. Their immobility forces investors to rely on local governments which not only provide the legal environment but also provide security and other local services. Other assets must also rely on local legal and security services, but if circumstances change, firms can shift production to other plants[12] or even abandon a plant, provided sunk costs are low. The lack or high cost of these options alters the risk profile of infrastructure assets.

GROWTH OPTIONS

Infrastructure assets have relatively few growth options.[13] Before we analyze the number and type of growth options and their importance, a brief description of options is in order. An option written on an asset confers on the buyer of the option the right but not the obligation to buy or sell the

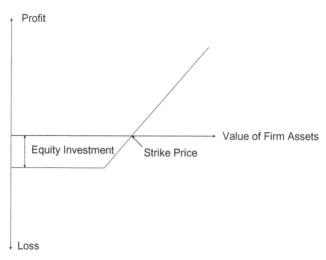

EXHIBIT 2.4 Call Option Payoff

underlying asset. A call option confers on the buyer a right but not the obligation to buy the underlying asset. The option buyer will exercise his right to buy the underlying asset only if the value of the asset exceeds the price at which he can purchase the asset, also called the strike price. If the underlying asset is trading below the strike price, the option buyer can purchase the asset in the market at a price cheaper than the strike price and consequently will not exercise the option. In other words, a call option purchaser only purchases the upside potential of the underlying assets.

Equity essentially is a call option on the assets of the firm, since the value of equity increases if earnings flowing to equity holders increase, while limited liability ensures that loss remains limited to their initial investment. Exhibit 2.4 shows the profit and loss profile of equity as a call option on the assets of a firm.

We may regard the present value of a firm's assets as a call option in the sense that their value equals the present value of future discretionary investments discounted at the firm's cost of capital.[14] Growth options comprise the population of future discretionary investments available to a firm. The value of a firm is higher if it has more growth options by virtue of its superior technology, differentiated products, well-known brands, market position, and/or research and development. Google, Apple, and Celgene are firms that are valued at higher price/earnings multiples compared to Consolidated Edison (an electricity utility) or gas utilities.

Exhibit 2.5 shows price/earnings (PE) ratios for infrastructure industries and technology industries from 2003 to 2008. The exhibit shows that

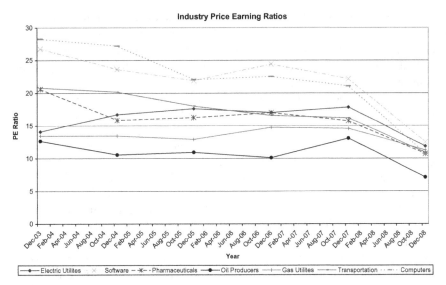

EXHIBIT 2.5 Industry Valuations: Price to Earnings Ratio
Source: Data from Bloomberg; author analysis.

the software and computer industries are consistently priced at an average of 20 and 22 times earnings while electricity and gas utilities are priced at 15 and 13 times earnings. Transportation industries, which comprise railroad companies and oil producing firms, are priced at 17 and 10 times earnings, respectively. It is interesting to compare Exhibit 2.5 with Exhibit 2.1. Although infrastructure industries produce far higher EBITDAs, they are valued at lower PE multiples. The difference is likely due to the larger number of growth options available to technology industries.

Growth options are essentially future positive net present value (NPV) investment opportunities. Investments in R&D, advertising, and brand building create future growth options to which the owners of these assets have monopoly access.[15] Investments in roads, mines, oil and gas pipelines, and utilities create relatively fewer such future investment opportunities. For example, an additional lane can be added to a toll road to generate additional revenues if traffic flow increases, or the capacity of an electric plant may be increased if demand increases, but the number and variety of such growth options is less than that created by a research laboratory at fuel cell producer Ballard Power Systems, or by solar power firm First Solar, or by a team of engineers in the wireless telecommunication industry at Motorola, Nokia, or Apple. Growth options from technology and knowledge assets are also qualitatively different since they tend to expand the option space by creating newer options. The acceleration of knowledge creation occurs because each new piece of technology invites further multiple directions for knowledge advancement. Exhibit 2.6 is a simple illustration of this logic.

Moreover, the present value of each knowledge and technology growth option is much higher than the present value of a growth option from infrastructure assets because the infrastructure option creates limited further options. Therefore, if we group alternative energy assets with traditional electricity generation, transmission, and distribution, and wireless telephony with fixed line communication, we are liable to focus on the wrong form of investment, using equity when debt would be more prudent.

Why are growth options important? The relatively fewer growth options leads to two important implications. The first relates to the free cash flows that infrastructure assets generate. Growth options with positive NPV are akin to in-the-money call options. In order to exercise these options, however, managers must buy the underlying asset at their strike price. In other words, investments are required to exercise in-the-money growth options. While managers can use internally generated cash flows from assets in place to exercise in-the-money growth options, infrastructure asset managers find themselves with surplus free cash flow since they do not possess similar growth options. Additionally, as noted earlier, infrastructure assets

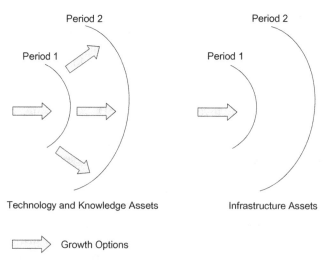

EXHIBIT 2.6   Growth Options from Different Assets

generate high free cash flows. This leads to agency conflicts that Jensen and Meckling[16] identify, which I examine in Chapter 4. The problem that infrastructure capital providers face is to limit how managers spend the cash to prevent value-destroying negative NPV investments.

The second implication deals with managerial skills. Managerial skills needed to manage firms with high growth options are different from skills needed to manage infrastructure assets. Managers of firms with high growth options must be skilled at creating, identifying, and funding in-the-money options. Managers are likely to possess significant information advantages over diffuse investors like shareholders and debt holders since assets as well as growth options are intangible, with high uncertainty and changing market conditions. The assets also require discretionary investments. Managers must be given far greater latitude to select growth options in which to invest. Therefore, capital providers must design governance structures that align managerial incentives with capital provider incentives. Managers of such firms are typically incentivized with stock options in addition to salaries, and equity plays an important role in governance.

A different dynamic operates in the case of infrastructure managers since assets are tangible limited-growth-option assets. Since infrastructure managers need to make few discretionary investments or evaluate multiple growth options, the governance problem for capital providers is different. Instead, infrastructure managers must ensure that high margins are preserved through maximizing the efficiency of operations. Capital providers therefore need to ensure that operations are run as efficiently as possible and that cash flows generated from these assets are returned to capital providers. Capital structure plays an important role in this governance function, particularly high debt. I examine the logic of governance structures in Chapter 4.

A third implication follows from the analysis of managerial skills. Infrastructure assets are easier for governments to expropriate than are high-technology assets. Governments find it difficult to mimic the skills needed for creating, identifying, and investing in growth options. Many governments including Japan, South Korea, and others have attempted to create technologically advanced, world-leading firms and have met with limited success. In these cases governments had the laudable aim of developing national champions and presumably encouraged the best people, processes, and knowledge to participate in the process. Still these efforts met with mixed success.

Imagine, then, a government attempting to take over or expropriate the assets of a firm that deals with intangible, knowledge-intensive assets. The prospects of such an expropriation providing the government with a steady revenue stream are not bright. In the case of infrastructure, however, governments can resort to expropriation and get to keep the revenues these assets generate. Infrastructure investors must therefore focus on managing the risks of government expropriation rather than managing traditional market risks.

Conversely, infrastructure asset managers must be skilled in designing and executing strategies that mitigate or hedge political risk. Henisz and Zelner (2006) make the point that firms cannot rely solely on financial engineering to manage political risk.[17] Similarly, investors cannot rely solely on insurance to hedge political risk since insurance only compensates for the replacement value of assets or the book value of assets, which may be even lower, and does not compensate for lost future cash flows. Firms in the infrastructure asset space must develop the capabilities to manage turbulence in policy environments within host countries. I examine this dynamic in detail in Chapter 6. For now, let us note that the options approach to examining the assets of a firm provides additional insights into their governance.

VALUE UNDER DEFAULT

We saw that infrastructure assets are tangible assets with stable cash flows. This makes them ideal as collateral for debt. We also saw that they possess few growth options and that the skills needed to manage them are operational skills. Both these factors affect their value under conditions of financial distress. Financial distress implies an inability to pay interest and principal payments to lenders. The components by which financial distress is measured are probability of default (PD), loss given default (LGD), and expected loss (EL).[18]

Probability of default is defined as the probability that a borrower will default within a year. The higher the PD, the lower the borrower's credit rating. Loss given default is defined as the loss incurred by the lender when the borrower defaults. Expected loss is defined as the mathematical product of PD and LGD.

In the event of default, lenders can foreclose on the assets that sponsors have pledged as collateral. Lenders can contract out operations and maintenance (O&M) to operate the asset and recoup their capital. A technology start-up, by contrast, may be difficult for lenders in possession to manage, particularly if key personnel, who carry the knowledge around in their head, leave or defect to competitors. Dymond (2003) points out that although lenders prefer to immediately sell foreclosed assets, lenders who wait for market conditions to improve and operate assets during the waiting period significantly enhance capital recovery.[19] As long as infrastructure assets produce output and generate revenues, their value even under conditions of default remains quite high. Of course, if the assets do not produce output and are idle they are liable to degrade and their salvage value is likely to be very low.

Beale et al. (2002) show that the median LGD for syndicated loans used in project-financed transactions that are typically used to fund infrastructure assets is only 25 percent, which means that on average 75 percent of the value of the loan is recovered by lenders.[20] In fact a majority of lenders recover 100 percent of their loan. The sidebar examines the case of Paiton power project in Indonesia, which fell into default after it was unable to meet its obligations to its lenders. However, this did not destroy the value of the assets. The project is currently producing power after a successful restructuring in which equity holders gave up some returns on their invested capital while the lenders essentially did not lose any capital.

THE PAITON POWER PROJECT, INDONESIA

The Paiton project is a 1,230-megawatt coal-fired power plant in Indonesia. The plant was tendered in 1991 and achieved financial closure in 1995 at a total capital cost of US$2.5 billion. The capital structure comprised $680 million in equity and $1.8 billion in debt, a leverage ratio of 72.8 percent. Equity holders in the project were Edison Mission Energy (40 percent ownership); Mitsui & Co. Ltd. (32.5 percent ownership); P.T. Batu Hitam Perkasa, an Indonesian coal supplier (15 percent ownership); and General Electric Capital Corporation (12.5 percent ownership). The debt was provided through a combination of multilateral agency support, syndicated lending, commercial loans, and capital market bond issue. Export-Import Bank of Japan (now Japan Bank for International Cooperation, JBIC) provided $900 million, the Overseas Private Investment Corporation (OPIC) provided $200 million, commercial banks provided $180 million, and investors in a bond issue provided $540m.

PT Perusahaan Listrik Negara (PLN), a state-owned power utility, contracted to purchase the entire output for the Java-Bali electricity grid that served the capital of Indonesia, Jakarta, for the next 30 years. The tariff that PLN agreed to pay for Paiton power included two provisions. The first was a *capital cost recovery tariff*, which basically increased the cost of power for the first 12 years and then halved it over the remaining duration of the contract. The second

(Continued)

provision indexed the tariff to the prevailing rupiah/USD exchange rate. The capital cost recovery tariff was meant to ensure adequate debt service coverage ratios, as well as an equity return that took Indonesian country risk into account. Paiton was required to use low-sulphur, low-ash, sub-bituminous coal from Kalimantan supplied by Perkasa, one of the equity partners, to meet environmental emission standards, which increased the costs for producing the power.

In 1997 the Asian financial crisis plunged Indonesia into a sharp recession. The rupiah fell from approximately 2,450 to the dollar to its worst level, 17,000 per dollar, before recovering to levels in the 8,000 to 10,000 range. The capital cost recovery tariff and rupiah/dollar indexation caused tariffs that PLN had agreed to pay to sky-rocket to over 9 cents/kilowatt-hour (kWh), while it could charge its customers about 1.7 cents/kWh. A comparable PLN plant cost 2.3 cents/kWh. PLN determined that it would pay for IPP power only at a rate equivalent to 2,450 rupiah/dollar, the rate the government had used for its 1997–1998 budget. The Paiton project could not meet its obligations to its lenders, and thereby became insolvent.

However, Paiton's lenders and sponsors completed the construction of the plant. Their judgment that a completed plant generating electricity was much more valuable than pieces of scrap metal was vindicated when PLN agreed to a new agreement. Paiton agreed to lower tariffs for PLN and the sponsors agreed to accept a lower, reasonable return on their investment. Paiton's sponsors had agreed to additional contingency equity commitments if the project ran into construction cost overruns. The sponsors agreed to pay lenders' interest payments through these equity commitments. Paiton's lenders agreed to a forbearance of their principal payments. U.S. Export-Import Bank agreed to extend its term loan commitment. However, the lenders' principal remained intact with no haircuts. The Paiton project retained its value even in extreme financial distress of bankruptcy.

The Paiton story is also instructive because it highlights several infrastructure characteristics: high up-front irreversible capital costs, risk of expropriation from the sole buyer, political risk, and value of equity versus debt. The story highlights how the attempt by Paiton's equity holders to address higher country risk by demanding a higher return through the capital cost recovery tariff was counterproductive. PLN renegotiated the contract, lowering the tariff that it agreed to pay, after the sponsors built the plant and incurred sunk costs.

CONCLUSION

To summarize, infrastructure assets are long-duration, capital-intensive assets with stable cash flows and limited growth options. Their cash flow distribution requires massive up-front investments which are irreversible and sunk. Since the assets are fixed to the ground in relative monopoly industries, they produce cash flows without relying on growth options. This makes them susceptible to managerial agency costs, expropriation from governments, and opportunistic counterparties. Chapters 3 through 6 argue that infrastructure assets are better funded by a higher proportion of debt in the capital structure. Debt is also a more efficient form of governance than equity because debt mitigates economic risks in infrastructure assets.

My analysis so far has been based on the underlying economics of infrastructure assets. From the portfolio perspective we need to examine infrastructure asset returns, risk, and correlations with other asset classes. In the next chapter I examine equity-based infrastructure indexes and in Chapters 4 and 8 debt based infrastructure investments, and analyze whether the underlying economics are reflected in the risk, return, and correlations. One may expect infrastructure investments to have low correlations with other asset classes. I begin the risk return and correlation analysis with equity-based infrastructure indexes.

CHAPTER 3

Equity Infrastructure Indexes

In God we trust, all others bring data.
—Dr. W. Edwards Deming

I analyzed infrastructure asset characteristics in Chapter 2 and showed that they possess unique economic properties. Long-duration, stable cash flow with low correlation to other asset classes and that is relatively immune to the business cycle is attractive to investors like pension plans and insurance companies who have long-duration liabilities. In this chapter I examine whether equity based infrastructure indexes fulfill the promise of infrastructure assets by providing low-volatility returns with low correlation to broader equity investments. The analysis shows that equity infrastructure indexes are strongly correlated with the broad equity market and that the correlation has increased since the indexes were introduced. The indexes are also riskier than the broad equity market itself. I also examine the impact of including these indexes on the efficient frontier. I begin the analysis by examining the different investment options available to investors.

INFRASTRUCTURE INVESTMENT OPTIONS

Investors can gain exposure to infrastructure assets through a slew of options based on their appetite for risk, their expertise, and their managerial resources. Exhibit 3.1 presents a simple framework that captures the various options.

Investors can invest in infrastructure assets directly or through intermediaries. Direct investments may be structured as equity or debt investments. For example, Ontario Teachers Pension Plan of Canada has built

EXHIBIT 3.1   Infrastructure Exposure Options

		Equity	Debt

Increasing investor expertise and attention	Indirect	Infrastructure indexes
		Infrastructure equity
		   funds
		Stocks of
		   infrastructure firms
			Infrastructure debt
			   funds
			Infrastructure bonds

	Direct	Individual project
		   sponsors
			Lenders to individual
			   projects (syndicated
			   debt)

up expertise in investing in electricity generating plants, airports, and containers in emerging markets.[1] The Plan takes direct equity stakes in plants along with partners. Direct debt investments in infrastructure assets can also be made by lending directly to specific assets or as part of a lending syndicate. Chapter 4 examines the implications of direct equity and debt investing for infrastructure assets. A direct investment in assets exposes investors to idiosyncratic business risk, or the unique risks arising from each individual asset, along with political, currency, and other risks. As noted previously, such investments are illiquid and investors must expect to be locked in for long durations. The investment also demands significant sectoral and geographical expertise in evaluating, monitoring, and managing assets. In return, investors achieve the asset class exposure they desire. They also gain asset concentration at the asset class level while maintaining diversification at the portfolio level. Ontario Teachers Pension Plan, for example, lost $12.5 billion in equities and $6.7 billion in fixed income but gained $200 million in infrastructure investments during the global economic meltdown in 2008.[2]

Investors can invest indirectly in infrastructure assets through equity and debt, as shown in Exhibit 3.1. They can invest in stocks of firms in the infrastructure sector or purchase equity-based infrastructure indexes. Investing in an infrastructure index is passive compared to stock selection; it is, however, less expensive. But do equity investments provide long-duration, low-volatility, stable returns? By investing in equities of firms, investors take on the firms' business risk, including the firms' management and financial risk, and are also exposed to the business cycle. Firms may not reproduce the unique benefits and relative immunity to the business cycle that infrastructure assets can deliver. Giliberto (1993), for example, shows that the equity real estate investment trust (REIT) index is correlated with the S&P 500 instead of the underlying real estate assets.[3] The focus of this chapter is to analyze equity infrastructure indexes and determine if they demonstrate infrastructure asset qualities and provide the exposure that investors are looking for.

Investors can also purchase bonds issued by infrastructure firms. Direct lending or syndicated lending to an individual asset differs from purchasing bonds. In Chapter 8 I analyze these differences and their implications for investing, and examine a portfolio of infrastructure bonds.

Alternatively, investors can invest in infrastructure funds, selecting funds that match their desired sectoral or geographic exposure and their equity or debt focus, although funds mostly focus on equity investments. An infrastructure fund provides expertise, experience, and active management for investors who perhaps lack the time, managerial resources, and experience of directly managing infrastructure assets. Funds also increase the pool of available capital through agglomeration, which may result in operating economies of scale and the capability of financing large assets where competition from other investors could be low. Infrastructure funds may also be able to exploit the *reputation effect* that protects investors from foreign government expropriation and which I examine in Chapter 7. In exchange for these benefits, investors give up a portion of their returns as fees. I examine the private equity model of investment adopted by a majority of infrastructure funds in Chapter 4. The next section analyzes equity infrastructure indexes.

EQUITY INFRASTRUCTURE INDEXES

The global size of firms in the infrastructure space in December 2007 was about $2.8 trillion.[4] During the same period, the global listed equity market was about $53.8 trillion. Standard & Poor's introduced the S&P Global Infrastructure Index (S&P GII) on November 16, 2001, with a base value of 1000. Macquarie Group and FTSE introduced their Macquarie Global Infrastructure Index (MGII) on December 31, 2003, with starting value of 5000.[5] Although the MGII was introduced in 2003, backdated index data is available from 2000. Credit Suisse First Boston (CSFB) introduced its CSFB Emerging Markets Infrastructure Index (CSFB EMII) on November 14, 2002, with a value of 100. Both the MGII and S&P GII are based on market capitalization. Stocks with the largest market cap are included in the indexes as long as they belong to index sectors and meet liquidity criteria. The CSFB EMII, however, selects stocks for inclusion through a proprietary methodology. All three indexes review their selection twice a year. Exhibit 3.2 compares the value of a $1,000 invested in the S&P 500, MGII, and S&P GII indexes from December 2001 to March 2009.

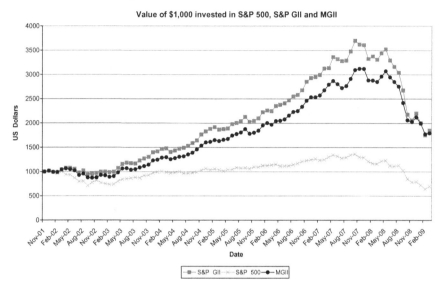

EXHIBIT 3.2   Value of $1,000 Invested in S&P 500 Index, MGII, and S&P GII
Source: Data from Bloomberg; author analysis.

We see the tremendous destruction of equity values over these eight
years, since an investment of $1,000 at the beginning of December 2001 in
the S&P 500 Index would be worth only $700.22 at the end of March
2009. The S&P GII and MGII fare much better, with an initial investment
of $1,000 worth $1,850.82 for the S&P GII and $1,793.36 for MGII at
the end of period. Exhibit 3.3 compares the value of $1,000 invested in the
three infrastructure indexes to the S&P 500 from December 2002 to March
2009, since the CSFB EMII was introduced only in December 2002.

Clearly, the CSFB EMII outperforms the other indexes by a considerable margin, with $1,000 growing to $4,480.35 by March 2009. The S&P
500 Index again loses money for investors. However, high returns may be
earned by taking on greater risk. We therefore examine the risk-return
relationship of the equity infrastructure indexes along with indexes for U.S.
government Treasuries, bonds, equities, and commodities. U.S. Treasury
indexes are the risk-free 30-day Treasury bills and 10-year Treasury bond
index. Bonds are represented by JP Morgan's Emerging Markets Bond
Index (EMBI) while commodities are represented by the Goldman Sachs
Commodity Index (GSCI). The risk of these indexes is measured by the
standard deviation over the measurement period from November 2002 to

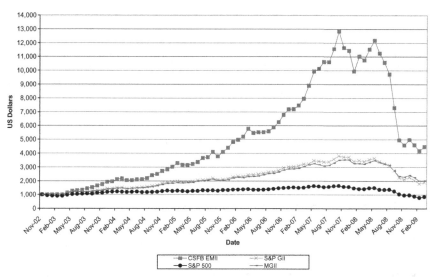

EXHIBIT 3.3   Value of $1,000 invested in S&P 500 Index, MGII, S&P GII, and CSFB EMII
Source: Data from Bloomberg; author analysis.

March 2009, while returns are the mean monthly returns over the same period. Exhibit 3.4 shows the relationship between index returns and index risk. The exhibit also includes consumer price index (CPI) mean and standard deviation for comparison.

The S&P 500 actually has negative mean return while still being fairly risky with a standard deviation of 4.15 percent per month. The negative mean monthly return, however, depends on the period under consideration since the equity market meltdown in 2002 as well as 2008–2009 contributes to the return. The S&P 500 returns 0.416 percent per month over a larger period, from 1992 to March 2009. However, the risk remains comparable with standard deviation equal to 4.25 percent.

Although the MGII and S&P GII indexes delivered higher returns they are also riskier. The CSFB EMII had the highest average monthly return of 2.33 percent but also the highest standard deviation of 7.91 percent. Commodities did not return as much as bonds although they had higher standard deviation, reflecting the volatility in commodity prices, particularly energy prices. Energy comprises the largest component in the GSCI with 76 percent of the total index at the end of 2005. The enormous run-up

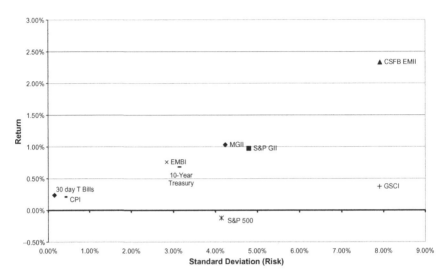

EXHIBIT 3.4   Risk versus Return: Monthly, November 2002 to March 2009
Source: Data from Bloomberg; author analysis.

in energy prices till July 2008 and the drastic fall-off after this time likely increases the standard deviation of commodity returns.

Exhibit 3.5 shows monthly return characteristics for different asset classes. The exhibit shows skew, kurtosis, and Sharpe ratio for these assets over the period November 2001 to March 2009.

I examine each of the infrastructure indexes in detail in the following sections.

MACQUARIE GLOBAL INFRASTRUCTURE INDEX

In December 2008 the MGII had 231 stocks in the index. Exhibit 3.6 shows the component sectors included in the index.

In order to be selected as an index component, a stock has to meet the following criteria:

■ The firm must be a constituent of the FTSE Global Equity Index Series. Therefore, only firms with market capitalizations greater than $250 million that are screened for liquidity and weighted for amount of free float are included in the index.

EXHIBIT 3.5 Monthly Asset Class Return Characteristics

Index	Infrastructure Equity Indexes			Stocks	Bonds	Commodities	Treasuries
	MGII	S&P GII	CSFB EMII	S&P 500	EMBI	GSCI	10-Year Treasury
Mean return	1.03%	0.97%	2.33%	−0.12%	0.76%	0.37%	0.68%
Standard deviation	4.24%	4.80%	7.91%	4.15%	2.84%	7.90%	3.15%
Maximum	8.41%	7.84%	13.78%	8.54%	7.77%	15.14%	12.33%
Minimum	−14.74%	−18.60%	−32.13%	−16.94%	−14.89%	−28.20%	−9.09%
Skew	−1.38	−1.53	−1.76	−1.27	−2.36	−0.79	0.14
Kurtosis	5.81	6.37	7.63	6.05	14.37	3.86	6.20
Sharpe ratio	0.19	0.15	0.26	−0.09	0.18	0.02	0.14

Source: Data from Bloomberg; author analysis.

- Share weighting of the individual constituents is the same as the FTSE Global Equity Index Series.
- The firm must be classified in a sector identified in Exhibit 3.6.
- Firms must obtain greater than 50 percent of their revenues from infrastructure-related activities.
- Firms whose investable market capitalization is equal to or greater than 0.05 percent of the investable market capitalization of the MGII are added to the index, and firms whose investable market capitalization is less than 0.02 percent of the investable market capitalization of the MGII are removed.
- The index is reviewed every six months.

The index does not limit the number of firms unlike, the S&P GII and CSFB EMII. The firm market capitalization criteria for inclusion, greater than 0.05 percent of the index market capitalization, implies that a large number of firms can become part of the index, and the index has regularly had more than 200 firms. Although the index is a global index, stocks with the largest market capitalization are likely to be from the developed markets of the United States and Western Europe and are therefore more likely to be part of the index. This also implies that the index is sensitive to the market capitalization of firms in a particular sector, since sectors are not weighted in the index. European and North American utilities, for example, have large market capitalizations. Consequently, the utilities sector dominates other sectors and composes a large portion of the index. Utilities carried a weight of 90 percent in the MGII 100 index, which comprises the top 100 firms by market capitalization from the MGII index. The index

EXHIBIT 3.6 MGII Sectors

Sector	Industries
Energy	Pipelines
	Gas distribution
Transportation	Airport services
	Highways and railroads
	Marine ports and services
Utilities	Electricity (generation and distribution including geothermal, nuclear, and solar)
	Gas
	Water
	Multi utilities
Telecommunications	Telecommunication equipment makers and distributors of high-technology communication products, satellites, mobile phones, fiber optics, switching devices, local and wide area networks, teleconferencing equipment, connectivity devices for computers like hubs and routers.

Source: FTSE "Ground Rules for the Management of the Macquarie Global Infrastructure Index Series," October 2008.

also includes telecommunication and computer sectors which I have argued do not possess infrastructure characteristics.

How do we interpret the returns from the MGII index? The MGII has outperformed the S&P 500, which includes all market sectors. Sectors included in the MGII have not been affected as badly as the financial, auto, airline, and retail industries except perhaps for the telecommunication industry, which has seen some bankruptcies—for example, that of Nortel. Investors were in favor of infrastructure sectors after 2003, driven by the explosive growth of the BRIC countries and the investments required to maintain and upgrade infrastructure in North America and Europe. Infrastructure funds raised billions of dollars during this period.[6] Even during the financial crisis of 2008, investments in infrastructure did not fall completely out of favor of investors, who perceived them to be defensive investments that would be stable during highly volatile and recessionary market conditions.

The infrastructure indexes have certainly given back a great chunk of their returns since the peak of November 2007, falling in tandem with the broader equity markets. The indexes therefore do not display the stability of returns that infrastructure assets should display based on their stable, long-duration cash flows. In fact, from a risk standpoint the returns of the MGII, S&P GII, and CSFB EMII all have higher standard deviations than

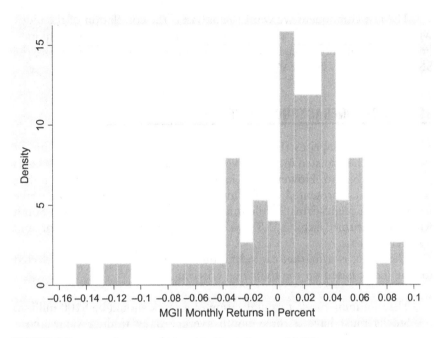

EXHIBIT 3.7   Distribution of Monthly Total Return: MGII
Source: Data from Bloomberg; author analysis.

the S&P 500, which makes them more risky and points to a disconnect between the behavior of these indexes and expected infrastructure asset behavior. This volatility of returns from a statistical viewpoint implies that equity infrastructure indexes could just as well underperform the equity markets if they fall out of favor from slowing growth, political crises, or regulatory tightening.

The return distribution shown in Exhibit 3.7 supplements this analysis. The monthly return distribution has a range from −14.74 percent to 8.41 percent, a negative skew of −1.38, kurtosis 5.81, standard deviation of 4.24 percent, and Sharpe ratio of 0.19.

The returns display *leptokurtosis*, or fat tails as compared to a normal distribution. MGII has kurtosis of 5.81. The leptokurtosis displayed by the returns implies that a larger proportion of the returns come from outliers. The distribution also has a negative skew, implying a higher likelihood of negative returns. Finally, the Sharpe ratio is 0.19, indicating low return per unit of risk. The Sharpe ratio shows that the MGII does not behave like the underlying economic assets with low standard deviation and relatively high returns.

The last component we want to analyze is the correlation of the index with other asset classes, particularly to a portfolio comprising equities, bonds, and commodities. I do this in the last section after analyzing the S&P GII and the CSFB EMII.

S&P GLOBAL INFRASTRUCTURE INDEX

The S&P GII comprises the equities of the 75 largest firms listed on 24 exchanges. The adjusted index market capitalization in December 2008 was US $733.72 billion. However, the index included only 14 firms from five countries that represented developing country infrastructure: Brazil (three firms), China (eight firms), Chile (one firm), Mexico (one firm), and South Korea (one firm). Exhibit 3.8 shows index composition by sector and number of firms.

The index is a market capitalization–based index. Stocks are selected for the index based on the following criteria:

- The minimum market capitalization of a stock should be $100 million.
- Stocks must have a three-month average daily trading value above US $1 million for developed markets and above US $500,000 for developing markets.

EXHIBIT 3.8   S&P GII Sectors, December 2008

Sector	Industries	Weight	Number of firms
Energy	Oil and gas storage and transportation	17.04%	15
Transportation	Airport services Highways and railroads Marine ports and services	38.73%	30
Utilities	Electric Gas Water Multi utilities Independent power producers and energy traders	44.23%	30
Total		100%	75

Source: S&P Global Infrastructure Fund fact sheet, accessed online at http://www2. standardandpoors.com/spf/pdf/index/SP_Global_Infrastructure_Index_Factsheet .pdf.

- Stocks must belong to one of the three groups in Exhibit 3.8.
- Initially 15 stocks from emerging markets are selected with the highest float-adjusted market capitalization. Of these, no more than 10 belong to a single group.
- Sixty stocks from developed markets are then selected with the highest float adjusted market capitalization.
- The index is completed with 30 stocks each in the transportation and utilities groups and 15 stocks in the energy group.
- The index is rebalanced every six months with the most recent float-adjusted market capitalization.

The S&P GII has a higher standard deviation than the S&P 500 and the MGII. It outperforms the S&P 500 yet the MGII has a better Sharpe ratio of 0.19 as compared to 0.15 for S&P GII over the period December 2002 to March 2009. The S&P GII does not include firms from the telecommunications sector, a sector included in MGII and one that has suffered in the equity market meltdown. Furthermore, the S&P GII contains 75 of the largest firms by market capitalization, as compared to the MGII which contains 231 firms. As such, the S&P GII is more sensitive to the equity price performance of the largest firms by market capitalization as compared to the MGII. The higher return from the S&P GII as compared to the S&P 500 likely shows that the large market capitalization firms in the infrastructure sector had strong equity price performances.

We next examine the distribution of returns from the S&P GII from December 2002 to March 2009. Exhibit 3.9 on page 60 shows distribution of monthly total returns. The distribution shows the number of occurrences over a range of −18.60 percent a month to 7.84 percent a month. Not surprisingly, the distribution has negative skew of −1.53, indicating higher likelihood of negative returns, and is more leptokurtic than the MGII. The kurtosis of 6.37 indicates fat tails with a large portion of returns generated from outlier events. The standard deviation is 4.80 percent while the Sharpe ratio is 0.15.

CSFB EMERGING MARKETS INFRASTRUCTURE INDEX

The CSFB EMII comprises 40 stocks listed on a regulated stock exchange that derive at least 15 percent of their income from emerging markets. The index has three themes: agriculture, power and utilities, and infrastructure, with a minimum of seven stocks in each theme. Stocks are selected through a proprietary valuation methodology that ranks stocks on three criteria: undervalued, market momentum, and corporate performance. Stock lists

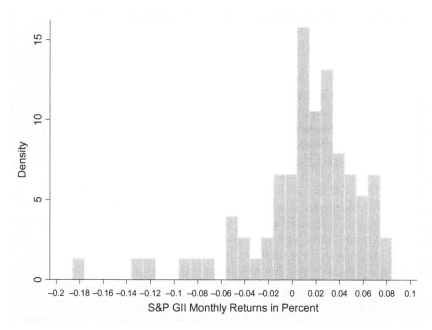

EXHIBIT 3.9   S&P GII Distribution of Monthly Total Returns, December 2002
to March 2009
Source: Data from Bloomberg; author analysis.

are reviewed at the end of each month and rebalanced every six months. Exhibit 3.10 on page 61 shows the regional distribution for stocks in the index as of March 31, 2009.

Although the CSFB EMII has only the three themes previously mentioned, a quick look at the industries included in each theme shows the diversity and range of firms that are eligible for inclusion in the index. Exhibit 3.11 on page 62 shows the composition of industries considered for this index.

Clearly the definition of infrastructure employed by the index comprises industries that do not correspond to the characteristics noted for infrastructure assets in this book. The returns from this index should therefore be more closely correlated with broad-based equity indexes like the S&P 500. Additionally, the index reflects the outcome of a stock selection process that is only loosely tied to the underlying economic fundamentals of infrastructure assets. The index also includes only 40 firms, which makes it exceptionally sensitive to the equity price performance of the individual firms, as compared to the MGII with its 231 firms, which is relatively less sensitive to the equity price performance of a single stock. These factors should be

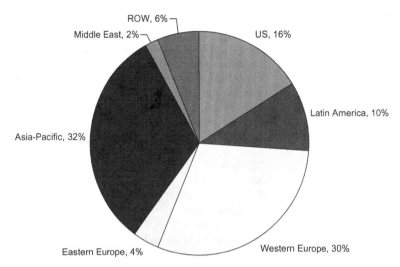

EXHIBIT 3.10   CSFB EMII: Geographical Distribution of Stocks

reflected in the distribution of returns from the index. Exhibit 3.12 on page 63 shows the distribution of the monthly returns from the CSFB EMII.

As we guessed, the return distribution is leptokurtic and shows very high kurtosis of 7.63, greater than the MGII and S&P GII. The fat tails indicate that a large portion of returns are generated from outlier events. The distribution shows the number of occurrences with a range of −32.12 percent a month to 13.78 percent a month. The distribution has negative skew of −1.756, indicating higher likelihood of negative returns. The index is the riskiest of the three indexes with a standard deviation of 7.91 percent. The Sharpe ratio is 0.26, higher than the S&P 500 and MGII, indicating that the stock selection process was able to generate higher return per unit of risk. The greater risk of the index, however, also points to the disconnect between expected infrastructure behavior and index behavior.

It is, therefore, hard to make the case that equity infrastructure indexes are a good proxy for investors seeking exposure to infrastructure assets that demonstrate low-volatility, stable cash flows over long periods of time. The equity indexes show highly volatile high returns. However, we are still missing the analysis of how these indexes perform as part of a diversified portfolio of equities and bonds. In order to analyze this aspect of investment, I first examine the correlations of these three equity infrastructure returns with broad indexes for equities, bonds, Treasuries, and commodities.

EXHIBIT 3.11 CSFB EMII Sectors

Sector	Industries
Agriculture	Fertilizers and agricultural chemicals
	Construction and farm machinery and heavy trucks
	Agricultural products
Power and utilities	Oil and gas storage and transportation
	Oil and gas equipment and services
	Electric
	Gas
	Water
	Multi utilities
	Independent power producers and energy traders
Infrastructure	**Transportation**
	Airport services
	Highways and railroads
	Marine ports and services
	Railroads
	Trucking
	Marine
	Materials
	Construction materials
	Steel
	Forest products
	Paper products
	Capital Goods
	Building products
	Construction and engineering
	Electrical components and equipment
	Heavy electrical equipment
	Industrial conglomerates
	Industrial machinery
	Technology Hardware and Equipment
	Communications equipment
	Computer hardware
	Computer storage and peripherals
	Commercial Services and Supplies
	Environmental and facilities services
	Telecommunication Services
	Alternative carriers
	Integrated telecommunication services
	Wireless telecommunication services

Source: Rules for the Credit Suisse Emerging Market Infrastructure Index, October 4, 2007, Version 1.

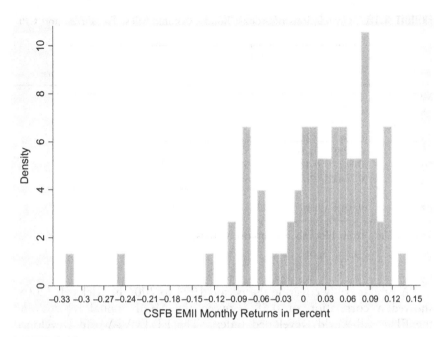

EXHIBIT 3.12 Distribution of Monthly Returns: CSFB EMII
Source: Data from Bloomberg; author analysis.

INFRASTRUCTURE EQUITY INDEXES CORRELATIONS

Exhibit 3.13 shows return correlations for the three infrastructure equity indexes—MGII, S&P GII, and CSFB EMII—to broad equities represented by the S&P 500, bonds represented by medium-term 7- to 10-year U.S. treasuries, high yield bonds represented by the Emerging Markets Bond Index (EMBI), and commodities represented by Goldman Sachs Commodity Index (GSCI). Exhibit 3.13 also shows correlations of these indexes with a monthly consumer price index (CPI) representing U.S. inflation rate.

The three infrastructure indexes are quite highly correlated with each other, which is not surprising. However, they are not perfectly correlated. The MGII has a higher correlation with the S&P GII of 0.9455 than with CSFB EMII, which is 0.8389. As we saw previously, the different sectoral composition of the indexes implied that the CSFB EMII was qualitatively different from the MGII and the S&P GII. The CSFB EMII monthly returns are correlated with monthly S&P 500 returns at 0.7991. The correlations of the MGII and S&P GII with the S&P 500 are also relatively high, at 0.7682 and 0.8175, respectively.

EXHIBIT 3.13   Correlations of Stocks, Bonds, Commodities, Treasuries, and CPI

	MGII	S&P GII	CSFB EMII	S&P 500	EMBI	GSCI	10-Year U.S. Treasury	CPI
MGII	1							
S&P GII	0.9455	1						
CSFB EMII	0.8389	0.888	1					
S&P 500	0.7682	0.8175	0.7991	1				
EMBI	0.6995	0.6868	0.6458	0.5548	1			
GSCI	0.3827	0.4303	0.5069	0.2837	0.2483	1		
10-Year U.S. Treasury	0.2261	0.1868	0.0318	−0.0125	0.5013	−0.042	1	
CPI	0.0908	0.107	0.1134	0.0551	−0.0106	0.4263	−0.3779	1

Source: Data from Bloomberg; author analysis.

A similar study covering the period 1994 to 2006 by Rickards (2008) showed a correlation of 0.58 between the MGII annual returns and the FTSE All-World Developed Index.[7] The FTSE All-World Developed Index is the aggregate of the large-cap and mid-cap stocks from the FTSE Global Equity Series that are located in the developed markets like North America and Europe. MGII monthly returns are available from July 2000 and the correlation with the S&P 500 monthly returns over this time period is 0.6198. The S&P GII correlation with the S&P 500 from December 2001 to March 2009 was 0.7809. The correlations between the equity infrastructure indexes and broad equity market therefore appear to be increasing.

The equity infrastructure indexes would have been valuable as vehicles of diversification if their correlations with the equity market had decreased during the turbulence and volatility of the financial crisis of 2008. The increase in correlation undermines the case for establishing these indexes as a proxy for investing in infrastructure assets with stable, long-term, low-risk returns and low correlations with other asset classes. Infrastructure assets are also expected to provide a good hedge against inflation when their cash flows are indexed to inflation.[8] How do these indexes perform against inflation?

Hedge Against Inflation

If infrastructure assets are expected to provide a good hedge against inflation, their returns should increase if inflation increases to compensate for the loss of purchasing power. As such, the three infrastructure index returns should be correlated with the CPI. The correlations between CPI and equity infrastructure indexes is, however, very weak at about 0.09, 0.10, and 0.11 for MGII, S&P GII, and CSFB EMII, respectively. In fact, these correlations are comparable to the correlation between CPI and the S&P 500 at 0.05, which is not surprising since the infrastructure equity indexes and the S&P 500 are highly correlated.

How does a portfolio comprising equity, bonds, and the infrastructure indexes perform? The next section analyzes different portfolios.

EFFICIENT FRONTIER

Portfolio theory teaches us that the risk/return profile of a portfolio is a function of the risk/return profiles of its constituent assets. The return of a portfolio is simply the weighted average of each individual asset return, with the weights equal to the proportional value of the portfolio invested in each asset. We use equation 2.3 from Chapter 2 to obtain historical portfolio returns.

The risk of a portfolio measured by its standard deviation is not equal to the weighted average or sum of the standard deviations of its assets since the assets comprising the portfolio are not perfectly correlated. Intuitively, the standard deviation of a portfolio comprising two assets with negative correlation, for example, will be lower than the standard deviation of each asset by itself. The risk of a portfolio incorporates the correlation between its constituent assets; we use equation 2.6 from Chapter 2 to calculate the historical standard deviation of each portfolio.

By varying the weights or proportion of the total portfolio invested in its constituent assets, we obtain a series of portfolios. The efficient frontier represents that set of portfolios that has the maximum return for every given level of risk, or the minimum risk for every level of return.[9] Exhibit 3.14 shows a set of portfolios comprising stocks and bonds represented by the S&P 500 and U.S. Treasuries. The monthly returns are plotted against the portfolio monthly standard deviation from November 2001 to March 2009. The plot is obtained by varying the proportion of stocks and bonds from 0 percent to 100 percent. At 0 percent stocks, the portfolio comprises only bonds, and at 100 percent stocks the portfolio comprises only stocks.

Exhibit 3.14 shows the negative returns as well as the high risk associated with holding a pure S&P 500 portfolio at the last point of the curve below the x-axis. The first point on the graph represents a pure bond portfolio (100 percent assets allocated to U.S. Treasuries), and different

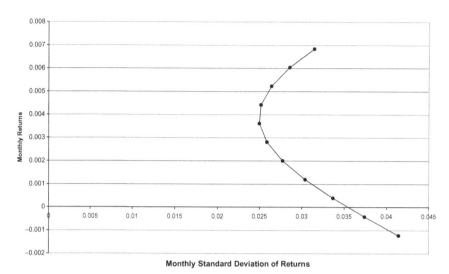

EXHIBIT 3.14   Efficient Frontier: S&P 500 and Bonds
Source: Data from Bloomberg; author analysis.

combinations of stock and bond portfolios are plotted in between. The point where the portfolio shows the highest return for the least risk is represented by an 80 percent bond and 20 percent stock portfolio. This efficient frontier has an unusual shape because of the negative returns from a pure S&P 500 portfolio resulting from the financial mayhem in 2008–2009 and the flight to safety of assets into Treasuries. A more usual efficient frontier with stocks and bonds displays higher returns and higher risk for stocks as compared to bonds.

We now add the infrastructure indexes to our stock and bond portfolios. We begin with the MGII and plot portfolios, keeping the MGII proportion constant at 10 percent, 20 percent, and 30 percent of the portfolio while varying the stock and bond proportions as we did for Exhibit 3.14. Exhibit 3.15 shows the resulting portfolios. When we add the MGII to the stock and bond portfolios, the resulting portfolios shift inwards and upwards. The exhibit shows that an inward shift represents a higher risk for the same return as long as the returns are positive. In other words, when the efficient frontier shifts inward *above* the x-axis, the portfolios represent higher risk for the same returns. However, the exhibit shows that an inward and upward shift *below* the x-axis represents less loss (or higher return) for

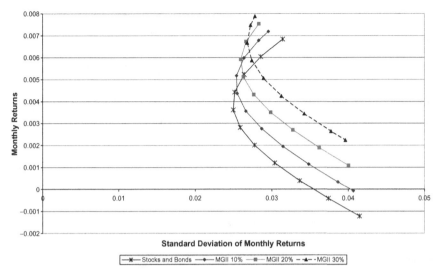

EXHIBIT 3.15   Efficient Frontier: S&P 500, Treasuries, MGII
Source: Data from Bloomberg; author analysis.

less risk. Adding the MGII therefore improves the risk/return profile for portfolios comprising stocks and bonds.

We perform the same analysis by adding the S&P GII to a portfolio comprising stocks and bonds. Efficient frontiers are plotted for 10 percent and 20 percent allocated to the S&P GII. Once again, the efficient frontier shifts out. The inward shift below the x-axis provides higher returns (through lower losses) for lower risk, while portfolios above the x-axis shift the efficient frontier out, showing that investors benefit by adding the S&P GII to a pure stock and bond portfolio. (See Exhibit 3.16.)

How does the CSFB EMII affect the efficient frontier, given that it has the highest correlation with the S&P 500? Exhibit 3.17 displays the shifts in the efficient frontier. The high returns and high risks from the CSFB EMII are reflected in the upward shift in the efficient frontiers. The high returns from the CSFB EMII help the portfolios that have been displaying negative returns. However, for portfolios with positive returns, the inward and upward shift that occurs upon including the CSFB EMII shows that high returns are obtained by taking on high risk.

The argument for including equity infrastructure indexes therefore needs to be revisited. These indexes have provided superior returns to stocks but with higher levels of risk.

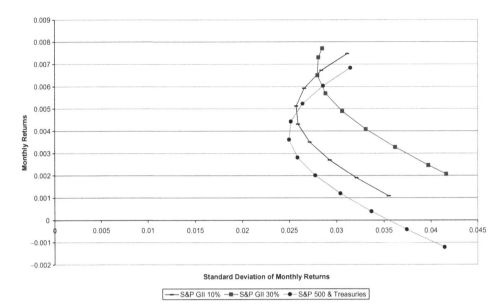

EXHIBIT 3.16 Efficient Frontier: S&P 500, Treasuries with S&P GII
Source: Data from Bloomberg; author analysis.

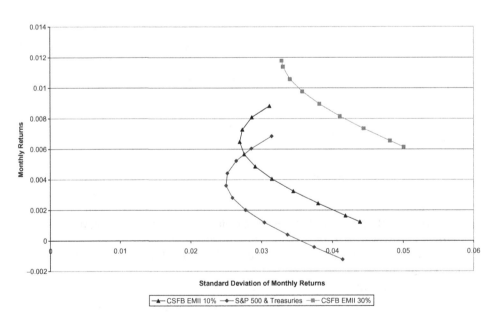

EXHIBIT 3.17 Efficient Frontier: S&P 500, Treasuries, CSFB EMII
Source: Data from Bloomberg; author analysis.

CONCLUSION

In this chapter I analyzed equity infrastructure indexes and historical returns, risk, and correlation with stocks and bonds. The MGII and S&P GII select stocks in sectors closely related to my definition of infrastructure, while the CSFB EMII includes sectors that represent a broader equity market. Although the indexes have outperformed the S&P 500 since their introduction, the volatility of the MGII is almost equal to the S&P 500, while the volatility of the S&P GII and the CSFB EMII are greater than that of the S&P 500. Their return distributions demonstrate a negative skew, indicating that negative returns are more likely, and high kurtosis, indicating that a large proportion of returns are obtained from outlier events. This is consistent with high volatility. The indexes are highly correlated with the S&P 500. Including the indexes in a portfolio of stocks and bonds and analyzing the efficient frontier demonstrates increased returns while lowering risk and shifting the frontier outside.

My analysis therefore indicates that investors expecting infrastructure exposure from equity infrastructure indexes did not find it. Investors following a strategy of indirect investment by selecting infrastructure stocks are also unlikely to find the desired infrastructure exposure because of high correlation with the broad equity market and susceptibility to the business cycle. In order to continue this analysis of the different investment options available to investors, I examine equity and debt investment characteristics in the next chapter. I also examine in Chapter 4 the private equity model of investing that most infrastructure funds have followed.

CHAPTER 4

Debt versus Equity
Mode of Investment

I shall make electricity so cheap that only the rich can afford to burn candles.

—Thomas Alva Edison

Chapter 2 outlined infrastructure assets' distinctive characteristics—long-duration stable cash flows, limited growth options, and threat of opportunistic expropriation from counterparties including governments—which differentiate them from other asset classes. These characteristics expose investors to unique risks and returns. We noted that equities represent residual claims on cash flows from assets and are implicit long call options. In this chapter we see that risky debt is an implicit short put option and examine its implications.

In Chapter 3 we saw that equity infrastructure indexes do not mimic the underlying infrastructure characteristics, instead resembling broad equity indexes. In this chapter I show that infrastructure characteristics influence the form of investment. Specifically I argue that debt investment is advantageous as compared to equity investment in increasing the value of infrastructure assets. Debt is a strategic tool in mitigating the unique infrastructure risks and consequently increasing the value of the investments. In order to make the argument, I first explore capital structure theory, which will help reveal the linkages between infrastructure asset characteristics and the optimal mode of investment, debt over equity.

THEORIES OF CAPITAL STRUCTURE

I begin with the seminal Miller and Modigliani theorem[1] about the irrelevance of capital structure to the value of the firm and a brief history of insights that have shaped our understanding of corporate finance. In a Miller Modigliani world, the value of the firm does not depend on how much equity and debt the firm uses. Of course, the result is based on assumptions of perfect functioning of capital markets and that investment strategies of the firm are fixed. Stiglitz (1969, 1974) argued that in addition to perfect capital markets, a necessary assumption for the Miller Modigliani theorem to hold was that the debt held by firms and individuals was default-free.[2] However, Miller and Fama (1972) argued that the theorem held even when the debt held by individuals and firms was not default-free, if stock-holders and debt holders protected themselves by seniority rules.[3] Miller and Fama called these *me-first rules*, and assumed them to be enforced costlessly and designed to protect existing debt holders by ensuring that the value of outstanding debt did not change if the firm altered its capital structure. For example, existing bondholders would insist on covenants that new debt remain junior to them. Me-first rules ensured that new financing did not undermine the position of existing debt. Fama (1978) argued that the assumptions for riskless debt or me-first rules were not necessary for the Miller Modigliani theorem to hold.[4] If stockholders wanted to issue unprotected debt (debt without me-first rules) then investors would be willing to hold them at the right price; in other words, investors acting rationally would price these securities assuming that stockholders would act opportunistically.

In a Miller-Modigliani world without taxation we should find a uniform capital structure for all firms. In a world with taxation we should find firms financed almost entirely with debt since debt provides tax shields. Firms would seek to minimize taxes and use high interest payments to shield their wealth from taxes. The financial innovations that have been such a vital part of modern capital markets would be absent since theoretically these do not matter. There would be no demand for different types of securities from investors and the financial services industry would consequently have no incentive to supply these innovations. Myers (2001) makes the point that the range and breadth of financial innovation found in capital markets proves that type of security does matter.[5] A primary assumption that makes financing choices irrelevant to the value of a firm is that investment strategies of the firm are exogenous. The rules that firms use to make current and future investment decisions are assumed to be independent of how the investments are financed.[6] Clearly this assumption is unrealistic since the costs of negotiation, monitoring, and enforcement of contracts are not negligible and agency costs influence the rules that firms use to make investments. Risky debt, for example, induces a suboptimal investment policy.[7]

What do we actually observe in the capital structure of different firms? We find that firms with intangible assets and high growth, such as pharmaceutical companies, Microsoft, and Cisco, are funded largely through equity and consequently have low debt ratios. Firms with high growth opportunities also tend to have low debt ratios.[8] Bradley, Jarrell, and Kim (1984) show that there is a significant inverse relationship between debt ratios and the level of advertising and R&D expenditure.[9] R&D investments and advertising are related to the acquisition of options for future growth. Therefore industries that invest heavily in R&D and advertising, like the drugs and cosmetics industry, have low debt to total value ratios at about 9.07 percent. Exhibit 4.1 lists industries and their debt to value ratios. Heavily

EXHIBIT 4.1 Industry Debt to Capital Ratios

SIC[a] Code	Industry	Number of Observations	Mean (Standard Deviation) Debt to Value
2830, 2840	Drugs and cosmetics	31	.0907 (.095)
3800	Instruments	27	.1119 (.086)
1000	Metal mining	23	.1347 (.099)
2700	Publishing	16	.1552 (.169)
3600	Electronics	77	.1579 (.121)
3500	Machinery	80	.1957 (.114)
2000	Food	50	.2056 (.128)
1300	Petroleum exploration	24	.2258 (.151)
1500, 1600, 1700	Construction	12	.2384 (.151)
2900	Petroleum refining	31	.2436 (.121)
3400	Metal working	33	.2502 (.139)
2800	Chemicals	47	.2544 (.135)
2300	Apparel	18	.2603 (.123)
2400	Lumber	7	.2605 (.182)
3700	Motor vehicle parts	52	.2714 (.138)
2600	Paper	24	.2895 (.114)
2200	Textile mill products	21	.3257 (.133)
3000	Rubber	26	.3262 (.167)
5300	Retail department stores	20	.3433 (.150)
5400	Retail grocery stores	16	.3460 (.187)
4200	Trucking	10	.3730 (.209)
3300	Steel	45	.3819 (.195)
4800	Telephone	10	.5150 (.097)
4900	Electric and gas utilities	135	.5309 (.081)
4500	Airlines	16	.5825 (.171)

[a] Standard Industrial Classification.
Source: Michael Bradley, Gregg Jarrell, and E. Han Kim, "On the Existence of an Optimal Capital Structure: Theory and Evidence," *Journal of Finance* 39 (1984): 857–878.

regulated infrastructure industries like electric and gas utilities with stable cash flows and limited growth options have the highest debt to capital ratios at about 53 percent. Moreover, the standard deviation at 0.081 is also low, indicating that most firms in the industry have similarly high debt to capital ratios. Exhibit 4.1 shows that other industries with infrastructure characteristics like telephone and transportation also have high debt to capital ratios.

Another empirical observation is that profitable firms have consistently low debt ratios, for example Procter & Gamble.[10] This observation is at odds with a view that the role of debt is merely to provide tax shields to the firm. Interest payments reduce the amount of income that is paid out as taxes, and since profitable firms have more income to protect from taxes, they should have higher debt ratios than average. Of course, the savings from taxes must exceed the payments made as interest in order for the transaction to add value. However, Graham (2000) found that profitable firms could add 7.5 percent to firm value by increasing debt ratios to conservative levels and protecting cash flows from tax payments.[11]

Clearly debt and equity contribute to value creation in different ways and are not mere financing methods. The prevailing theories of capital structure—chiefly the pecking order theory, free cash flow (agency cost) theory, and trade-off theory—outline the functions that debt and equity play in creating value for the firm. I examine each in turn, followed by the theory of financing as a governance structure, to examine the implications for infrastructure investing.

PECKING ORDER THEORY

The pecking order theory of capital structure refers to the order in which managers choose debt and equity when investing in new projects. The pecking order theory posits that managers prefer using internally generated funds first, followed by debt, and issuing new equity last. The logic for the order of financing is based on information asymmetry between managers and new capital (debt or equity) providers and the inferences that rational capital providers draw from the method of raising new capital.[12] Managers are assumed to possess better information than outside investors about the true value of the assets of the firm and the value of growth opportunities. Investors must therefore infer the value of assets and growth opportunities from the signals that managers send to the capital markets. Raising new equity sends a signal to outside investors that managers believe that the assets of the firm are overvalued. If existing shares are undervalued (i.e., new investors pay less for the new equity issue than the actual shares are worth) then value is transferred from existing investors to new investors. In this instance the firm would not want to issue new equity. Managers will issue new equity when debt is available only if they have reason to believe that the existing shares are overvalued and if they can convince investors to pay more than the shares are worth.

A new equity issue therefore implies that the managers possess information that leads them to believe that the firm is overvalued. In this equilibrium, therefore, new investors will not buy the shares. Firms therefore prefer internal finance to external finance. If internal finance is not available they prefer to issue new debt instead of equity. Managers choose to issue new equity only if the firm is highly levered and additional debt is likely to cause the firm to go into financial distress.

The pecking order theory therefore posits that each firm's debt ratio reflects its cumulative requirement for external financing. The theory explains why profitable firms issue less debt. Profitable firms generate more internal capital and consequently have more capital to invest. Less profitable firms need to use external capital to invest in positive net present value (NPV) projects, in which case they prefer to issue debt over equity. Less profitable firms therefore end up with more debt.

Pecking Order Theory and Infrastructure

How does the pecking order of financing theory apply to investment in infrastructure assets? The pecking order theory relies primarily on information asymmetry between managers and investors. The pecking order theory and its predictions therefore become particularly relevant in conditions when information asymmetries are large and vital. Managers are likely to possess greater information than external investors about operations when the firm deals in intangible products and processes, and when the capabilities of the firm are a function of tacit knowledge embedded either within the firm or within the firm's network of suppliers, partners, and subsidiaries. Managers are likely to know more about future growth options in conditions of great uncertainty from rapid technological changes or market turmoil. These conditions occur in industries like software engineering, pharmaceuticals, and other intangible, R&D-intensive industries.

By contrast, infrastructure assets are tangible stable assets that are not opaque to investors. Outside investors can simply examine comparable firms in the market and gain a fairly clear picture of an asset's likely cash flows and relative value. Chapter 7 examines the financing structure of project finance in which investors spend considerable time examining future cash flows and other operating details of an asset and essentially eliminating any vestiges of informational asymmetry between internal managers and external investors. The pecking order theory therefore is of limited value in the context of infrastructure assets.

The pecking order theory assumes that managers act in the best interests of existing equity holders. This is an important assumption and one that is not borne out by empirical observations. The second theory of capital structure focuses on conflict between the different stakeholders of the firm.

FREE CASH FLOW THEORY

The free cash flow theory of capital structure uses the concept of *agency costs*. Agency costs are related to the agency problem that occurs when cooperating parties have different goals and require a division of labor. The agency relationship between two parties is a relationship where one party (the principal) delegates work to another (the agent) who performs the work. The agency problem arises when (1) the goals or aim of the principal and the agent conflict and (2) it is difficult or expensive for the principal to verify what the agent is actually doing. In the context of a firm, the shareholders are principals who delegate work to the managers, who are agents. When a firm throws off free cash flow, managers may undertake unwise investments or resort to profligacy and wasteful expenditure. Jensen and Meckling (1976) refer to these costs as the agency costs arising from conflicts between owners and managers of a firm.[13]

Consider the first case when interests of the firm's managers and shareholders are not perfectly aligned. This may occur because agents or managers desire above-market salaries, perquisites, job security, and sometimes appropriation of assets and cash flows which is detrimental to shareholders' interests. Managers may also seek to make *entrenching investments*, investments that maximize their particular knowledge and skill set. By undertaking investments that rely on their specialized skill sets, managers make it difficult for shareholders to replace them and consequently improve their bargaining power over investors.[14] In this case shareholder and managerial incentives are not aligned, and shareholders must find a solution to force managers to act in the interests of shareholders.

Consider the second instance when it is difficult or expensive for principals to monitor their agents. Independent boards are expected to safeguard shareholder interests by reviewing managerial compensation and investment policies and monitoring the operations of the business. A related option available to shareholders is the market for corporate control—the threat of takeover of the firm by outside investors who replace inefficient managers. Outside investors must compensate existing shareholders in order to take over control and are likely to do so if they can extract greater efficiencies from the operation by replacing inept or inefficient managers. However, attempts to align managerial incentives through monitoring by independent boards or threats of takeover are costly and also subject to decreasing returns.

Shareholders could in theory write contracts that describe managerial actions in great detail and thereby monitor them by ensuring that the contracts are observed. In practice, complete contracts rewarding managers for good decisions, hard work, and commitment cannot be written because these are hard to measure. Such contracts are also unenforceable because it is difficult for disinterested third parties like the courts to observe breach of contracts. Such contracts are incomplete in the sense that they cannot apprehend every possible state of the world and the correct managerial response to protect shareholder interests in each state of the world. Since it is difficult and in many cases expensive for diffuse shareholders to monitor managers, managers may misuse their control over the assets of a firm, particularly when the assets create large amounts of free cash flow. The problem is how to motivate managers to disgorge the cash rather than investing it below the cost of capital or wasting it on organizational inefficiencies.

The free cash flow theory suggests that the solution to the agency conflict between shareholders and managers is the use of debt. Debt forces managers to meet contractually mandated payments as per a prearranged schedule. An extreme form of this capital structure is the leveraged buyout (LBO). We saw in Chapter 2 that an LBO is found only in certain industries with high, stable cash flows. The extreme amount of debt in an LBO is used to retire equity and force managers to improve operational efficiency in order to make the required debt payments. High debt levels also give large tax shields and create additional value.[15]

Free Cash Flow Theory and Infrastructure

How does the free cash flow theory of capital structure apply to infrastructure assets? As we saw in Chapter 2, infrastructure assets create large amounts of free cash flow due to their low variable costs and high margins. The opportunity exists for managers to overinvest in negative NPV projects. The opportunity for overinvestment implies that the firm does not have a sufficient number of positive NPV growth options in which free cash flows can be profitably deployed. In this instance, the firm is better off returning cash to investors rather than wasting it on negative NPV projects. Infrastructure assets, as we saw, possess relatively few growth options and cash flows are better off returned to investors. Free cash flow theory suggests that a high level of debt forces managers to disgorge free cash flows because they need to meet contractually mandated interest and principal payments.

The opportunity for managers for self-aggrandizement through perquisites, above-market salaries, and so forth, also exists when large free cash flows are combined with low growth options. The relative ease of monitoring assets, since these are tangible assets with clearly defined suppliers and buyers, attenuates this opportunity. Another option available to investors is the separation of cash flows from individual assets. When multiple assets are part of a firm's balance sheet their cash flows are commingled. In this instance it is more difficult for investors to monitor cash flows, and separation of the asset in a different entity makes cash flows transparent and improves monitoring. There are certainly advantages both to combining assets on a single balance sheet and to separating out their cash flows, and Chapter 7 explores this aspect of structuring investments.

Nevertheless, the free cash flow theory provides a strong rationale for using debt as a mechanism of forcing managers to disgorge free cash flows. Not only do investors force managers to disgorge cash flows but they also create a mechanism for monitoring performance by creating high contractually obligated payments. Managers must operate the assets efficiently to meet interest and principal payments, and late or missed payments that are immediately brought to investors' attention reveal that managers are not performing optimally.

Clearly, high debt increases the risk of bankruptcy and comes with its own set of problems. The next section examines the trade-off theory of capital structure, which considers the risks and rewards of debt.

TRADE-OFF THEORY OF CAPITAL STRUCTURE

The trade-off theory of capital structure is based on the trade-offs between the benefits and costs of debt. The theory predicts that firms will borrow till the marginal value of tax shields from additional debt equals the increase in the present value of costs from financial distress. What are the costs of financial distress? We can analyze two kinds of costs: costs that a firm and its stakeholders incur after the firm declares bankruptcy and costs before the firm becomes insolvent. A firm's customers, workers, and suppliers suffer when a firm goes out of business. Titman (1984) shows that these costs are highest when a firm has relatively unique products that need further service.[16] Customers are unlikely to buy from firms that are in financial distress, and costs from lost revenues add to other costs. Costs of bankruptcy include transaction costs of reorganization (for example, legal and administrative expenses), costs of liquidating assets, costs of renegotiation between the creditors and shareholders, and reorganization of the firm, including the opportunity costs of lost revenues when the firm is in bankruptcy court.

However, there are significant costs from financial distress even before actual default occurs. As a firm moves towards default, its debt becomes riskier. Agency costs arise between the firm's debt holders and equity holders when the firm's creditworthiness is in doubt. Since debt holders are paid before shareholders, shareholders have incentives to take actions that transfer wealth from creditors. If managers hold stock options and we assume that managers act in shareholders' interests, managers can take the following actions:

- Managers undertake riskier investments akin to a double-or-nothing bet. If a risky investment pays off, stockholders get to keep the upside. If the bet goes sour, shareholders are no worse off than before. Debt holders, however, gain nothing from the risky bet since their payoff is limited to interest and principal payments. If the bet fails, debt holders are worse off since the probability of default increases. Jensen and Meckling (1976) called this action *risk shifting* and named it as an agency problem between equity and debt holders. The problem is also called an *asset substitution* problem because managers replace the firm's low-risk assets with high-risk assets.[17]
- Managers can attempt to exploit information asymmetries, borrow even more capital, and pay cash to shareholders. In this instance the increased leverage makes existing debt holders worse off for two reasons. First, the increased leverage actively pushes the firm towards default and the probability of default increases. Second, the loss given default for existing debt holders might increase because they may have to share the proceeds from a liquidation of the firm's assets with the new lenders.
- Managers can choose to forego positive NPV projects or underinvest.[18] This problem arises when the value of a new discretionary positive NPV project is less than the sum of new investment and present debt payments:

Value of project < Equity investment required + Existing debt payments

In this case, cash flows from the new project go towards existing debt payments. In other words, the effect of the new investment is to transfer wealth to existing debt holders (who contribute nothing to the new project) from stockholders who take the risk. Thus, risky debt induces a suboptimal investment policy for the firm. This problem is also called a *debt overhang* problem.

▪ Managers can play for time. They can conceal problems with the aim of preventing creditors from forcing the firm to declare bankruptcy and seizing the assets of the firm. This lengthens the effective maturity of the debt, and debt holders lose while stockholders gain.

Firms incur these costs of financial distress because the threat of a default feeds back into a firm's investment and operating decisions. The trade-off theory predicts that these costs must be offset by the tax shields that debt provides. The trade-off theory predicts moderate levels of debt since an increase in debt increases agency costs.

Impact on Infrastructure

How does the trade-off theory apply to infrastructure assets? As previously noted, infrastructure assets are large, indivisible, lumpy, and transparent with relatively few growth options. The goods and services they provide are not differentiated or unique, and they do not require great support after sale to the end user.[19] In this sense, costs of financial distress after default are likely to be quite low for infrastructure assets. The customers of a utility continue to buy electricity, gas, or water even if the utility is at high risk of bankruptcy. The costs of a bankruptcy therefore remain mostly limited to the transaction costs of legal and administrative fees during the renegotiation or reorganization period.

Moreover, we have also seen that the value of infrastructure assets is quite high even under default since lenders can manage the assets relatively easily and continue to generate cash flows. What about agency costs between creditors and shareholders before default? Creditors are certainly exposed to the risk that shareholders can make high-risk investments, borrow additional capital and use it to pay shareholders, forego positive NPV projects, or conceal problems and play for time. Although infrastructure assets may not suffer loss in value from foregoing positive NPV projects, the other costs impair the value of these assets. Shareholders may use the revenues from ongoing operations to fund highly risky investments instead of making interest and principal payments. From an economic standpoint this is not the most efficient use of capital.

A governance mechanism must therefore be found to mitigate these risks. Chapter 7 examines the governance and financing structure of project finance that promises to mitigate these agency costs. Debt plays a central role in project finance. A complementary perspective that builds on capital structure as a mechanism for governance comes from transaction cost economics. Although I discuss transaction cost economics in Chapter 5, let me briefly examine this view of capital structure in the following section.

GOVERNANCE AND CAPITAL STRUCTURE

Williamson (1988) draws attention to the nature of the asset and its relationship to the type of financing.[20] In this perspective the financing decision
or the capital structure decision of using debt and equity is determined by
the governance functions that each performs. Equity is risk capital because
it entitles providers to residual cash flows. Equity holders are paid after all
other stakeholders are satisfied, and in return equity holders obtain ownership and control rights.[21] Debt, by contrast, has first rights on cash flows
from assets it finances and in return earns a fixed rate of return without
ownership or control rights. The required return for equity capital providers
is usually higher than debt because of the residual nature of equity returns;
equity is therefore more expensive than debt. Equity control rights allow
equity holders discretionary powers to make operational, investment, and
funding decisions concerning the firm. As long as debt holders receive their
promised payments, they do not have much say in how the firm is managed.

Equity is an intrusive form of capital because equity holders elect the
board of directors through which they exercise their control rights. The
board decides on the hiring of key management positions, decides on their
compensation, makes investing decisions and capital structure decisions,
and determines the strategic direction of the firm. Because equity holders
can manage the business directly and returns accrue to them only after all
other stakeholders are satisfied, equity focuses on maximizing the upside
potential from assets. This is why equity holders are more flexible than debt
holders under conditions of financial distress. Debt holders prefer liquidation if liquidation guarantees the recovery of their capital. Debt holders
therefore have incentives to sacrifice future value that may be possible by
keeping the firm as a going concern.

Equity holders have greater incentives to make sure the asset's upside
opportunities are given sufficient time, managerial attention, and investment for payoff to occur. Equity therefore is an economically superior
governance structure for assets with high upside potential which require
intrusive, discretionary decision making, and which have uncertain payoffs.
Debt is economically more efficient where discretionary, intrusive decision
making is unnecessary, where assets have limited upside, and where cash
flows are stable.

This perspective on financing as a mode of governance reveals that
equity should be used in assets with high growth opportunities where discretionary investment is needed. Equity better governs intangible assets
whose value depends on tacit knowledge, because financial distress leading
to liquidation can destroy such asset value while equity is more likely to
devote the attention necessary to unlock the value in these assets. Equity

also better governs assets with volatile cash flows and a high degree of uncertainty. We see that technology firms, knowledge-intensive firms (biotech, consulting partnerships), and high growth opportunity assets are almost always financed with equity. In these firms managerial compensation frequently takes the form of stock options since managers get to share in the upside that they are charged with creating.

Debt capital, which is cheaper than equity capital, is economically more efficient for financing low growth option, tangible assets with stable cash flows, like infrastructure assets, that are susceptible to agency cost problems and have low growth opportunities, less volatile cash flows, and less uncertain business risks. We have already alluded to the use of debt as a means of forcing managers to disgorge free cash flow and monitoring managerial behavior. In addition we will see that debt has certain attributes that make it more suitable for infrastructure assets. We now examine a final perspective on financing that uses option theory.

OPTIONS APPROACH

We have already seen that equity is a long call option on the value of the underlying assets. I now show that debt is the sale of a put option on the value of the assets of the firm.[22] Exhibit 4.2 shows the payoff from the sale of a put option on the value of the assets of the firm. Point S on the x-axis shows the point where asset value (present value of cash flows) equals interest and principal payments required to debt holders. The maximum benefit that debt holders can receive is their interest and principal payments, shown by the horizontal line above the x-axis. However, if asset value falls below point S, the level at which interest and principal payments must be made, then the value of the outstanding debt begins to fall. This payoff profile is exactly like the payoff profile from the sale of a put option. Debt is therefore a short put option.

What determines option value? Option theory teaches us that the volatility of the underlying asset price determines the value of options written or bought on the asset. Exhibit 4.3 shows the change in the Black-Scholes value of a European call option with a fixed expiration date and strike price for a change in volatility of the underlying asset price.*

---

*A European call option allows the option holder to exercise the option (i.e., buy the underlying for a call option) only on the option expiration date. The Black-Scholes value of an option is computed by using the formula derived by Professor Fisher Black and Myron Scholes.

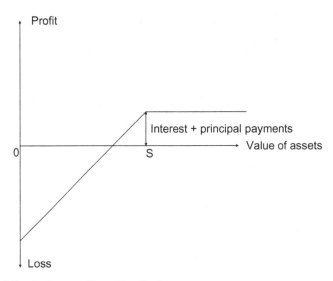

EXHIBIT 4.2   Debt as a Short Put Option

At σ volatility, the Black Scholes value of a European call option is C(σ). As the volatility increases, the option value increases at an increasing rate.

The greater the volatility, the higher is the value of the option. This makes sense because of the asymmetric payoff that option buyers and sellers experience. For example, a call option buyer makes a profit on his investment only when the price of the underlying asset exceeds the strike price. When the volatility of the asset price is high (i.e., the price takes a wide

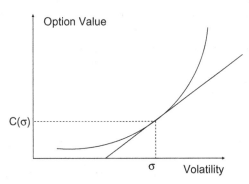

EXHIBIT 4.3   Option Value and Volatility

range of values), the probability that the asset price will exceed the strike price is high. Therefore the chance that the option buyer will profit from his investment is also high and consequently he is willing to pay a higher price to buy the call option.

We know that buyers benefit when the price of their asset increases. Since the price of call options depends on the volatility of the underlying asset price, an increase in asset price volatility increases the value of the call option on the asset. Call option buyers therefore benefit when the volatility of the underlying asset price increases. Similarly, the options perspective shows us why equity holders have an incentive to increase the volatility of the assets of the firm. High volatility increases the value of their holdings. We have seen that equity holders invest in risky assets and pass up low-risk positive, NPV projects when a firm is under financial distress. Such behavior is consistent with a desire to increase the volatility of the firm's assets.

We also noted that equity is a better governance structure for high growth option assets where the future payoffs are uncertain. The options perspective shows us that high growth option assets with uncertain payoffs are high-volatility assets. Consequently equity, will be the preferred instrument for funding these assets. The options perspective is consistent with empirical observations and our prior analysis that equity mostly funds high growth option assets. Equity is long volatility; equity holders gain when volatility increases and lose when volatility goes down.

We now apply the options perspective to debt. We saw that debt is the writing or sale of a put option. Sellers benefit when the price of the asset they have sold falls. Short-sellers can borrow the asset and sell it in anticipation of a fall in the price of the asset. If the price falls, they can buy the asset back at a lower price, return the borrowed asset, pay interest for the period over which the asset was borrowed, and keep the profit (the difference between the higher sale price and the lower purchase price) from the transaction. If the price rises, however, short-sellers incur a loss when they buy the asset back. The same logic applies to sellers of put options. The value of the put option depends on the volatility of the underlying asset. Debt holders benefit when the price of the put option falls because of their short position. Therefore a fall in the volatility of the underlying asset causes a fall in the price of the put option and benefits the option sellers. Debt holders are short volatility; in other words, they gain when volatility falls and lose when volatility increases.

We now apply our discussion of the options perspective to infrastructure assets. We know that infrastructure assets have limited growth options and stable cash flows. They operate in monopoly-like industries with low elasticity of demand. Infrastructure asset returns should therefore show low volatility. The probability that infrastructure returns will have very high

EXHIBIT 4.4 Infrastructure Life Cycle

Phase	Time Period	Governance
Due diligence	Varies with project complexity and regulatory regime	Equity and debt
Construction	Varies with project complexity	Equity
Operation	Asset life	Debt

returns or very low returns is quite low. Call options written on these assets should not be very valuable. This implies that the value of equity is likely to be low while value of debt is likely to remain high.

So far throughout the analysis we have not considered the different phases in an infrastructure asset's life. Exhibit 4.4 shows the different phases.

Life Cycle of Infrastructure Assets

During the construction phase the project needs to have intrusive governance since unexpected problems and situations frequently arise during construction. The construction phase needs to be managed decisively and innovatively to complete the project on time, without cost overruns, while meeting technical and design specifications.[23] Cash flows are volatile not in a revenue sense but in a cost sense, since the probability of cash outflows either exceeding or coming in under budget are high. Infrastructure assets do not behave like traditional infrastructure assets during the construction phase. For example, a majority of the problems encountered with the Eurotunnel project arose during the construction phase.[24] Equity is the correct governance structure during this phase because ownership provides the correct incentives, intrusive inspection, and decision-making rights to use capital efficiently. Once the asset is built and cash flows are stabilized, debt becomes the correct structure. This implies that the capital structure of infrastructure assets must change from the construction to the operational phase. The desire to maintain high leverage may also explain the practice of refinancing.

Finnerty notes that equity investors in infrastructure projects are "those parties who will directly benefit from the operation of the project: the purchasers of the project's output, the owners of any natural resource reserves the project will utilize, and the suppliers of essential products and services to the project, including engineering firms."[25] I attempt to explain this interesting fact in Chapter 5, which examines the risk of holdup in infrastructure projects based on recent theoretical work.[26] However, notably absent from this list are private or public equity investors. Infrastructure assets should be funded through a high proportion of debt. Debt is cheaper than equity, provides tax shields, aligns managerial and investor incentives, and is an economically superior form of governance for infrastructure assets. Debt also plays a role in mitigating other risks like threat of holdup from major buyers/suppliers and political risk, and is an important feature of the financing structure of project finance. Yet a majority of infrastructure funds prefer the private equity model of investing.[27] What are the implications for the private equity model in infrastructure? The next section examines this approach to investing.

PRIVATE EQUITY MODEL OF INVESTING

Megginson (2004) defines *private equity* as a professionally managed pool of money raised for the sole purpose of making intermediate-term, actively managed, direct equity investments in rapidly growing private companies, with a well-defined exit strategy.[28] Private equity implies the use of private equity capital in lieu of public equity capital and is used for venture capital, leveraged buyouts, mezzanine debt, and distressed debt investing.[29] Economically these are very different animals, and mezzanine debt is the use of debt with equity characteristics. Although a detailed exposition of each of these forms of private equity is beyond the scope of this book, I examine their common characteristics and their relevance to infrastructure investing.

A venture capital (VC) fund takes equity stakes in start-up firms before they acquire assets. VC funds invest in people and ideas and take on business risks in return for the upside. VC funds generate returns when they convince public equity markets about the growth potential of businesses they have invested in, since VC returns are mostly obtained from exiting their investments through initial public offerings (IPOs). VCs have the highest risk/return profile and are pure equity plays aiming for the maximum upside for their initial investment. As expected, VCs are found in information technology, biotechnology, and other industries that promise explosive growth with the downside limited to the initial investment of the fund. VC funds have generated a quarterly average return of 4.13 percent with 11.00 percent standard deviation, which indicates high risk and high return.[30]

An LBO involves purchasing the outstanding public equity of a firm with private equity and borrowed funds. The new capital structure of the former public firm comprises high leverage, up to 80 to 90 percent, with low equity contributions.[31] Unlike VC funds, LBOs are not used for greenfield ventures. Ideal LBO candidates are firms with a history of profitability, stable earnings, low debt on the balance sheet, and poor governance from diffuse shareholders who do not monitor management very well. LBOs add value to the firms they invest in with these strategies: improving operating efficiency, divestiture of noncore businesses in a conglomerate, merger and acquisition of synergistic companies, and incentivizing managers to innovate. Divestiture of nonsynergistic businesses in a conglomerate or a strategy of mergers and acquisitions, of course, does not require an LBO. The distinctive feature of LBOs is the use of high leverage to improve operational efficiency by focusing managerial incentives and forcing them to disgorge excess free cash flow that would be unwisely invested.[32] LBO funds earn returns for investors through fees and capital appreciation of initial equity boosted by leverage when the firm's shares are sold to public shareholders. LBO funds have generated average quarterly returns of 3.49 percent with lower standard deviation than VC funds of 5.66 percent.[33]

Mezzanine private equity funds are funds that provide debt. The name derives from the fact that mezzanine debt is placed ahead of equity but below senior and subordinated debt in the cash flow distribution ranking, as shown in Exhibit 4.5. It acts like a hybrid security of debt and equity

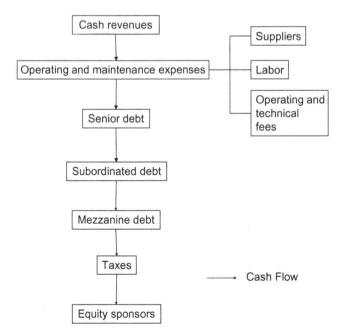

EXHIBIT 4.5 Cash Flow Distribution Ranking

for middle market firms. Firms to whom the high-yield debt market is closed use mezzanine debt. The size of mezzanine debt is small, at around $400 million, and pre-IPO firms use it to clean up their balance sheet while waiting for suitable market conditions.

Mezzanine debt providers therefore demand much higher coupon than regular debt since their position is more risky than senior debt. Mezzanine is also not considered as a lien on assets of the firm since senior debt has first rights on those assets. Mezzanine is considered an investment in the firm especially because mezzanine debt holders almost always receive additional warrants that entitle them to equity stakes on conversion. Mezzanine providers usually accept lower coupons for more warrants. Mezzanine debt therefore earns returns from high coupons and equity upside since mezzanine is mostly provided to firms that are likely to grow fast from a small base (middle-market firms, pre-IPO firms) and are not large enough to access the high-yield market. In this sense mezzanine compares well with VC and LBO firms, whose return profile is based on capturing the upside of equity. Mezzanine debt has generated average quarterly returns of 3.00 percent with standard deviation of 4.50 percent, lower returns than LBO funds with lower risk.[34]

Private equity in distressed debt involves buying the debt of distressed firms and converting it to equity. Investors seek to profit from firms with a good business model but a short-term cash flow problem. They pick up distressed debt that might trade at pennies on the dollar, convert the debt into equity, turn the company around through superior management, and exit the investment by taking the firm public. Similar to VCs, distressed debt investors take on significant business risk and are compensated when the firm's economic condition improves and the public equity markets buy the equity during an IPO or private placement. Distressed debt generated an average monthly return of 1.11 percent with a standard deviation of 6.05 percent for investors from 1990 to 2005.[35]

Our quick examination of private equity reveals that returns are generated from the exit event of selling equity to public shareholders from an IPO or private placement, or to strategic investors (this is called a secondary sale), or to other private equity funds (called a trade sale). Public investors are willing to pay a higher earning multiple for the equity of these firms for a number of reasons. They may believe the rejuvenated business growth story and upside potential of the firm or believe that the strategic fit of the firm results in synergies. The initial equity investments in LBO funds are boosted through leverage.

What are the implications for infrastructure assets? During the construction phase we saw that mezzanine debt and equity investments add value by mitigating construction risk and creating appropriate incentives to prevent cost overruns and encourage timely project completion. Once construction is complete and the project starts generating cash flows, exiting with a high return on equity is difficult because of illiquidity and the lack of growth options. As noted earlier, the assets are wasting assets and the cash flows are stable. Consequently the likelihood that existing equity investors can sell their stakes at high earning multiples is low. Also, the lack of a transparent high-volume market for these assets makes pricing difficult, and an exit may be achieved with minimal gains.

If capital gains from the initial investment is problematic due to the difficulty of exit, what options do equity holders have? Equity holders can certainly generate returns from dividend payments. But cash flows from the asset could equally well be paid as interest payments instead of dividend payments. Wells and Gleason (1995) note that debt obligations are more likely to be paid than equity obligations during expropriatory actions by countries even when the same party holds the debt that owns the equity.[36] For example, Exhibit 4.6 shows the distribution of cash flows from Aguas Argentinas and those accruing to equity holders.

During the nine-year period 1993 to 2001, Aguas Argentinas equity holders received US $109 million as dividends for four years, from 1996 to 2000. This represented a return over capital employed between 5 and 6 percent, insufficient to compensate for the cost of equity in Argentina. Over the same period, debt holders received interest payments of US $300 million, the government of Argentina received taxes of US $1.3 billion, and employees received wages of US $1.1 billion. Moreover, detractors charged that these equity payments were unreasonable and proof that Aguas profited by exploiting the consumers of Buenos Aires.

Interestingly, shareholders protected themselves in other ways. Aguas Argentinas's largest shareholder, the French group Suez, was also the operator of the project and entitled to 6 percent of gross operating margin as per its contract, in effect elevating its cash flow rights ahead of debt holders and the government while boosting its actual equity returns.[37] A similar class of equity investors, chiefly engineering and construction contractors like Bechtel and Asea Brown Boveri (ABB), take equity stakes in infrastructure assets. These firms consider equity investments akin to marketing investments that generate their main business of engineering, procurement, and construction (EPC). For example, Bechtel was an equity investor and the EPC contractor in the Quezon electricity project.[38] The EPC contracts in these projects are typically much larger than the individual equity investments (Bechtel had $12.5 million of equity at risk for a $465 million EPC contract in the Quezon project); the investments make sense as long as the net profit margin from the EPC contracts exceeds the equity investment.

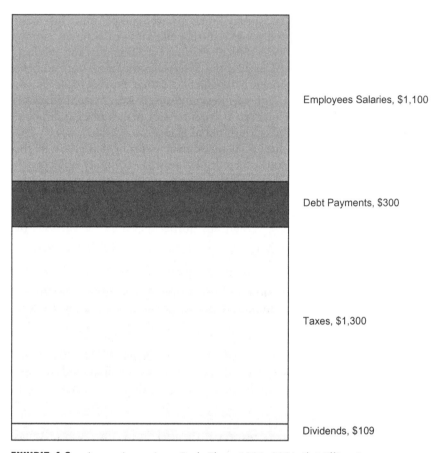

Employees Salaries, $1,100

Debt Payments, $300

Taxes, $1,300

Dividends, $109

EXHIBIT 4.6   Aguas Argentinas Cash Flow, 1993–2001 ($ Millions)

Such specialized equity investors enjoy cash flow rights ahead of debt holders' interest, principal payments, tax payments, and dividend payments to purely financial equity investors. The advantage of holding equity for the purely financial equity investors lies in control rights and future growth prospects, for which equity investors subordinate their cash flow rights to all other stakeholders. Interest payments, for example, are paid before taxes. If tax rates change, interest payments are not at risk while dividends are liable to be reduced. Not only is political risk and creeping expropriation a significant risk for infrastructure assets, but the value of equity holder control rights and claim to future growth is minimal. Chapter 6 examines creeping expropriation and political risk in detail.

Is it possible to find strategic buyers who may pay a premium because of strategic fit reasons? Although it is certainly possible to find firms with infrastructure asset portfolios, individual infrastructure assets are highly idiosyncratic with unique market and regulatory risks. For example, Intergen, with a portfolio of power plants in developing countries like China, Philippines, Mexico, and Turkey, along with the United Kingdom and the Netherlands, has changed ownership twice over a 13-year period. Intergen was started in 1995 by Shell (68 percent) and Bechtel (32 percent).[39] The firm was bought by Ontario Teachers' Pension Plan (OTPP) and AIG Highstar Capital for $1.75 billion in 2005 with equal contributions of $0.875 billion each. OTPP and AIG Highstar also took over $3.6 billion in debt. After OTPP and AIG Highstar took over Intergen, the firm increased its power plant portfolio from 10 to 12 plants.

AIG Highstar exited from Intergen in June 2008 with a $1.1 billion sale to GMR Infrastructure Limited, an Indian infrastructure company.[40] GMR Infrastructure paid an average price of $360,000 per megawatt of generating capacity, which was less than half the replacement value of the assets. GMR Infrastructure needed the additional generating capacity to increase its electricity generating portfolio to 4,000 megawatts, allowing it to meet the minimum threshold established by the Indian government for bidding on ultra megawatt power plants planned across India. Although I cannot extrapolate the distribution of returns that a private equity model is likely to generate from a single example, my analysis suggests that returns are unlikely to mimic those available to traditional private equity assets.

The Intergen example shows the use of leverage at two levels: at the level of Intergen's balance sheet and at each individual power plant's level. Cash flows from Intergen's assets must repay debt on Intergen's balance sheet, and the high leverage boosts equity returns. Intergen's assets are project financed with high debt. Each power plant is an independent entity with no recourse to Intergen's balance sheet. The leverage at each plant is also around 75 percent. This means that dividend payments from the power plants must service Intergen debt.

The analogous private equity structure can use debt both at the fund level and at each individual investment level. If leverage is employed at the fund level, the strategy levers up returns to fund investors and allows the fund to seek larger capital investments competing for deals larger than what the fund could otherwise have access to. In the infrastructure space, however, equity returns from individual assets, chiefly in the form of dividends, flow through to the fund. The infrastructure fund relies on these cash flows to repay debt at the fund level and generate returns to fund investors. Later chapters show that returns to equity holders in infrastructure are particularly risky. Exhibit 4.7 shows debt at the fund level and equity cash flows

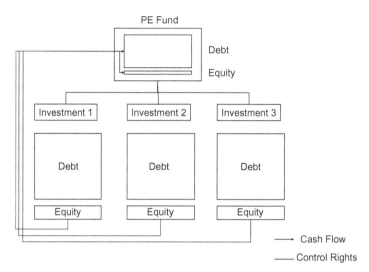

EXHIBIT 4.7   Debt at Fund Level versus Debt at Individual Asset Level

from each investment flowing to fund-level debt holders before reaching equity fund investors.

Infrastructure funds have about 40 percent leverage at the fund level in addition to leverage at the investment level.[41] Some Australian-listed infrastructure funds carried higher leverage. For example, Babcock and Brown Infrastructure (BBI) supported A\$14.18 billion in assets with A\$2.9 billion in equity. In 2009 BBI was forced to sell its assets to reduce its debt burden and at last count had written off A\$920 million in impairment charges.[42] Its share price dropped from A\$2.00 in 2007 to A\$0.02 and has recovered since to A\$0.06. Admittedly the financial crisis of 2008 played a role in BBI's troubles, yet leverage at the fund level is risky for infrastructure funds.

Our analysis so far suggests that the traditional private equity strategy of high leverage in each individual investment actually fits infrastructure characteristics. However, equity investors in infrastructure with specific economic interests in the assets rather than purely financial equity interests, like the asset operators, EPC contractors, and buyers from or sellers to the infrastructure assets, mitigate the political risks they face by either altering their cash flow seniority or improving their bargaining positions. Traditional private equity investors who are purely financial equity investors are unlikely to possess these capabilities. It is of course possible that purely financial equity holders like private equity could mitigate political risk through superior political risk management. To add value through risk mitigation, private equity investors need to broaden their traditional skill sets.

I noted in Chapter 2 that infrastructure assets are vulnerable to political risk and that firms must mitigate or hedge these risks. Apart from hedging through insurance and using financial engineering to mitigate political risk, asset managers need to design and execute political risk management strategies. I examine these strategies in Chapter 6 and note that these strategies are difficult for debt holders to execute without legal rights to direct management, although debt holders do influence the probability and outcome of expropriatory holdup. Skilled managers and equity owners are necessary for building relationships with the community, influencing government policies, and selecting and aligning with suitable local partners in order to mitigate political risk. This suggests that equity holders have a role to play in selecting, motivating, and monitoring managers to fulfill the function of political risk mitigation. The private equity form of governance may have some advantages in infrastructure investing in developing countries. Even though most infrastructure funds focus on investing in North America and Western Europe where political risk is perceived to be low, infrastructure engenders political risk and consequently this particular function of equity is valuable. However, most infrastructure funds are unused to unstable political environments and consequently need to develop political capabilities.

Guillen and Garcia-Canal (2009) analyze the growth of new multinational enterprises (MNEs) from the BRIC countries and their great inroads into the global economy.[43] They note that the new multinationals lack the resources and capabilities of established MNEs but make up for it with political capabilities, acquired in dealing with their own discretionary and/or unstable governments. These capabilities allow multinationals from the emerging countries to succeed in countries characterized by a weak institutional environment. In sum, the private equity model of investing where equity holders add value through superior political capabilities is appropriate for infrastructure investing in developing countries. For now the analysis suggests that the private equity model of infrastructure investing needs to be reevaluated. Apparently this reevaluation is in progress, since Gravis Capital Partners launched the first infrastructure fund exclusively investing in UK infrastructure debt in June 2009.[44]

Finally, infrastructure investment horizons are around 15 years or more. The concession period for the City of Chicago's parking meters taken over by Morgan Stanley Infrastructure Partners is 75 years,[45] while the concession period for the Chicago Skyway Toll Bridge is 99 years.[46] Traditional private equity investment horizons are about five to seven years since that is the time it takes to take over assets, improve their performance, and exit. The same is not true of infrastructure.

CONCLUSION

This chapter drew on insights from capital structure theories to determine the optimum structure for infrastructure asset governance. Infrastructure asset characteristics tend to favor debt over equity because debt and equity engender different incentives for managers. Debt helps solve the problem of monitoring managers by forcing operational efficiency in order to meet scheduled and legally binding interest and principal payments. Debt also helps force free cash flow to be paid out to capital providers and prevents managerial waste and perquisites. The governance and options perspectives on capital structure showed us that debt matches infrastructure asset characteristics and is a less costly form of governance since these assets have limited growth options which do not require intrusive and discretionary management. However, during the construction phase, equity is a better governance mode since its intrusive nature and control rights engender the right incentives needed to handle the risk of time and cost overruns. For investors considering the private equity model of infrastructure investing, we advise caution because infrastructure assets are illiquid, growth options are limited, and purely financial equity investments face risks from creeping expropriation or political risk. Chapter 6 explores how capital structure helps mitigate political risk.

But first, Chapter 5 examines the difficult problem of holdup that affects infrastructure assets and in which capital structure also plays an important part.

CHAPTER 5

Infrastructure and the Threat of Holdup

It sometimes happens that one man has all the toil, and another all the profit.

—Aesop's Fables

In Chapter 4 I examined debt and equity as financing forms and examined their relationship to infrastructure characteristics. I argued that financing forms serve as governance structures and that debt is a superior governance structure to equity in the case of infrastructure assets. The result was based on infrastructure characteristics of stable cash flows, low growth options, the tangible nature of assets, and the agency costs arising from these characteristics.

In this chapter I examine the risks arising from these characteristics that investors are exposed to. In addition to basic business risks that all investments face, infrastructure investors bear the risk of holdup from opportunistic suppliers/buyers and political risk in the form of creeping expropriation. I first examine these major risks. The following section examines the risk of holdup and begins with a brief description of the theory of transaction cost economics that helps us understand how the threat of holdup arises and how it is mitigated. Chapter 6 examines political risk.

TRANSACTION COST ECONOMICS

Transaction cost economics traces its roots to Coase (1937), who asked a deceptively simple question: Why do firms exist when production can be carried on without any organization?[1] Since then the theoretical and empirical research on transaction cost economics has been extensive, and Coase received the Nobel Prize in economics in 1991 for his pioneering work.*

A firm begins when an entrepreneur hires employees who are compensated for producing goods and services. The same goods can be produced by contracting out the individual labor of the employees and renting the machines instead of owning them. Firms produce goods and services through transactions that occur within the firm. These transactions can be replicated through a market mechanism; in other words, production can be contracted for directly from the market. Firms certainly buy goods and services from the market as well as make goods and services internally.

How do firms decide which transactions to conduct internally and which transactions to contract out? The analysis proceeds from the observation that the cost of goods bought and sold in the market is not just the price of the good. Individuals transacting through a market incur additional costs, or *transaction costs*. These costs include information costs, search costs, bargaining costs, monitoring and contract enforcement costs, and, vitally, costs from the threat of holdup. Information costs relate to the cost of establishing the veracity of the seller's claims and costs from information asymmetry between the buyer and the seller. Search costs relate to the costs of searching for the best price, the right product, or the right person with the required qualifications. Bargaining costs relate to the costs of negotiating and reaching agreement on the terms of the trade. Monitoring and enforcement costs relate to the cost of ensuring that the seller follows the terms of the contract and enforcing the contract when the seller does not. Firms internalize transactions when transaction costs make market transactions costlier than production within the firm.

When would transaction costs outside the firm exceed costs inside the firm? Williamson (1975) establishes that the determinants of these costs are frequency, specificity, uncertainty, limited rationality, and opportunistic behavior.[2] Clearly, if the entrepreneur needs recurring transactions, it is more expensive to negotiate multiple contracts when a single employment contract will achieve the same result. The frequency with which the contract needs to be negotiated therefore determines whether a transaction is internalized within the firm.

The most important transaction cost is the cost of holdup, which arises from the nature of the transaction. Infrastructure assets are susceptible to costs from holdup because of asset specificity. I examine asset specificity and the costs from holdup in greater detail in the following section.

---

* The Nobel Prize was awarded to Ronald Coase for "The Nature of the Firm" and "The Problem of Social Cost."

Asset Specificity

Firms internalize transactions when transactions have high asset specificity. Asset specificity is present when transactions require specialized investments—in other words, investments have small or no value to alternative users or uses. The concept of asset specificity lies at the heart of the holdup problem.

Consider a gas supplier building a pipeline that supplies its gas to an electricity plant. The gas supplier can use the pipeline only for supplying gas to the electricity plant. Its value to any other user or for any other use is essentially zero. The gas supplier may have other customers for its gas and the electricity plant could obtain its inputs through contracts with other suppliers. The gas supplier and the electricity plant need not be operating as monopolists. However, once the gas supplier builds the pipeline, it is locked into a bilateral monopoly relationship with the electricity plant.

The investment creates what Williamson calls a *fundamental transformation* between the parties to the transaction.[3] An ex ante large-numbers bidding competition is transformed into a bilateral trading relationship ex post. The noteworthy aspect of this analysis is the effect of time and the transformation of the relationship between the two parties. Ex ante, or before the investment is made, a large number of buyers are competing to buy the gas from the gas supplier. Similarly, there may be a large number of suppliers willing to sell to the electric utility. However, ex post, or after the pipeline is built, the supplier and the utility are locked into a bilateral negotiating relationship. Instead of a large number of buyers or sellers, they must bargain with each other. In this instance the asset-specific transaction results in a bilateral relationship; other instances may result in a very few players bargaining among themselves. Such a situation is a small-numbers bargaining situation. What is the effect of small-numbers bargaining?

First we note that the investment itself is sunk since it cannot be reversed easily and it can only be recovered through the revenues generated from transportation of gas. The utility must pay the gas supplier as per the terms agreed upon before the pipeline is built and continue to do so over a long period of time to enable the gas supplier to recoup his investment. The utility, however, may not adhere to the terms it agreed to before the pipeline was built. It may resort to opportunistic behavior. Opportunistic behavior extends the motivation of self-interest that is expected to guide the actions of economic agents. Self-interested agents, while seeking to maximize their utility, obey rules and keep promises. Opportunistic behavior is the seeking of self-interest with guile.

Guile relates to false promises. It is defined by Williamson as "the making of false or empty, that is, self-disbelieved, threats and promises in

the expectation that individual advantage will thereby be realized."
Opportunism is the proclivity of the agent to resort to opportunistic behavior and in Williamson's model is a result of human nature. He does not specify the mechanism by which it can be created or reduced. For now let us ignore the moral, behavioral, contextual, and cultural dimensions of opportunism and how these reduce or aggravate opportunistic behavior.[4] To further this analysis we do not need to assume that the electric utility will resort to opportunistic behavior, only that it *can* resort to such behavior. We do not even need to assume that the electric utility is prone to immoral behavior; changing business conditions over the course of the pipeline's lifetime can cause a change in the utility's behavior. The utility can ask for and pay a lower rate than the promised rate for the gas.

Why should the gas supplier accede to this behavior? Note that the gas supplier incurring the sunk costs finds it economically feasible to continue using the asset as long as revenues are equal to variable costs. Even when revenues are less than fixed costs, as long as they are greater than variable costs, the difference (revenues – variable costs > 0) reduces total fixed costs. The gas supplier therefore suffers a greater loss of total fixed costs if he closes the pipeline than if he remains open. This does not include the costs of constructing the pipeline, however, since these costs are sunk. The utility can therefore reduce payments to the gas supplier till they equal the variable costs of the pipeline and can thereby *hold up* the gas supplier. Thus the electric utility using the asset can behave opportunistically and appropriate all the revenues in excess of variable costs, leaving the gas supplier with very poor returns on its sunk capital.[5]

Exhibit 5.1 shows a stylized representation of holdup. Notice that our analysis falls apart absent small-numbers bargaining, because if the gas can easily be sold to other buyers the electric utility cannot hold up the supplier. The situation would be very different, for instance, if the gas supplier could use tankers to supply the gas instead of using a pipeline. Tankers can be diverted to other buyers with little cost, and therefore tankers have low asset specificity. They can also be resold, and therefore an investment in tankers is not a sunk investment. Certainly the ex post incentives of the electric utility are known to the gas supplier ex ante. Therefore, unless a solution is found to prevent holdup, the investment will not be made. The gas supplier will either forego the investment or use tankers, which are more expensive and economically inefficient for transporting the gas.

We note that a lack of investment is socially undesirable because it prevents welfare-enhancing trade between the gas supplier and the electric utility from occurring. Firms internalize transactions in order to prevent holdup. In our example, the gas supplier and electricity plant merging under common ownership (internalization) can solve the holdup problem. There

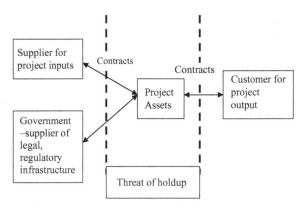

EXHIBIT 5.1   Threat of Holdup

are certainly other solutions to the holdup problem. I examine these solutions for mitigating holdup in a later section.

Incomplete Contracts

Holdup problems are essentially contract violations, which are more likely to occur under conditions of asset specificity, sunk costs, and small-numbers bargaining. Williamson (1985) notes that firms internalize transactions under conditions of uncertainty and limited rationality.[6] Under these conditions, firms eschew market-based contracts since they are likely to be incomplete. The term *incomplete* means that the parties to the contract are ex ante unable to incorporate every eventuality that may affect the transaction ex post.[7] In other words, the parties to the contract cannot anticipate the future and consequently cannot address every eventuality at the time of writing. Therefore, when unanticipated eventualities crop up in the future, the parties to the contract need to renegotiate the original terms of the contract. Contracts are likely to be incomplete when the future is highly uncertain. When conditions are uncertain and a renegotiation is highly likely, it makes sense for the firm to internalize the transaction rather than relying on an external contract.

The final condition necessary for incomplete contracts relates to the condition of the contracting parties' limited competence in contract design. In this situation the contracting parties cannot anticipate the future eventualities simply because of limited cognitive capabilities and consequently cannot write the contracts to cover these eventualities. The contracting parties, however, do realize that their cognitive abilities are limited and prefer to internalize the transaction instead of relying on market contracts.

In the case of infrastructure assets, we have seen that operational uncertainties are low while political uncertainties are high. The guiding principle in recognizing asset specificity is that it occurs when an investment creates a lock-in for the investor because the investment cannot be redeployed to another user or another use.

Infrastructure assets are particularly prone to holdup problems because of large sunk costs, low variable costs, asset specificity, small-numbers bargaining situations, and the long duration of payback required to recoup the initial investment. Oil and gas pipelines, electricity plants supplying electricity to a monopoly distribution company, and electricity plants receiving fuel supplies from monopoly suppliers are susceptible to holdup because low variable costs create incentives for the counterparty to hold up the investor. Infrastructure assets like transportation, fixed line telecommunications, and water supply networks are tied to fixed locations. They are susceptible to holdup from governments since governments are suppliers of legal infrastructure like law and order, regulatory infrastructure like taxes, restrictions on toll increases, reporting policies, repatriation rules, and so on. Interestingly, roads, rails, and fixed telecommunication lines are not susceptible to holdup from users because small-numbers bargaining is absent. In fact, users can be subject to holdup if the road or rail links are the only available means of transportation, a fact that governments take quite seriously. I examine the case of governments holding up investors in the next chapter under the rubric of political risk, since there are significant differences between sovereign holdup and counterparty holdup, even though government expropriation is a form of opportunistic behavior.

A number of empirical studies demonstrate the problem of small-numbers bargaining. Lieberman's (1991) empirical study of the organic chemical industry uses supplier concentration or small number of suppliers as a proxy for the existence of the holdup problem.[8] Small-numbers bargaining is more likely when there is a small number of suppliers as well as buyers since these parties can potentially appropriate revenues arising from sunk investments.

It is difficult to identify and measure the extent of the holdup problem, especially because it is difficult to measure asset specificity. Lieberman measures supplier concentration by using the reciprocal of the total number of upstream suppliers for every firm in his sample. Lieberman (1991) uses two measures of asset specificity: total plant investment costs as a measure of sunk costs and the need to invest in input pipelines. He finds that vertical integration is strongly supported when sunk costs in the form of total plant investments are high and when the inputs are supplied through pipelines built specifically for that purpose. A small number of suppliers is also positively related to vertical integration, although the results are not strongly supported. These findings are consistent with the analysis that lock-in is created by the investment in the pipelines along with sunk costs. The sidebar shows the example of transaction cost economics (TCE) and Standard Oil.

TRANSACTION COST ECONOMICS AND STANDARD OIL

It is instructive to examine the economic strategy of John D. Rockefeller and Standard Oil in the nineteenth century. In 1865, after oil was discovered in Pennsylvania and Ohio, Rockefeller invested $4,000 in a refinery that refined crude oil into kerosene for illumination instead of investing in oil production. His Standard Oil Company of Ohio consolidated refining capacity and by 1880 controlled 90 percent of U.S. refining capacity. Standard Oil's preferred competitive strategy was to drop prices and buy up competing refiners who could not match the lower prices.

How could Standard Oil offer lower prices while its competition could not? By focusing on two aspects of the emerging oil industry. First, Standard Oil extracted economies of scale from its refining operations, and as it increased its scale it drove hard bargains with the upstream oil extraction companies. The oil extraction companies could have fought off Standard Oil's demands if they could have transported their oil to other refiners. They could not because oil producers were small, fragmented suppliers.

Second, Standard Oil concentrated on transportation of oil from the oil wells. Initially oil was transported by the railway companies. Standard Oil began to invest in pipelines instead, foreseeing that pipelines were far more economical than railways in transporting oil and thereby also preventing the railways from holding them hostage to high freight rates. Instead, Standard Oil struck secret bargains with the railway companies, agreeing to pay them for oil transported on Standard Oil–owned pipelines in return for setting high freight rates for Standard Oil's competition. The railway companies accepted this arrangement, collecting bountiful fees from Standard Oil for oil they did not even transport, and helping Standard Oil drive its competition into bankruptcy by setting high freight rates.* By the beginning of the 1880s Standard Oil owned 35,000 miles of the 40,000 miles of oil pipelines in the United States.

(Continued)

An examination of Standard Oil's net profits between 1891 and 1911 shows that of the $1,280 million in profits, $532 million came from transportation of oil, $307 million came from marketing, $259 million came from refining, and a paltry $170 million came from extraction.[†] Standard Oil's success owes much to its understanding of opportunistic behavior, holdup, and transaction cost economics.

[*]See Alfred D. Chandler, Jr., *The Standard Oil Company—Combination, Consolidation, and Integration* (Abridged) (B), HBS Case #9-391-244 (Boston, MA: Harvard Business School Publishing, 1993), 5.
[†]See Rondo E. Cameron, Valeri Ivanovich Bovykin, and B. V. Anan'ich, eds., *International Banking and Multinational Enterprise: 1870-1914* (New York: Oxford University Press, 1991), 444.

Investors must therefore discourage opportunistic behavior before they commit to large sunk costs. This is true even for assets that are in operation, since returns on invested capital require the counterparties to honor their ex ante contractual obligations. The next section examines the mechanisms for discouraging opportunistic behavior.

SOLUTIONS FOR THE HOLDUP PROBLEM

Klein, Crawford, and Alchian (1978) point out that the holdup problem arises because of investment by one transacting party in assets that are specific to the second transacting party—in other words, the investing party's alternative to replacing the transaction or the counterparty is too costly. Theoretical and empirical research presents three distinct solutions to the holdup problem:

- *Long-term contracts that rely on enforcement by third parties like the courts.* This solution approaches the holdup problem from the incomplete contract perspective. Because contracts do not account for all states of nature, a party to the contract may end up with unfavorable terms of trade and therefore be subject to holdup or be forced to trade. Now the party can renegotiate the contract by threatening to sue, or it can force the courts to intercede by filing suit. This strand of research explores the conditions under which contracts can be completed by renegotiation or by court intervention.

- *Vertical integration.* In this case, the possibility of opportunistic behavior is eliminated if both the transacting parties are combined under single ownership. The vertical integration solution assumes that contracts between the transacting parties will not be sufficient to prevent holdup.
- *The use of capital structure, particularly debt.* Debt is presented as a means of reducing the cash flow available for expropriation. It is also presented as a means of improving the ex post bargaining position of the investing party by making credible threats of bankruptcy in some models and threats of underinvestment in others.

I examine each of these solutions in the following sections in the context of infrastructure assets.

Long-Term Contracts

Investors can discourage opportunistic behavior by long-duration contracts, extending up to and beyond 25 years. Long-term contracts make economic sense only between bilateral monopolists, a situation created by durable transaction-specific investments (Joskow, 1985).[9] To see this, let's examine the incentives of a monopoly supplier with multiple buyers and the opposite situation of a monopoly buyer with multiple suppliers. When multiple buyers exist (i.e., specific investments are not required to sell output), a monopolist supplier firm has little incentive to enter into a contract and sell most of its output to only one buyer among the many. When a firm competes with other suppliers to sell to a single buyer, the buyer has little incentive to enter into a contract. Long-term contracts therefore make economic sense between bilateral monopolists created through durable transaction-specific investments. Long-term contracts prevent the counterparties from easily changing the terms of trade to their advantage.

Long-term contracts are a solution because the analysis of the holdup problem follows from an analysis of incomplete contracts. We know that contract incompleteness means that the contract is insufficiently contingent and the parties to the contract are unable to anticipate and account for every state of nature in the contract. However, specific investments are required to be made *before* the state of nature is revealed, and this investment is either fully or partially unrecoverable. As a result, the party making the investment faces a holdup problem if it must contend with unfavorable terms of trade. In this situation the contract can be breached or renegotiated. A successful renegotiation, in the sense that the parties agree to trade and realize the social return on investment, solves the holdup problem. A breach of contract occurs if the renegotiation fails. In this instance, the parties approach the courts and the courts grant a remedy. Exhibit 5.2 shows the sequence of events over time.

Among the most common remedies awarded by courts for breach of contract are the *expectation damages* remedy and the *specific performance* remedy. As described by A. S. Edlin and S. Reichelstein, under expectation damages a buyer (seller) can unilaterally breach a contract if she pays the seller (buyer) an amount equal to what her profits would have been under performance of the contract, measured ex post.[10] Under the specific performance remedy, unilateral breach of contract is not possible since either party can insist that the contract be performed according to its terms.[11] The expectation damages remedy is the more common remedy while the specific performance remedy is usually awarded for the sale of heirlooms or priceless works of art when the courts require a defaulting seller to deliver the work of art to the buyer. Each of these remedies results in different incentives depending on whether a single party makes the specific investment or whether both contracting parties need to make specific investments.

Let us first consider the case of one party making the specific investment. The ex ante contract is likely to be breached when it is no longer optimal for the contracting parties to trade the agreed-upon quantity. The two conditions or states of nature are either (1) it is optimal to trade less quantity than the contract stipulates, or (2) it is optimal to trade a greater quantity than the contract stipulates. Let us analyze first that state of nature when fulfillment of the contract is socially harmful and it is efficient to trade less quantity than the contract requires. When courts grant the

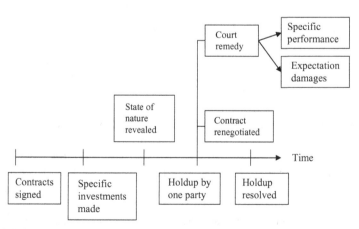

EXHIBIT 5.2   Holdup as Incomplete Contract

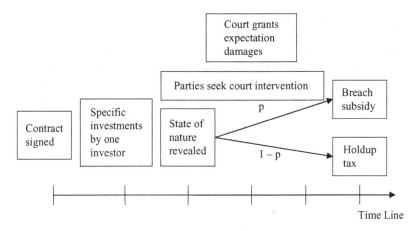

Investor's expected value = p * (Breach subsidy) + (1 − p) * (Holdup tax)

Where p = Probability of state of nature

EXHIBIT 5.3   Expectation Damages Remedy for Breach of Contract

expectation damages remedy, the remedy may encourage parties to overinvest because this remedy causes a higher return to the investing party than is socially valuable. In this situation the expectation damages remedy compensates a party even when an investment creates no social value and it is inefficient for the parties to trade. This excess of realized return over the socially desirable return is, in effect, a breach subsidy and it encourages overinvestment.[12]

We know that the holdup problem leads to underinvestment because parties making asset-specific sunk investments are, ex ante, aware of the threat of ex post opportunistic behavior and choose to forego these investments. In contingencies where it is efficient to trade higher quantities than the contract requires, parties must bargain over the return from the excess quantities not specified in the contract. The investing party in this instance faces a holdup tax, which discourages investment. If legal enforcement of specific performance or expectation damages is costless and information is symmetric, then contracts provide efficient investment incentives for one investing party because the holdup tax is balanced against the breach subsidy. See Exhibit 5.3 for two states of nature and the efficient investment incentives arising from the remedy of expectation damages.

In some states of nature the investing party gets a breach subsidy and in other states he gets a holdup tax. But on average, for a risk-neutral investor the breach remedy of expectation damages solves the holdup problem.

What happens when both parties must make specific investments? The remedy of expectation damages in this situation does not provide efficient investment incentives. When the court awards expectation damages to one party it penalizes the second party, thus jeopardizing its specific investment. The expectation damages remedy is not symmetrical for both parties and, ex ante, does not provide correct incentives for optimum investment. The second remedy of specific performance, however, forces a party demanding the holdup tax to renegotiate with the party facing the holdup tax. The specific performance remedy allows the parties to solve bilateral investment problems provided that both parties get a constant share of the bargaining surplus.

Edlin and Reichelstein argue that vertical integration as a solution for the holdup problem is efficient when courts do not grant specific performance as a breach remedy. In this instance, an integrated firm will be able to facilitate efficient trade between the divisions with the headquarters negotiating interdivisional transfer pricing which the specific performance remedy governs.

The use of long-term contracts to solve the holdup problem, however, depends on the intervention of a court or a legal regime with well-established breach-of-contract remedies that parties to the contract can reasonably rely on. Such a legal regime with enforcement powers is either inefficient or weak in a host of developing countries. As we saw in Chapter 1, the demand for infrastructure is highest in developing countries. It is unlikely that investors can rely solely on long-term contracts to prevent opportunistic behavior.

The second issue with long-term contracts governs the relationship of the investing parties with sovereign entities like governments. I analyze the challenges of long-term contracts between firms and sovereign entities and firms that sovereign entities own in Chapter 6. Moreover, even when investors can rely on the legal regime, contracts are not costless to enforce. Lawsuits are not effective when there are large delays and when legal costs are high. Tirole (1990) points out that there is substantial empirical evidence on the costs of litigation.[13] The solution of long-term contracts, therefore, has drawbacks when investing in countries with weak legal institutions and when legal costs are significant. In the next section I examine the solution of vertical integration and analyze its applicability for infrastructure assets.

Vertical Integration

Single ownership of specific investments or vertical integration solves the holdup problem because all possibilities for opportunistic behavior are eliminated by eliminating the contract counterparty. In our previous example, combining the gas supplier, pipeline, and electricity plants under single ownership eliminates the incentives of the electricity plant to appropriate the revenues of the pipeline in excess of variable costs. Exhibit 5.4 shows backward integration. Vertical integration is effective when contracts are no longer sufficient to prevent opportunistic behavior. This is likely to be the case when cash flows available for expropriation by one party are large, increasing incentives for opportunistic behavior.[14] In this instance, contracts may not be sufficient to prevent opportunistic behavior. We noted that infrastructure assets generate large amounts of free cash flow due to low variable costs, monopoly-like positions, and inelasticity of demand. The attraction for opportunistic behavior is therefore likely to be strong.

However, there are costs to vertical integration, too. For example, coordination costs increase with the size of the firm. Administering and controlling unrelated businesses[15] (e.g., electricity generation with natural gas extraction) might impose costs of learning, operating dissynergies, increased complexities leading to diseconomies of scale and scope, and problems of moral hazard among divisional managers. Grossman and Hart (1986) argue that a vertical integration only makes sense if the increased control over the asset arising from ownership is economically efficient.[16] Vertical integration is economically efficient when the benefits from vertical integration outweigh the costs. Single ownership essentially transfers control rights for both sets of assets to the single owner. The owner whose asset has been purchased sells his control rights. If a division of control rights could have been specified precisely in the original contract, then vertical integration is not efficient because the contract would function like a vertical integration without taking on the costs of vertical integration.

We assume that we can enforce such a contract through the courts. However, we know that some specific rights are too costly to be included in contracts, because they are noncontractible or inefficient to monitor. In

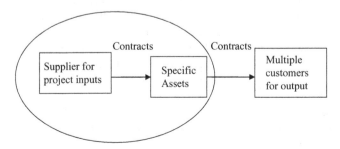

EXHIBIT 5.4 Backward Vertical Integration

particular, Grossman and Hart point out that control rights for future investments and managerial inefficiencies are two elements of performance that cannot be written into an ex ante contract without incurring costs from inflexibility and rigidity. Their key insight is that in a vertical integration, *residual rights* are transferred to the owners—that is, rights not specified in the contract are transferred to the owner. This reallocation of residual rights increases the rights of control for the owners and reduces the rights of control for the nonowners.

The transfer of residual rights of control to one of the contracting parties improves efficiency when the increase in productivity of the buyer due to increased control is greater than the decrease in productivity of the seller due to loss of control. The increase in productivity is likely to be high when the assets under consideration have high future growth options or when it is difficult to monitor managers of the separate firms. We know that infrastructure assets have limited high future growth options. Also, the problem of monitoring managers of infrastructure assets has other solutions, like high debt, that do not assume the costs of vertical integration. As such, theoretically, vertical integration may not be the most efficient solution to the holdup problem that plagues infrastructure assets. Empirically we observe that electricity generators rarely purchase their coal, gas, or oil suppliers or own the fuel transmission assets, such as pipelines. Joint ownership of pipelines and generating plants is more common. Chapter 7 examines the structure of joint ownership in the context of project finance. However, electricity generation firms own transmission and distribution assets. Forward integration is more common possibly because the benefits of integration are higher than the costs.

There are other instances when vertical integration is economically more efficient than relying on contracts. In a complex environment of cost as well as revenue volatility, the vertically integrated firm is more efficient than long-term contracts. High volatility implies that contracts are more likely to remain incomplete since the parties cannot incorporate all the possible eventualities in their contract. This leaves room for renegotiations and holdup. Under these conditions, Wiggins (1990) shows that long-term contracts are able to handle either input cost shocks or shocks to revenues from output price shocks but not both simultaneously.[17] Suppliers have an incentive to inflate cost shocks to inputs, thereby reallocating profits or holding up the firm. Additionally, artificial input cost inflation causes the firm to set output incorrectly.

Vertical integration surmounts the incentive to reallocate profits by breaking the link between compensation and the performance of a particular stage of production. Divisional managers in an integrated firm are compensated on the basis of the overall firm's performance and therefore have no incentive to distort the true nature of the cost shocks. Information flows also improve under integration.

A similar logic operates on the buyer's side. Buyers have an incentive to inflate demand destruction, thereby appropriating profits through revenue discounts in conditions of demand volatility. Forward integration allows the firm to observe demand shocks accurately. The firm can therefore set output to incorporate cost shocks as well as revenue shocks efficiently. Better information flows make the vertically integrated firm better able to handle upstream shocks to input costs as well as downstream shocks to output revenues. Riordan (1989) also shows that vertical integration solves the holdup problem because it facilitates improved information flow between the supplier and the downstream firm. In his model the downstream firm is better able to observe the input price.[18]

In the context of infrastructure assets we need to analyze the probability of input and output shocks. Electricity generation, refining, and petrochemical industries are susceptible to input shocks while toll roads, railways, and telecommunications are susceptible to demand shocks or output shocks. Wiggins notes that long-term contracts handle one type of shock quite well. We noted that demand inelasticity and regulated environments make infrastructure assets less volatile. Additionally, the probability of asymmetric information flows distorting output is limited for infrastructure assets. Vertical integration therefore seems to add more costs than benefits.

How does the empirical evidence stack up for vertical integration as a solution for holdup? There is a large body of empirical work on vertical integration; I examine two studies here for a flavor of the approaches and methods used by researchers. MacDonald (1985) empirically tests for vertical integration as a solution to the threat of opportunistic behavior by using seller and buyer concentration to measure small-numbers bargaining and capital intensity to measure sunk costs.[19] He uses a special report of the 1977 Census of Manufacturers, "Distribution of Sales by Class of Customer," that provides detailed information about the sector and ownership of buyers of shipments from manufacturing plants. The report details the proportion of industry shipments, in total and by sector of buyer, that are allocated internally or to other establishments of the firm and externally through market exchange. MacDonald finds that vertical integration increases as seller and buyer concentration increase. He also finds that capital-intensive industries have a greater extent of vertical integration.

Levy (1985) tests for vertical integration as a response to reduce costs from small-numbers bargaining arising from transaction specific capital.[20] His model, however, incorporates internal costs of management of firms and tests whether firms integrate only when market transaction costs outweigh costs of internal management. He measures vertical integration by the ratio of value added to sales. He measures small-numbers bargaining by the four-firm concentration ratio at the firm level; sunk costs with the minimum efficient size divided by industry sales at the plant level; and asset specificity by the distance between plants, with co-location and close plants signifying high asset specificity. He also uses R&D intensity, measured as the firm's research and development expenditure per dollar of sales, to measure asset-specific investments in human capital as well as specialized inputs; and advertising intensity, measured as the firm's advertising expenditure per dollar of sales, to measure asset-specific investments in product differentiation. Levy finds that there is a positive relation between vertical integration and firm concentration, and between research intensity and vertical integration. We now turn to the solution of capital structure and the use of debt.

Capital Structure

The solution of capital structure uses leverage as a strategic tool to reduce the probability of holdup before it occurs and to increase the probability of favorable post-investment renegotiations after holdup occurs. Bronars and Deere (1991)[21] and Baldwin (1983)[22] show that debt shields wealth away from a supplier, reducing the revenues available for appropriation and, ceteris paribus, reducing the propensity for opportunistic behavior. Subramaniam (1996)[23] and Perotti and Spier (1993)[24] argue that debt improves the bargaining position of investors in ex post negotiations. In Subramaniam's model, the mechanism by which debt improves equity holders' bargaining positions is to make the threat of project abandonment credible. In Perotti and Spier's model, debt makes threats of future noninvestment credible.

Baldwin models a firm's rational response to the possibility of holdup by an employee union. She argues that long-lived capital investments are necessary in industries like steel, mining, and autos before production can begin. This is also particularly true in the context of the petrochemical and oil and gas industry. Baldwin argues that once these sunk investments are made, it is economically advantageous to continue production as long as revenues are greater than ongoing costs. This fact can be exploited by an opportunistic union to hold up the firm and demand increased wages. As long as the increased wage demand does not result in marginal costs becoming greater than marginal revenues, the firm will continue to produce. The returns to the invested capital are therefore vulnerable to exploitation by the employees union.

Knowing this rationale, investors have an incentive to maintain an inefficient plant so that ongoing costs are high enough that an increased wage demand increases ongoing costs to the point of exceeding revenues, which would result in plant closure. In Baldwin's model the union is also aware of this fact and its rational response is to forego increased wages. This practice of deterrence by maintaining an inefficient plant is of course wasteful and costly in that it increases the average cost of production. In addition, Baldwin argues that it also increases the incentives for capital providers not to invest in new capacity or in cost-reducing R&D. Investors have a number of mixed strategies of maintaining differing proportions of efficient and inefficient plants.

Baldwin goes on to show that the potential losses from these strategies can be avoided through ex ante contracts that are ex post enforceable. One form of ex post enforceable contracts is contracts enforced by a third party. Baldwin cites these third parties as the force of law, a disinterested arbitrator, and debt holders. She shows that if a portion of equity is replaced with debt the result is an increased marginal cost across all plants. Consequently, debt payments increase the threshold of productivity without increasing the propensity for increased wage demands. Workers bear a portion of bankruptcy costs and the firm can reduce the costs associated with maintaining an inefficient plant. Of course the strategy is self-limiting because bankruptcy costs prevent debt from forming 100 percent of the firm's capital.

Bronars and Deere model the use of debt to prevent holdup by an employees union. Their model is based on the threat of unionization, and shareholders use debt before formation of a union. Debt allows shareholders to commit the potential union members' share of net revenues to creditors in return for funds acquired before the union exists. If a union is formed it must decide if an increased wage demand will drive the firm into bankruptcy. In the case of bankruptcy the union must bargain with the creditors to the firm. Since bankruptcy is costly for the firm the union is unlikely to get increased wages. Therefore, existing debt increases shareholder value because it reduces the surplus available for expropriation by the union and credibly threatens the union with firm bankruptcy that reduces the wages that the union can obtain. However, in this model Bronars and Deere do not consider investment as a variable. Perotti and Spier as well as Subramaniam consider the effect of investment policy and debt to prevent opportunistic behavior by concentrated suppliers.

Perotti and Spier model the strategic use of debt to reduce opportunistic behavior by an employee union. In particular, if the firm is dependent on earnings from future investments to pay its obligations, then the equity holders' control over investments serves as a bargaining mechanism to prevent holdup. Perotti and Spier model two investment decisions over two periods. They show that after the returns from the first investment are known, equity holders can retire equity in exchange for debt. This exchange then causes Myers underinvestment due to debt overhang problem in which equity holders choose to forego investments because returns are captured by debt holders instead of equity holders. Thus equity holders can credibly threaten to forego the next investment and extract wage concessions from the union. Additionally, debt repayments also shield a part of the surplus away from union demands. Perotti and Spier therefore show that seniority of claims offers only a limited degree of financial security. Control over the investment and financing decisions emerges as the crucial factor in the ex post allocation of firm value.

They additionally point out that after the wage concessions are extracted, the firm's capital structure can be altered again by replacing its high leverage with equity. They link their model to the leveraged recapitalizations in LBO financings. Perotti and Spier assume that adjustments to the capital structure are costless. In their model, therefore, debt rises initially to force wage concessions, and once these are obtained, debt is drawn down quickly by issuing equity. Although Perotti and Spier's model applies particularly well to leveraged recapitalizations in LBO financings, infrastructure does not need earnings from future investments to pay its obligations. This considerably weakens the bargaining position of equity holders that is premised on their control of financing and investment decisions. A threat of noninvestment is not always credible. In the infrastructure context, Subramaniam's mechanism of the use of debt works better.

In contrast to Perotti and Spier, Subramaniam models a change in the capital structure from equity to debt after the investment is made. Subramaniam argues that allowing the firm to replace equity with debt ex post actually makes the ex ante investment efficient. Debt is advantageous to the firm because only the equity holders receive the value of the debt up front but debt is repaid out of the end-period surplus of which the suppliers are also stakeholders. Debt therefore shields wealth away from suppliers. Debt also lowers the probability of holdup by suppliers because equity holders can credibly threaten bankruptcy and abandon the project if suppliers demand a greater share of the revenues. In the absence of debt such a threat is not credible and suppliers can demand a greater share of revenues, knowing that the firm has sufficient cash flow to pay them.

Subramaniam points out that debt also imposes costs on equity holders. It reduces the status quo payoff to the equity holders during the ex post bargaining process, but this is bounded above due to limited liability. Debt also increases expected bankruptcy costs. Therefore equity holders ex ante increase investment, knowing that they will replace their equity for debt and thereby alleviate the possibility of holdup from the suppliers. This model seems very well suited to the sequencing of infrastructure investments in which equity is typically used to build the assets and debt funds are committed only after the assets are in place. The high debt levels are then used to mitigate the ex post bargaining anticipated by investors before they make the investment. Moreover, we know that infrastructure assets have high value even under conditions of default, which implies that they have low bankruptcy costs.

What about the evidence for the use of debt as a means of mitigating hold-up? Sawant (2009) shows that the financing and governance structure of project finance mitigates holdup in the oil, gas, and petrochemical industry. Among other mechanisms mitigating holdup, project finance is characterized by high leverage, with average leverage greater than 70 percent.[25] He uses the size of the investment to measure sunk costs and buyer and supplier concentration as a measure of asset specificity. He finds that the propensity for project finance is high when sunk costs are large and buyer and supplier concentration is high. The gas industry, which has high asset specificity from pipelines due to inability to store natural gas, also shows a high propensity for project finance. Chapter 7 examines project finance as a mode of investment.

CONCLUSION

Holdup is one of the most important sources of risk in infrastructure investing. It arises because infrastructure investments are capital-intensive investments which investors can recover only by using the assets for their specific purpose. The capital is therefore sunk in assets with high asset specificity. Counterparties to the investments must honor their promises over long periods of time in order for the investments to generate returns. Infrastructure assets therefore face the risk of holdup from asset counterparties like suppliers and buyers.

Among the means for mitigating holdup are the methods of long-term contracting, vertical integration, and capital structure. Long-term contracts rely on third parties like the courts to enforce the contracts. We saw that the type of remedy a court prescribes for a breach of contract and whether both contracting parties make investments affects the ex ante incentives for investment. When a court does not impose the remedy of specific performance on the defaulting party, the solution of vertical integration is more efficient. Long-term contracts also require the existence of a stable legal environment with remedies that investing parties can rely on. Legal remedies are costly and may be lacking in countries with weak legal enforcement.

Vertical integration is favored in volatile environments and when the firm has high growth opportunities. In this situation the benefits of vertical integration tend to outweigh the costs because of improved flows of information and the control rights of common ownership. The costs of vertical integration arise from attempts to integrate dissimilar businesses. Since infrastructure assets tend to have few growth opportunities and operate in low-volatility environments, vertical integration is perhaps not an ideal method of mitigating holdup.

Capital structure or the use of high leverage removes cash flows available for appropriation by counterparties since the firm is legally obligated to make payments. A demand for an increased share of revenues by asset counterparties can cause the assets to default. Debt therefore improves the bargaining position of capital providers in ex post renegotiations since the threat of bankruptcy is credible. All these solutions have empirical support. Among the counterparties that can resort to opportunistic behavior, sovereign entities like governments are especially important. Sovereign opportunistic behavior is qualitatively different. Chapter 6 examines the sources, manifestations, and risks arising from political risk.

CHAPTER 6

Infrastructure Assets and Political Risk

Why, sir, there is every possibility that you will soon be able to tax it!
—Michael Faraday (1791–1867) to UK Prime Minister William Gladstone on the usefulness of electricity

In Chapter 5 we examined the risk of holdup in infrastructure investments. I showed that holdup arises from sunk costs, asset specificity, and opportunistic behavior of counterparties. I also alluded to political risk as the risk of holdup by sovereign governments. Definitions of political risk focus on the risk of loss to investors arising from political factors. Lessard (1993) defines political risk as "the risk of political discontinuities resulting in losses through expropriation or major policy shifts."[1] Howell and Chaddick (1994) define political risk as "the possibility that political decisions, events or conditions in a country, including those that might be referred to as social, will affect the business environment such that investors will lose money or have a reduced profit margin."[2]

The characterization of political risk as sovereign holdup allows us to use the opportunistic behavior construct to classify political risk into two categories for ease of analysis and management. The opportunistic behavior construct imputes guile and intent to mislead the counterparty. While this may or may not be the case in relations with sovereigns or, for that matter, with other counterparties, the possibility of opportunistic behavior allows us to identify risk and fashion strategies that mitigate and hedge political risk.

POLITICAL RISK TYPOLOGY

We obtain a broad classification of political risk by using opportunistic behavior as the analytical factor. I classify political risk as sovereign holdup when investors are exposed to loss due to actions taken by host governments against specific assets, arising from a proclivity for opportunistic behavior. Examples include increase in prices for inputs that sovereign-owned suppliers supply or nonpayment for output that sovereign-owned buyers purchase, increase in taxes/royalties affecting the specific assets in a discriminatory fashion, changes in repatriation rules, outright expropriation, creeping expropriation, interference in operations which could include harassment or intimidation of the firm's officers, incitement of labor unrest, incitement of violence against assets, nonprovision of utilities, increase in utility rates affecting assets, and so on. Sovereign holdup is akin to holdup by investment counterparties that we analyzed through the transaction cost economics lens. Although sovereign holdup differs in important ways from counterparty holdup, we can apply transaction cost analysis profitably towards mitigating sovereign holdup.

The second category of political risk is events of a political or social nature that expose investors to loss. Although these events may result from host government actions, host governments do not direct their actions against specific assets. For example, precipitous currency devaluations, hyper-inflation, civil war, violence within a host country, social unrest, breakdown in law and order, and so on, are political and social incidents that occur even though government actions are not directed against the investments. These risks arise from socioeconomic and political factors that affect all businesses in the host country without discrimination. Their nature is more akin to acts of God, albeit political in nature.

Political risk insurers, of course, pay great attention to the language by which they define the conditions under which they are liable to pay insureds. *Force Majeure* or "act of God" has definite legal and financial implications in the insurance context, but I use these terms in the generic publicly understood sense. My classification is also a tool to help us analyze which methods are likely to mitigate these risks. I use *political risk* to mean these types of events and *sovereign holdup* to refer to the other category of political risk.

How important are these risks? The results of research by Standard & Poor's on sources of risk leading to rating downgrades in project finance debt over a period of 10 years show that although overall downgrades are just 4.1 percent of the total rated portfolio, counterparty and sovereign risk are responsible for over half (51.5 percent) of the downgrades.[3] Technical risk, which includes construction, technology, and operations risk, causes just 4.5 percent of downgrades. Improper structuring—for example, not separating assets from sponsor balance sheets—causes another 18.5 percent of downgrades. I examine the requirements of structuring in detail in Chapter 7.

Guasch (2004) analyzed a data set of more than 1,000 concessions in electricity, telecommunications, water, and transportation in Latin America between 1985 and 2000.[4] In a concession model, investors do not own the underlying assets; they get the rights to operate the assets and recoup their investments from user fees. The term of the concession is usually 15 to 30 years and after that period the assets devolve back to the state. The concession model is used when there are legal or political problems for private ownership of public assets.

Guasch found that, excluding telecommunications, 41 percent of the concessions were renegotiated. Renegotiations affected a whopping 74 percent of water concessions and 55 percent of transportation concessions. Moreover, renegotiations occurred on average within 1.6 years and 3.1 years, respectively, after the concession award. Holdup therefore occurs almost immediately after capital is sunk even though the concession terms extend out to 15 to 30 years. Guasch, Laffont, and Straub (2007) further found that renegotiations are initiated by the firms operating the concessions as well as by governments.[5] Firms typically initiate renegotiations due to macroeconomic shocks like massive devaluation, which we have seen reduces the foreign currency value of the local currency, thereby reducing the value of local currency–denominated revenues and increasing the value of foreign currency denominated debt payments. In their sample, governments unfortunately initiate opportunistic renegotiations, reneging on contracts to please political constituencies typically after and before elections. Guasch et al. show that an independent regulator significantly reduces the probability of renegotiations in conditions of political opportunism.

Interestingly, investors are aware of this *election effect*. Vaaler (2008) shows that multinational corporations perceive higher risk and announce fewer investments when right-wing political incumbents are likely to be replaced by left-wing political challengers.[6] Even credit rating agencies reflect the importance of elections in determining political risk, broadly defined. Vaaler, Schrage, and Block (2006) show that credit rating agencies are more likely to downgrade country sovereign risk ratings when right-wing incumbents are likely to be replaced by left-wing political challengers.[7] Counterparty and political risk are therefore among the most important sources of risk that investors must manage.

Investors can manage sovereign holdup either by deterring or mitigating the incentives to resort to sovereign holdup or by hedging the risk. Hedging is a method of reducing loss typically caused by price fluctuations. The hedger buys or sells equal quantities of the same or similar commodities in two different markets at about the same time with the expectation that a future loss or gain in one market will be offset by an equal and opposite change in the other market.[8] Investors in infrastructure assets can hedge by purchasing insurance in the political risk insurance (PRI) market. The insurance contract compensates investors if their investments suffer losses arising from sovereign holdup and political risk, although insurance contracts compensate losses up to the book value of assets or the replacement value of the assets. Political force majeure risks can only be hedged, while sovereign holdup can be mitigated as well as hedged. Exhibit 6.1 displays the options available to investors.

Although I listed the investment treaty arbitration (ITA) mechanism under hedging in this exhibit, including the provision in infrastructure contracts likely also mitigates the threat of holdup. Similarly, we shall see that project finance mitigates sovereign holdup by deterring holdup as well as increasing the likelihood that a renegotiation is favorable to investors once holdup occurs. The rest of this chapter follows this exhibit and develops the different strategies available to investors.

EXHIBIT 6.1   Hedging and Mitigation Strategies

Strategy	Sovereign Holdup	Political Force Majeure
Hedging	1. Insurance for expropriation, breach of contract, creeping expropriation, inconvertibility. 2. Investment treaty arbitration.	1. Insurance for riots, revolution. 2. Protection against devaluation.
Mitigation— Deterring holdup	1. Financial structure like high leverage in project finance. 2. Management's political capabilities. 3. Aligning with host government objectives. 4. Competitive rates of return. 5. Local partners. 6. Local community support. 7. Front-loading cash flows.	NA
Mitigation— Increasing investor bargaining power during renegotiations	1. Long-term contracts. 2. Project finance. 3. Joint ownership. 4. Deployment of investor-controlled technology.	NA

Source: Author analysis.

I should emphasize that investors in infrastructure assets are exposed to sovereign holdup and political risk even in developed countries. Instances where providers of basic services are seen to profit at the expense of tax payers attract government attention. An example is the proposal of the U.S. Congress to impose a windfall gains tax on oil and gas firms.[9] Similarly, the sidebar "California's Abrogation of Contracts" examines the state of California's unilateral abrogation of contracts after the electricity crisis of 2000–2001.[10]

CALIFORNIA'S ABROGATION OF CONTRACTS

In February 2002, the California Public Utilities Commission filed a complaint with the Federal Energy Regulatory Commission (FERC) that long-term contracts signed between power producers and the California Department of Water Resources (CDWR) for purchase of electricity were unjust, unreasonable, and should be thrown out. After deregulation of the California electricity market, wholesale electricity prices exploded during the period November 2000 to June 2001, and the state's investor-owned utilities went bankrupt. CDWR took over power purchases for the state, buying almost 80 percent of all of California's electricity. During the height of the crisis CDWR bought electricity on the spot market at prices that rose over $308 per megawatt-hour (MWh). In January 2001 CDWR signed 20-year contracts agreeing to purchase power at a price of $69 per MWh from electricity generating companies. At the end of the crisis, in January 2002 electricity prices dropped to $33 per MWh. Clearly $69 per MWh no longer looked attractive. In its complaint, CDWR alleged that the contracts should be abrogated because CDWR had entered into the contracts during a market environment dominated by exercise of market power and the contracts contained burdensome provisions, like requiring that California maintain a certain credit rating or face penalties, preventing the FERC from reviewing the contracts, and so on.

In addition to complaining to the FERC, in March 2002 California also filed a petition with the FERC for a refund of rates charged to the state before October 2, 2000, to the tune of $1.8 billion to $2.8 billion, claiming that the generating companies had overcharged the state. In addition, California filed lawsuits against Dynegy, Williams, Reliant, and Mirant, claiming $150 million in penalties and alleging

(Continued)

that the firms were in violation of the state's Unfair Competition Act by double-selling emergency power that they were supposed to hold as an emergency reserve.

The story illustrates breach of contract or sovereign holdup risk arising from perceptions of outsized returns at the expense of taxpayers. Although the drop in electricity prices triggered CDWR actions, perceptions that power producers caused the initial market run-up through market manipulation did not help. The story also illustrates the arsenal of tactics available to government entities for forcing renegotiation of contracts.

The next section examines how and why infrastructure assets are susceptible to sovereign holdup.

SOVEREIGN HOLDUP

I have touched on the importance of governments in infrastructure sectors. Infrastructure provides basic services or social goods that are politically sensitive. Users typically believe that they are entitled to basic infrastructure services like uninterrupted electricity, reliable transportation, smooth roads, clean water, and sanitation services. I pointed out that infrastructure possesses monopoly-like characteristics. Attempts to increase user fees therefore seem exploitative to users even when the increase is economically justified. Users perceive attempts to restrict access to services as an encroachment on rights. An attempt to earn large returns from infrastructure assets also seems exploitative and provides ammunition to opposition groups within host countries. Users vent their outrage on governments as well as on the offending firm. In these situations governments have strong incentives to find scapegoats, and private investors become easy targets. The Cochabamba water war in Bolivia (see sidebar) is a case in point.

EL AGUA ES NUESTRA CARAJO! (THE WATER IS OURS, DAMN IT!)

In September 1999 the Bolivian government granted a 40-year concession to Aguas del Tunari to supply water and sanitation services to the city of Cochabamba. Aguas del Tunari was a consortium of

International Water (British subsidiary of U.S. construction giant Bechtel) with 55 percent equity stake, Spanish company Abengao with 25 percent stake, and the remaining 20 percent stake equally divided between five local firms, including a politically influential firm, ICE Ingenieros. The Bolivian government cancelled the concession six months later amid escalating and violent protests that took the life of one protestor and injured scores of protestors and police. The riots were so furious that the Bolivian government had to call in the army to quell protestors, who rioted over four days.

Cochabamba, a city of 600,000 nestled in a valley in the Andes Mountains, experienced severe water shortages due to an exploding population and lack of natural water sources. In response the Bolivian government began the Misicuni project connecting the Titiri river system, which entailed the building of a dam, a 19-kilometer-long pipe, a five-meter-high tunnel through the surrounding mountains, and an aqueduct to bring water into city. Cochabamba's municipal water company, Servicio Municipal de Agua Potable y Alcantarillado (SEMAPA), was able to provide water to only 57 percent of the population. The rest sank wells, lowering the water table, or relied on tanker water supplied by *tanqueros*. SEMAPA had an upside-down tariff structure with heaviest water users paying the least amount. This prevented the highest users from having any incentive for conserving water. Tanker water was at least 300 percent more expensive than the highest tariff levied by Aguas del Tunari (10 bolivianos per cubic meter to 2.4 bolivianos per cubic meter).* SEMAPA also lost about 55 percent of its water through leaks and poor maintenance.

The aim of Aguas del Tunari was to connect 95 percent of the population to piped water and 100 percent to sewerage by 2019. However, Aguas del Tunari had to incorporate into its water tariffs the half-built Misicuni assets, a new expensive treatment plant, and $35 million in debt that SEMAPA had accumulated. Within five months of operations the company increased water rates by 35 percent, from 10 percent for the lowest user to 106 percent for the highest users. About half the tariff increase came from the additional requirements previously cited. Additionally, Cochabambinos used far more water than before because of service improvements and consequently got a larger bill.

A Bolivian law unrelated to Aguas del Tunari designated all water wells as national resources and gave the exclusive rights to the utility

(Continued)

providing the service. This meant that people could no longer use their self-constructed wells free of cost. Local farmers feared they would be charged for water used for irrigation. The low-income households had none of their usual water vendor options until they were connected to the Aguas del Tunari network. The *tanqueros* wanted to protect their business. These interests coalesced into the opposition to Aguas del Tunari.[†]

Epilogue: Bechtel sued for $25 million in the World Bank's International Centre for the Settlement of Investment Disputes (ICSID) and, in an unprecedented move, dropped the suit under pressure from NGOs.[‡] The Bolivian government bought 80 percent of the firm for 2 bolivianos (0.25 cents). Local firms still own 20 percent of the firm and some assets. SEMAPA took over the contract but mostly provides water to the wealthy at low rates and still loses 50 percent of its water to leakage, theft, and provision of water to politically connected users.[§]

---

[*]Bechtel statement re Aguas del Tunari, accessed at University of California, Hastings College of Law, Prof. N. Roht-Arriaza, law and development class web site at http://www.uchastings.edu/faculty-administration/faculty/roht-arriaza/class-website/docs/law-and-development/law-and-development09-bechtel-statement-re-bolivia.pdf (accessed on August 15, 2009).
[†]Nicholas Miranda, "Concession Agreements: From Private Contract to Public Policy," *Yale Law Journal* 2007, 510.
[‡]"NGOs: Public Pressure Forces Bechtel to Drop Water Case—Bolivia," *The America's Intelligence Wire,* January 19, 2006.
[§]Franz Chávez, "Bolivia: Cochabamba's 'Water War,' Six years on," Inter Press Service News Agency, 2006. Accessed at http://ipsnews.net/news.asp?idnews=35418 on August 15, 2009.

Governments therefore remain intimately involved with infrastructure assets as regulators, as direct input suppliers, as output buyers, and as direct suppliers of security and legal environments. Additionally, governments have traditionally provided infrastructure services and may regard private capital with suspicion and as a necessary inconvenience that must be highly regulated.

Infrastructure is also susceptible to sovereign holdup because of the nature of cash flows and managerial skills needed to manage infrastructure assets. We noted that infrastructure assets have stable cash flows and that managers focus on operational requirements and not on managing growth options. The implications from these characteristics are as follows. First, assets with stable cash flows are more attractive for expropriation than assets with volatile cash flows. Governments can increase taxes or royalties and expect them to be paid when cash flows are stable. Volatile cash flows that swing from large surpluses to large deficits are not as attractive. Second, governments find it difficult to manage firms with high growth options like technology and consumer brand companies. Governments can manage infrastructure assets comparatively easily. This reduces the bargaining power of infrastructure investors if sovereign holdup occurs.

We have also noted that infrastructure assets are fixed to the ground and investors cannot relocate them. Moreover, investors cannot deter sovereign holdup by threatening to shift their output to locations outside the host country.[11] The firm must generate revenues from the assets in order to recoup the investments. These conditions also serve to reduce the bargaining power of investors.

In addition, sovereign holdup differs from counterparty holdup. Sovereign holdup can be hidden and more difficult to recognize for outside observers because the sovereign has regulatory oversight over the assets. A government can legitimately claim that actions of an expropriatory nature like imposition of fines, taxes, surcharges, back taxes, increases in royalties, and so on, are part of its regulatory duties. In many instances this is indeed the case, but the problem lies in differentiating between genuine regulatory need and expropriatory tendency. Governments also control the business and financial environment, ranging from fiscal policy to monetary policy, exchange rate policy, taxation policy, foreign trade policy allowing imports and exports, repatriation rules, customs duties and the legal policy, and so on. Even in the present conditions of global capital flows and integrated markets, the sovereignty of governments over these levers of power largely remains unchallenged. This makes it difficult for investors to rely solely on two of the solutions discussed in Chapter 5 that mitigate the holdup problem, namely long-term contracting and vertical integration.

Long-term contracts between sovereigns and investors are difficult to enforce against the sovereign. Although investors could rely on courts within the host country to enforce these contracts, the host country courts may not be inclined to be sympathetic to foreigners. Although an unbiased, independent third party with coercive authority against a sovereign is an oxymoron, investors have some options. Investors can seek to be compensated for losses arising from host government actions by seeking the intervention of their home governments or choosing the international treaty arbitration mechanism.

Traditionally, investors approached their own sovereign governments to intervene on their behalf and sought *diplomatic protection* to enforce their claims. Although this method of seeking compensation for investor losses is time honored, it has a number of drawbacks. Investors must possess significant influence over their own governments to convince them to exert influence over the host government. The investor's government then must be able and willing and have sufficient political capital to convince the offending government to undo its breach of contract or provide compensation in lieu. The U.S. government, for example, did not fulfill investor expectations when Indonesia rescinded contracts for power projects in the 1990s because it was unwilling to pressure Indonesia to honor contracts made by former President Suharto.[12] The mechanism therefore relies on factors that are outside most investors' control, a fact that does not inspire confidence in investing.

This mechanism is also time intensive, taking years before a resolution happens. It took 14 years of U.S. and Mexican government diplomatic exchanges before a settlement was reached between Mexico and U.S. investors after Mexico expropriated U.S. landowners as part of agrarian reform in 1929.[13] It is interesting to note that among private investors, the pension funds analyzed in Chapter 1 are likely to have a strong ability to influence their own governments and seek diplomatic protection.

The second option we considered was the mechanism of international treaty arbitration for enforcing contracts. Insofar as the ITA mechanism is reliable and timely long-term contracts can be used by investors, investors then face the challenge of proving expropriation when it may be cloaked as regulation. I examine the ITA mechanism later on in the chapter.

The solution of vertical integration is unavailable because ownership over some sovereign functions is not possible. Infrastructure asset owners, for example, could buy a concentrated state-owned supplier or buyer if the host government privatizes them. But governments will usually not permit private ownership of security enforcement. The two mechanisms available to investors for risk mitigation are the use of debt and a structure that permits joint ownership with governments or government-owned/controlled entities. I examine these in the next chapter when I examine project finance. I examine hedging options in the form of political risk insurance available to investors in the section titled "Hedging Sovereign Holdup." In the next section I examine the different types of sovereign holdup.

TYPES OF RISK

We can organize sovereign holdup into the following categories as a function of decreasing government appropriation of revenues and interference:

- Expropriation or outright nationalization.
- Creeping expropriation.
- Breaches of contract with expropriatory consequences.

These categories differ from traditional political risk categories used by the political risk insurance industry. Insurers traditionally placed political risk into three categories of expropriation, inconvertibility, and political violence. I examine these categories and their evolution through time in the following sections.

Expropriation

We have noted that infrastructure assets are fixed to the ground and that they provide essential services that governments used to provide and which users widely believe encompass fundamental rights. Governments therefore have incentives and can find political justification for taking over infrastructure assets. However, outright expropriation over the past 25 years has become rare.[14] Exhibit 6.2 shows the decline in direct expropriations and in the number of countries indulging in direct expropriation from 1960 to 1992.

Governments recognize that global capital flows are essential for raising the living standards of their countries and that outright expropriation is costly and ultimately counterproductive. Unfortunately, as we have seen from transaction cost economics theory, incentives for appropriation of revenues arise from the very nature of infrastructure assets. Infrastructure asset characteristics have not undergone any change and neither have government incentives. The forms of sovereign holdup have evolved to include subtle forms of expropriation like changes in tax or royalty rates. The risk of creeping expropriation therefore probably exceeds the risk of expropriation. Creeping expropriation is hard to detect and harder to mitigate, as described in the next section.

Creeping Expropriation

Creeping expropriation has also been termed regulatory risk or policy risk. Schnitzer (2002) characterizes creeping expropriation as follows: "The returns on the investment may be adversely affected by sovereign acts of the host country, such as changes in the tax law, specific import or export duties, or other charges which the investor has to pay."[15]

Oseghale (1993) lists measures that lead to creeping expropriation like operational restrictions, restrictions on the repatriation of profits, breaches of contracts by the host government, and discriminatory taxation.[16] Creeping

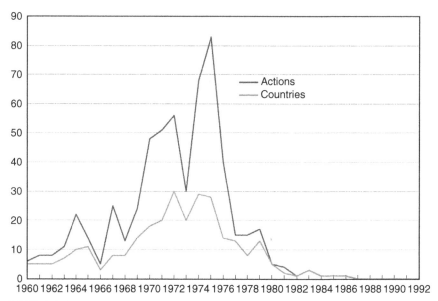

EXHIBIT 6.2   Expropriations from 1960 to 1992
Source: Michael S. Minor, "The Demise of Expropriation as an Instrument of
LDC Policy, 1980–1992," *Journal of International Business Studies* 25, no.1
(1994): 180.

expropriation is hard to detect since it tends to remain hidden unlike an
outright expropriation. In today's highly networked and information-rich
environment, an outright expropriation is likely to immediately garner
headlines and create a public relations problem for the host country. Small
changes in tax rates over extended periods of time are unlikely to create
the same dynamics even if the ultimate effect remains the same. Apart from
this ability to calibrate the expropriation, governments can also actively
cloak their actions under regulatory authority. This ability differentiates
creeping expropriation from simple breach of contracts that have an expropriatory effect.

Creeping expropriation differs from breach of contract in two additional respects. First, government regulations have the force of law and are
a legitimate sovereign right. When governments change regulations they can
do so for legitimate reasons like enhancing public safety or enhancing public
welfare. Governments can cloak creeping expropriation under their regulatory rights. A breach of contract lacks the inherent legitimacy of a regulatory action. Second, a breach of contract is easier to determine because, by
definition, a breach occurs when governments do not fulfill their obligations

as per clauses clearly specified in the contract. It is very difficult for third parties like insurance providers to determine if a government takes a regulatory action with the intent of expropriation. It is also difficult to determine a priori which actions a government can take and include them in the insurance contracts, provided insurance sellers are willing to take on the risk. This distinction has implications for political risk insurance contracts. I examine breach of contract in the next section.

Breach of Contract

A breach of contract is simply nonperformance of contractual obligations by host governments or state-owned entities. We know that governments can be concentrated suppliers of inputs or buyers of output from infrastructure assets. They can therefore demand higher prices for inputs or pay lower prices for output. Clearly, complying with such demands will cause economic hardship to projects and reduce the return available to investors. Typically such an expropriatory action is likely under conditions of economic hardship to the government, in instances of severe economic contraction, currency devaluations, and budgetary deficits. For example, the Indonesian government refused to pay the contractually agreed rate for electricity from the Paiton project when the rupiah devalued drastically during the Asian financial crisis of 1997 and the dollar-indexed price of electricity soared. How do investors handle breach of contract risk?

I alluded earlier to the existence of the international treaty arbitration (ITA) mechanism. I examine the ITA system briefly in this section but the vastness of the subject precludes me from examining it in any great detail here. ITA is a relatively new development in international law.[17] It came into existence after sovereign countries executed bilateral and multilateral investment treaties among themselves to promote investments and, in effect, willingly constrained their sovereignty. The investment treaties typically contained provisions that allowed investors from the signatory countries to settle disputes with the host countries through a binding arbitration process.

The first bilateral investment treaty (BIT) was executed in 1959 between the Federal Republic of Germany and Pakistan. In 1966, the Convention on the Settlement of Investment Disputes between States and Nationals of other States (ICSID Convention) established the International Centre for the Settlement of Investment Disputes (ICSID) under the auspices of the World Bank. The ICSID Convention was initially ratified by 20 countries and now has over 140 signatories. The international investment treaty regime consists of a network of over 2,500 BITs and 241 bilateral or trilateral free trade and investment agreements.

The ITA system therefore amounts to a voluntary surrender of sovereignty by states to an arbitration panel since parties agree to abide by the ruling of the panel. The signatory parties lay down the arbitration process in the investment treaty; the important components are the method of selection of the panel, number of members, method of filing complaints, time periods of the process, review of awards, and so on. For example, the Dabhol partners GE and Bechtel launched arbitration proceedings against the Government of India under the India-Mauritius Bilateral Investment Treaty since GE and Bechtel had set up subsidiaries in Mauritius to invest in Dabhol.[18] The treaty provided for a three-member arbitration panel. Each party appointed one arbitrator within 60 days of dispute filing and the BIT specified that the third arbitrator would be appointed by the two selected arbitrators. The decision of the panel is binding on the Government of India and on Mauritius. Other BITs allow for arbitration to be conducted under ICSID.

Of course, countries can withdraw unilaterally from these treaties or frustrate the proceedings.[19] Such an action will likely damage future investment flows to the country, but countries might choose to withdraw if the benefits of withdrawal outweigh the future costs of investment. For example, Ecuador has threatened to withdraw from nine bilateral investment treaties with El Salvador, Cuba, Guatemala, Honduras, Nicaragua, the Dominican Republic, Paraguay, Uruguay, and Romania because it did not want to remain subject to ICSID arbitration.[20] Ecuador initially notified the ICSID that it would not submit to arbitration proceedings concerning nonrenewable resources. However, such a notification probably fell short of its intent since the nine BITs it had signed allowed for ICSID arbitration. Ecuador needed to withdraw from every treaty.

Moreover, most BITs include provisions that even if the country withdraws from a BIT, agreements with investors when the BIT is in force continue to remain in force. Investors should and are indeed considering the protection provided for foreign investors in bilateral investment treaties. For instance, in the case of Ecuador, although Japan does not have a BIT with Ecuador, Japanese nationals can incorporate in any of the nine countries with Ecuadorian BITs and take advantage of protections afforded by the BITs. Over 150 claims have been filed in the past decade, mostly against developing countries by investors from the developed countries.[21] However, investors cannot rely completely on the ITA system because the system has not developed a coherent body of international law and it is not open and accountable.[22]

The ITA system is not coherent because arbitration panel judgments sometimes reach opposite conclusions for the same BIT provisions and the same set of facts. For example, LG&E filed a claim against Argentina at

ICSID, under the ICSID Convention and the BIT between the United States and Argentina, for a breach of contract which prevented LG&E from increasing prices for gas distribution and which, in 2000, converted all dollar obligations payable into pesos. The Argentine government took these actions because of the recession in 1998–1999 and the devaluation of the peso. In this case the tribunal ruled that Argentina was not liable because of the international law defense of necessity.[23] However, similar claims by CMS Gas Transmission Company were judged differently and the claimants awarded monetary damages.[24] The tribunals in the latter case determined that the customary international law defense of necessity did not protect Argentina.

The system does not have an appellate body, which has prevented the formation of a coherent body of international law. The system is also not accountable because arbitration awards are more widely enforceable with almost no opportunity for judicial review. This of course favors investors if the arbitration tribunal rules in their favor, because once the tribunal concludes arbitration, governments cannot delay payments through judicial reviews. Among the enforcement mechanisms of arbitral awards, the Convention on the Recognition and Enforcement of Foreign Arbitral Awards is the most important. Also called the New York Convention, it entered into force on June 7, 1959. Presently 144 nations are signatories to the convention.[25]

Finally, the ITA system is not open because arbitrations are usually conducted outside public scrutiny. Although these shortcomings are likely to be reduced over time, investors must rely on additional mechanisms to hedge and mitigate the risk of sovereign holdup. Let us now examine the category of political risk and examine currency inconvertibility.

Political Risk: Inconvertibility

Inconvertibility refers to the inability of investors to convert host country currency into home country currency due to restrictions on currency exchange. The risk of inconvertibility due to capital controls has diminished recently, quite like the risk of expropriation. Countries realize that blocking capital from moving out of the country prevents capital from entering the country, too. The floating-exchange-rate regimes followed by a large number of countries and the globalization of the economies imply that countries place fewer restrictions on currency conversion than before. Investors are and should be more concerned with devaluation risk. When the host currency devalues sharply against the U.S. dollar, for instance, dollar cash flows drop sharply. If the investment has U.S. dollar–denominated debt on its books, dollar cash flows may be insufficient to pay interest and principal payments. If the host country cash flows are indexed to the U.S. dollar, the price of the output increases to equal the currency devaluation. This can trigger breach of contract, as we saw in the Paiton project in Indonesia when the off-taker refused to pay the increased price of electricity. The government of Maharashtra, the state in India purchasing power in the Dabhol project, also cited the dollar indexation of output price as one reason for project cancellation. Devaluation risk can therefore threaten project viability.

In most developing countries, currency hedging instruments like forwards and futures are not available over the long tenors of project cash flows, which can extend out to 15 years or more. Since devaluation risk is not a sovereign holdup risk, only hedging remains a viable option. Although financial market instruments like forwards, futures, options, and currency swaps are widely developed for mitigating foreign exchange risk, these instruments may not be available for long-term infrastructure exposure and, in some underdeveloped foreign exchange markets, may be completely unavailable. Moreover, transferring devaluation risk to the project's buyers increases sovereign holdup risk. Investors can instead consider a money market hedge in which investors match their foreign currency assets by creating an offsetting foreign currency liability.[26]

Political Force Majeure

Political force majeure refers to the risk of catastrophic loss due to political events like politically motivated violence, war, civil disturbance, and so on. Investors usually hedge by purchasing insurance. Recently terrorism has been added to the list of dangers threatening investors with catastrophic loss. Unfortunately insurance sellers generally do not cover terrorism, and if they do there are likely exclusions for chemical, biological, and nuclear catastrophes. The next section examines the hedging tools available to investors in the form of insurance.

HEDGING SOVEREIGN HOLDUP

We have noted that investors can hedge sovereign holdup and/or mitigate it—that is, reduce the probability of occurrence. Hedging typically does not affect the probability of occurrence. It compensates investors if the hedged event occurs and the investors suffer loss. In this section I examine the traditional form of hedging in the form of insurance. Insurance is only meant to cover an actual loss caused by specified risks. This implies that the insurance company must observe the occurrence of the specified risks, must observe actual loss, and must also determine that the loss occurred directly due to the occurrence of the specified risk, before it pays for a claim against the risk. The language determining the risk specification is therefore very important. Insurance contracts in the political risk insurance (PRI) industry are frequently customized and boilerplate language varies among insurers.

Traditionally, political risk insurance covered three types of risks: expropriation, inconvertibility, and political violence. Political risk insurance is provided by public as well as commercial risk insurers. Public agency insurers are ideally suited to cover sovereign risk; commercial insurance firms can take on less risky projects and markets and act as coinsurers to the public agencies. The following are among the most active public insurance entities: Overseas Private Investment Corporation (OPIC); World Bank's Multilateral Investment Guarantee Agency (MIGA); and other regional multilateral development lenders like Asian Development Bank (ADB), European Bank for Reconstruction and Development (EBRD), Japan Bank for International Cooperation (JBIC), and others. The list is not meant to be exhaustive but illustrative.

OPIC was established in 1969 through amendments to the Foreign Assistance Act of 1961 and offers commercial insurance to U.S. firms only. OPIC does not provide insurance for a country in which it does not have a bilateral *investment incentive agreement*. The agreement provides for binding international arbitration between the host country and OPIC in the event of a dispute between them in connection with a claim. OPIC therefore attempts to recover any insurance claims it pays out from the host country through the investment incentive agreement. OPIC's statutory authority for insurance is limited to expropriation, inconvertibility, and political violence. MIGA was established in 1988 and provides political risk insurance under the auspices of the World Bank.

In the pages that follow, I examine how insurance providers handle the different risks enumerated in the preceding section.

Expropriation

Expropriation insurance coverage is designed to cover outright expropriation when a host government takes over assets without any compensation or actively interferes with operations. Expropriation without compensation usually violates international law, although international law permits such acts for certain public purposes like public safety. This definition leaves open the question of whether a forced sale of assets with rudimentary compensation is also considered expropriation and consequently whether the insurer will honor a claim. Expropriation coverage sometimes requires the host government to be *ultra vires* (in breach of international law). This requirement is problematic in some cases, and if possible investors should exclude the requirement from the insurance contract.[27] Insurance firms are, however, unlikely to deviate from the *ultra vires* standard because they need a legal basis for recovering claims that they have paid out to investors from the host country.[28] Such recoveries are a vital part of the PRI business. We have already noted that expropriation is no longer as prevalent and is a much lower risk as compared to creeping expropriation.

Creeping Expropriation

OPIC defines *creeping expropriation* as a series of actions taken by the host government that, in aggregate, have the effect of a total expropriation.[29] This raises the problem of interpretation and effect on claims if government actions stop short of total expropriation. The insurance contract also needs to determine when the expropriation took place, when the waiting period began and ended, and finally, when creeping expropriation became total expropriation. These questions must be answered to determine if investors will be covered. Creeping expropriation is difficult to write into insurance contracts, which means insureds will not be certain about which claims will be paid and which denied until the actual event occurs. In addition, host government actions must be distinguishable from their regulatory responsibilities, which we have noted is not always clearly the case. Creeping expropriation therefore remains exceptionally difficult to hedge against. Chapter 7 discusses project finance as a structure that helps investors mitigate creeping expropriation.

Breach of Contract

As we have noted, breach of contract is easier to observe than creeping expropriation and therefore easier to incorporate into language in the insurance contract. Traditional expropriation coverage normally does not cover breaches of contract like nonfulfillment of promises made to investors, such as price for input supplied or output bought by state-owned firms, because sovereign breach of contract is not a violation of international law.[30] Products from OPIC and MIGA offer coverage for breach of contract; however, there are additional requirements that investors must fulfill. OPIC reimburses losses incurred if host governments violate contractual agreements only after investors have followed the arbitration process and failed to obtain resolution of their claims. This can be because the host government can refuse to participate in international arbitration, can prevent international arbitration from moving forward, or can withhold payment if it loses the arbitration proceedings. MIGA follows a similar policy with an additional condition that claims are not reimbursed if the host government frustrates the arbitration. Private insurance companies offer "non-honoring of guarantee" insurance which pays if the host government defaults on guaranteed payments, without requiring investors to go through arbitration.[31] Investors can also buy additional insurance which pays if governments refuse to honor arbitration awards against them. This form of coverage is called arbitral award default (AAD) coverage.[32]

Another form of insurance available to investors is the partial risk guarantee for breach of contract, from the World Bank. Although the World Bank cannot lend to projects sponsored by private investors and lenders, it can guarantee commercial loans against specific breaches of contract by a host government, provided that the host government has a backup agreement with the World Bank, agreeing to reimburse the World Bank for any such payments. The amount of the guarantee counts towards the country's overall borrowing limit with the World Bank, which makes countries that reach the limit of their borrowing ability unable to participate in these guarantees. Unfortunately, these countries are the ones most in need of investments, and the partial risk guarantee program has not been a great success. Partial risk guarantees are available only for loans from the World Bank. The European Bank for Reconstruction and Development (EBRD) is the only multilateral development lender that provides partial risk guarantees of equity.

It is important that investors carefully consider the exclusions under which insurers will not pay insurance claims for breach of contract. Exclusions for "commercial acts of government" and "bona fide actions" of government can make certain breaches of contract invalid, and although the investors buy the coverage they may not receive what they pay for. Breach of contract due to currency fluctuations may also be excluded. This can be problematic if breach of contract occurs due to more than one reason. Insurers could deny claims under the currency fluctuation exclusion. Investors should be careful of such exclusions that lead the insurance company into attempts to uncover the underlying causes of breach of contract, which can be complex with numerous linkages.

I mentioned that insurance for breach of contract may require investors to go through the process of international arbitration. The insurance contract, however, should not include recognition of this arbitration by a forum within the host country, nor should it require local arbitration. Host country forums can throw out international arbitration awards and consequently block investor claims with the insurance companies.

Political Force Majeure

Insurance firms require political force majeure claims to cause catastrophic loss. The event must cause termination of the project, or of the contract, or abandonment. It is important for investors to note that insurance does not cover losses that occur due to political violence stemming from actions taken to achieve "labor or student" or other nonpolitical objectives. Therefore insurance firms may not compensate for loss from such social events.

Moreover, insurance at most pays for the replacement cost of assets or the book value of assets, which after depreciation is likely to be quite low. Investors cannot recoup future cash flow losses, which are usually far more valuable than the replacement cost. Insurance is therefore a blunt instrument for hedging the risk of sovereign holdup, and investors would be wise to supplement it with risk mitigation strategies, which are examined in the next section. We can broadly classify risk mitigation strategies as those that reduce the probability of sovereign holdup or, in the event of a holdup, increase the probability of a favorable outcome for the investors.

RISK MITIGATION STRATEGIES

The first group of strategies aims to reduce the probability of sovereign holdup. Some strategies reduce the probability of holdup by relying on financial structure while others rely on political capabilities outlined in Chapter 4. I have already alluded to the use of debt as a means of reducing the probability of holdup. A simple mechanism by which high debt mitigates the probability of sovereign holdup is by precommitting free cash flows. We have seen that large free cash flows attract attention. Large reported profits attract even more attention. High leverage not only precommits cash flows to debt holders but also reduces reported profits. I examine this mechanism in detail in Chapter 7. For example, after Bougainville Copper reported the largest profits in its history, the government of Papua New Guinea in which Bougainville Copper mined its copper announced that it would reexamine all contracts signed with Bougainville Copper.

In this section I examine strategies that rely on investors political capabilities. In my preceding analysis of holdup, opportunistic behavior was a necessary condition for the sequence of events leading to holdup and its resolution. I pointed out in Chapter 5 that the opportunistic behavior construct ignores factors that affect the *propensity* for opportunistic behavior, like culture, trust, relationships, and institutional context. Ghoshal and Moran (1996) note that "the context in which social relations and economic exchange are embedded can induce self-aggrandizement or trust, individualism or collectivism, competition or cooperation among participants."[33] The implication is that we cannot consider opportunistic behavior in a vacuum. The nature of the relationships between suppliers, buyers, and investors, along with the cultural and institutional context of the transaction, influences the propensity for opportunistic behavior. These insights are particularly useful in investor relationships with host governments and the threat of sovereign holdup. We know that sovereign holdup is extremely difficult to hedge or mitigate. The realization that investors can influence the nature and context of the interaction and generate trust and a sense of shared purpose allows investors to design strategies for mitigating this risk.

These strategies require a deep and sophisticated understanding of a country's political, social, cultural, and economic realities as well as the historical context in which these realities have evolved. Although gaining such an understanding may seem onerous, the payoffs can mean the difference between success and failure of an investment. In addition, such an understanding has increasing returns to scale since investors can leverage the knowledge across multiple projects within the host country and gain access to future investments.

Alignment with Government Objectives

One strategy is to make sure that investors align their investments with the stated as well as hidden policy objectives of the host government. These typically comprise poverty reduction, employment generation, technology transfer, and reliable provision of services with either a positive environmental impact or a minimal negative impact. It is also important for investors to be sensitive to hidden agendas, which can range from favored treatment to political sympathizers during job selection, building additional supporting infrastructure, providing below-cost service to politically sensitive or economically disadvantaged consumers, and so on. Although some of these objectives may not make commercial sense, investors can think of them as loss leaders, helping them meet the goal of overall returns on investment.

Aligning investment objectives with government objectives can mitigate government incentives to expropriate revenues. For example, in 1998 AES bought Telasi, the newly privatized power distribution company supplying electricity to Tbilisi in Georgia.[34] Tbilisi, the capital of Georgia, suffered from chronic power shortages especially in its harsh winter, when power was routinely available a few hours a day. In 2003 AES sold Telasi to a Russian firm, Inter RAO UES, for $26 million after paying off $60 million of AES-Telasi debt, which essentially meant that AES *paid* Inter RAO UES $34 million while relinquishing the assets. Within five years AES shareholders lost $300 million in the transaction. AES-Telasi CFO Niko Lominadze was murdered in 2002, and threats against other company officials escalated.

Initially AES-Telasi started off well, dramatically improving revenues by 91 percent from residential households by 2001 and another 42 percent by 2002. Importantly, AES-Telasi relied on improved collection, increasing collection rates from 44 percent in 2000 to 86 percent in 2002 (the break-even collection rate was 70 percent), rather than increased tariffs to achieve these results.[35] AES-Telasi improved revenues by installing new meters in households, targeting subsidies for poor households, and by launching a high-profile public relations campaign in which AES-Telasi CEO Mike Scholey debated government officials on television and convinced customers that they needed to pay for their electricity.

Unfortunately his successor, under pressure from AES corporate head-quarters to deliver financial profits, focused on the financial results, reduced payments to the government, eliminated the public relations program, suspended investments, and cut off power to nonpayers. Public and government support for AES-Telasi dwindled and ultimately turned into active hostility, culminating in the tragic death of the CFO and AES withdrawal from Georgia.

Local Community Support

I mentioned the importance of investors sharing host government interests in infrastructure assets. A related strategy for investors is to develop and nurture strong local community support. Infrastructure assets are highly idiosyncratic and localized. Since they provide local services, a strong relationship with the local community isn't just good public relations but is also good customer service, which is a basic principle of good business. Unfortunately, investors tend to focus on political leadership at the country level because initial licenses, permits, and negotiations are usually conducted with federal or central authorities.

Local political and social conditions can be markedly different. For example, in the Cochabamba case, Aguas del Tunari worked with the president of Bolivia and top central ministers but relied on the local municipality SEMAPA to inform its customers of the new water rates. Aguas del Tunari did not reach out and communicate the reasons for the tariff hike, how the hike would affect water bills, or the advantages vis-à-vis *tanqueros* water. Strong local community support can sustain an investment's returns through long periods of time by preventing sovereign holdup.

Local Partners

A third strategy that investors can adopt involves aligning with influential local partners. Local financial institutions are usually a good idea since a host government should be understandably reluctant to expropriate its own firms. Local partners are also likely to possess the relationships with host governments and local communities that allow investors to make their arguments to policy makers. Influential local partners can help influence policy in favor of investors while making investors aware of culture, business customs, government idiosyncrasies, and potential risks and opportunities.

However, politically influential partners can also become liabilities if they fall out of power. For example, Indonesia abrogated contracts signed with foreign power producers that included President Suharto's kith and kin after President Suharto fell from power, alleging corruption.[36]

Competitive Returns

A fourth strategy in infrastructure investing relates to estimating the level of returns that are deemed to be *fair and reasonable* to the host government and local customers. The strategy is to calibrate returns so as to match these fair and reasonable returns. In simple words, investors should not aim to make what could be considered *too much* money. Investors demand higher returns for high country risk. However, higher returns are obtained through higher output prices. There is a positive feedback effect between higher returns and increased risk of sovereign holdup, because high output prices, as we noted, can seem exploitative and trigger holdup. Therefore, by raising output prices, investors end up increasing political risk. Wells and Gleason (1995) term this phenomenon the "paradox of infrastructure investment."[37] Exhibit 6.3 shows the feedback effect.

By matching the fair and reasonable return expectations of the host government, investors can actually reduce the risk of sovereign holdup and thereby justify accepting lower returns in the first place. Although the

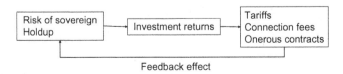

Feedback effect

EXHIBIT 6.3 The Feedback Effect

evidence for this strategy is anecdotal, it is growing. AES-Telasi also initially focused on collection but lost its investments when it attempted to focus on tariffs and rely solely on its contractual rights with the Georgian government. Later on in this chapter we take a look at Manila Water Company, which focused on increased collection of bills while raising tariffs gradually, unlike Aguas del Tunari, which tried to meet revenue targets by increasing tariffs.

A preliminary approach to estimating reasonable and fair returns can begin by comparing current prices for similar output in the country and in similar countries in the region. Investors can also consider infrastructure prices as a percentage of user incomes. For example, Manila Water's fees comprised 1.5 percent of their users' income, while Aguas del Tunari's fees in Cochabamba reached 20 percent of users' income. Manila Water is generating positive returns for investors while Aguas del Tunari sparked violent protests. Investors can then estimate the positive externalities, like creation of ancillary jobs, attracting further investments to the region, creation of new skills among the population, creating a positive reputation for the country, and so on, that the project is generating, and add these to the beginning price of output. Investors can commission local surveys of potential users, government officials, and opinion leaders to determine their perceptions of a fair and reasonable return on investment. This process not only gives investors a good estimate of fair pricing but it also allows them to decide on a communication strategy that points out the value addition of the investment and justifies the negotiated output price. The fair and reasonable price also becomes a valuable input for the initial economic analysis determining project viability. Although infrastructure assets typically do not need marketing, investors should not underestimate the importance of communicating the value proposition of the investment and shaping public opinion to prevent sovereign holdup.

The next challenge for investors is to forecast the evolution of output prices over the term of the investment. Determining current prices is relatively easy compared to modeling the possible paths along which output prices can evolve within the host country under the constraints of appearing reasonable and fair. Building such a model requires modeling macroeconomic indicators like inflation rates, exchange rates, GDP, per capita income growth rates, as well as project-specific indicators like operating and maintenance expenses, capital expenditures, debt repayments, and so on. Rather than relying solely on point estimates of output prices, investors would be wise to consider using a tool like Monte Carlo simulation to generate a distribution of output prices with mean and variances. Such an exercise likely provides insights into the evolution of future output prices that local consumers will support and prevents problems down the road.

Front-Load Cash Flows

A related strategy that investors can use to avoid long-term exposure and manage high political risk is to front-load cash flows from the project. Investors can front-load cash flows through a variety of mechanisms, usually by setting up-front fees in the form of management fees, royalty fees, commitment fees, and so on, or by setting high initial prices. For example, in the Aguas Argentinas case, the largest shareholder Suez, received a 6 percent of gross margin fee for technical know-how and operating the assets. The Paiton Energy project set very high initial tariff rates of 182 rupiahs per KWh with rates declining over the next six years.[38]

This strategy, however, can generate backlash from host countries and actually increase the risk. Front-loading communicates to the host country that investor interests are not aligned with the interests of the host government. Host country suspicions about investors are usually at their highest at the start of projects and host governments are likely to scrutinize investors' actions very closely. Project beginning is the time to lay the foundation of the long-term relationship that infrastructure investing demands. The sidebar examines the case of Manila Water Company that demonstrates these risk mitigation strategies.

MANILA WATER COMPANY

In 1997 Manila Water Company, Inc., took over from the government-owned Metropolitan Waterworks and Sewerage System (MWSS) the responsibility of providing water and sewerage services to approximately 5.3 million people living in 23 cities and municipalities over 1,400 square kilometers.[39] MWSS, with 8,000 employees, was overstaffed and inefficient, made piped water available to only 60 percent of the households, lost about 67 percent of the water to leaks and theft, and provided sewerage services to only 5 percent of the population. Moreover, the per capita income of the Philippines was only $1,156 and about 850,000 residents in Manila lived in abject poverty. Poor residents would trek for hours for water, leaving at midnight and returning by the morning.

The Ayala group, the oldest and largest business group in the Philippines, owned 60 percent of Manila Water; United Utilities, the largest private operator of water utilities in the United Kingdom, owned 20 percent; and Bechtel owned the remaining 20 percent.

(Continued)

Manila Water achieved enormous success after taking over the concession in 1997. From 1997 to 2006, Manila Water increased the number of households connected to reliable clean water from 325,000 to 909,000, representing about 5 million people. Water losses decreased from 67 percent to less than 30 percent, volume of water sold more than doubled to 992 million liters per day, percentage of areas with 24-hour water increased from 26 percent to 98 percent, percentage of people connected to the sewer system doubled albeit from a low 5 percent to 10 percent, and sewerage treatment capacity more than doubled from 40 million liters per day to 85 million liters per day. The company invested $475 million, raised $75 million through an IPO in March 2005, and made cash profits for every year after 1999 with over 50 percent EBITDA (earnings before interest, taxes, depreciation, and amortization) per dollar of sales and net income margin averaging about 30 percent. How did Manila Water succeed?

Antonino Aquino, Manila Water's president, says that the biggest reason for the success was the ability of the organization to align its sustainable development initiatives with its business objectives. The company did not lay off employees, focusing instead on retraining them and building a culture of accountability and performance through employee programs (called *Lingap Manggagawa*). The firm reduced head count through attrition and retirement while focusing on employee health and safety through its *Lingap Kalusugan* (Caring for Health and Safety) program. The other areas of focus for Manila Water were as follows:

> *Lingap Kabuhayan (Caring for Livelihood)*. The company is estimated to have generated 12,000 jobs in nine years through a policy of selecting local vendors, encouraging entrepreneurial activity, and creating jobs. Manila Water's livelihoods program partnered with Bank of the Philippine Islands to offer microfinance loans to 350 low-income households.
>
> *Lingap Barangay (Caring for the Community)*. Manila Water organized water distribution for the poorest low-income customers by using a community cooperative model. Instead of providing an individual water meter to each dwelling, Manila Water provided one mother meter for an entire community, with five or six submeters. Manila Water collected revenues from a community representative as per the mother meter

while the cooperative collected bills from individual households internally as per the submeters. The community representative was paid by the Philippine government. This method reduced collection costs, reduced illegal connections, and reduced the tariffs that individual low-income consumers had to pay, all the while delivering clean, safe water to customers and ultimately increasing goodwill.

Lingap Kalikasan (Caring for the Environment). Manila Water selected a sewage service model based on desludging trucks. Instead of building a centralized giant system of pipes connecting millions of individual households through slums that lacked space, which would be enormously costly and create land acquisition disputes, disruptions, and conflicts, Manila Water chose to use a decentralized model. The existing sewage system, if it existed at all, relied on communal septic tanks.[40] Desludging these was costly and users put it off because the large one-time expense was prohibitive. Manila Water desludges regularly by charging users a small fee on their monthly water bill. The company has set up 27 sewage treatment plants all over the city which produce treated water used for watering public green spaces, biosolids that are used for fertilizing selected land, and biogas used for power generation. Although Manila Water could dump the sewage in the sea as per their contract, the company chose to stop dumping in 2001.

When Manila Water rebased its tariff to adjust for inflation in 2003, the tariff hikes were unanimously approved by the government. In fact, community leaders and 90 *barangay* captains showed up for the hearing and asked for the hikes to be approved. Water tariffs for users consuming less than 30 cubic meters per month comprised just 1.1 percent of average monthly income, increasing as water usage increased.

Manila Water demonstrates the following strategies that mitigate the risk of sovereign holdup and political risk: The firm had a strong, influential local partner; was able to align the government's interests with its own; built employee and community support; and focused on a fair and reasonable return on invested capital.

Investors can also exploit ex ante strategies that improve investor bargaining power in the event of holdup. We have noted that sunk costs, location specificity, inability to shift production, and government ability to manage infrastructure assets all reduce investors' bargaining power in infrastructure assets. If available, investors can deploy technologies that only they can control. This naturally increases the bargaining power of investors in the event of a holdup. We have also touched upon the traditional strategy of requesting investors' home countries to lobby with the host country on investors' behalf. Another strategy that investors can adopt exploits the reputation effect that countries need to maintain with rating agencies, multilateral banks, and private lenders. In Chapter 7 I examine how these mechanisms improve investors' bargaining power in ex post renegotiations.

CONCLUSION

Among the risks that infrastructure investments face, sovereign holdup and political risk are the most important in determining investment outcomes. Infrastructure assets are susceptible to holdup because of sunk costs that can be recouped only over long periods of time; because the assets remain fixed to the ground; because investors cannot shift production; and because governments can manage infrastructure investments relatively easily. Governments remain highly involved in regulating infrastructure assets because infrastructure provides politically sensitive services. Infrastructure investments are also prone to creeping expropriation because of stable cash flows and limited growth opportunities.

Investors can mitigate and hedge these risks with political risk insurance, but it has traditionally been available only to guard against expropriation, inconvertibility, and political violence. We noted that expropriation has been replaced by creeping expropriation and breach of contract risk, while investors seek to hedge devaluation rather than inconvertibility. Creeping expropriation is particularly difficult to hedge because it can be cloaked in the regulatory authority of the host government. It is also hidden, unlike outright expropriation. Insurance as a hedging mechanism requires well-defined events that can be observed by the insurers, with waiting periods and losses that can be attributed directly to the event. These conditions make it difficult to write language defining creeping expropriation as an insured risk in insurance contracts.

Breach of contract is relatively easier to insure. However, we noted the conditionality of international arbitration that public insurance agencies like OPIC and MIGA impose before paying breach of contract claims.

Among the risk mitigation tools available to investors, we saw that while vertical integration is not possible, joint ownership is possible, while long-term contracts against sovereigns can be enforced only with difficulty. Traditionally, investors relied on their home governments to influence host governments to compensate investors for losses. The relatively recent development of international treaty arbitration is another mechanism available to investors for reclaiming losses caused by sovereign holdup. Although the ITA mechanism is increasingly popular with investors, it suffers from lack of coherence as a body of law, along with accountability and openness problems.

We also examined risk mitigation strategies that investors can adopt within host countries. Investors can reduce the probability of sovereign holdup by ensuring that their investments help fulfill host government policy goals, by building local community support rather than relying solely on distant federal authorities, and by partnering with politically influential entities. However, partnering with politically influential entities has the drawback of creating the risk of backlash if these entities lose power. Investors can also reduce the probability of holdup by reducing free cash flows available for expropriation and by avoiding the feedback effect of high returns. We noted that since host governments are apt to characterize high returns in infrastructure as exploitative, the risk of holdup increases with an increase in returns. Risk of sovereign holdup is likely to be reduced if investors determine a fair and reasonable return from the investment. Investors also need to effectively communicate the value of their investment to the community and avoid strategies that demonstrate lack of commitment to the community.

Investors can also use the strategy that exploits the host government's need to maintain its reputation among international lenders, multilateral banks, rating agencies, and prominent investors. I examine this strategy and other strategies embodied in the financing and governance structure of project finance in the next chapter.

CHAPTER 7

Project Finance
and Infrastructure

The objects of a financier are, then, to secure an ample revenue; to impose it with judgment and equality; to employ it economically; and, when necessity obliges him to make use of credit, to secure its foundations in that instance, and for ever, by the clearness and candor of his proceedings, the exactness of his calculations, and the solidity of his funds.

—Edmund Burke

Among the risks that infrastructure investors face, counterparty and sovereign holdup pose the greatest threat and are also the most difficult to hedge and mitigate. Investors can deploy mitigation strategies that reduce the probability of holdup and that increase the probability of a favorable outcome during renegotiations after a holdup. Strategies that increase the probability of a favorable outcome after a holdup try to increase the ex post bargaining power of investors. Long-term contracts, vertical integration, the strategic use of leverage, and investor-controlled technology are such strategies. Vertical integration aims to reduce the probability of holdup, while long-term contracts and leverage aim to do that as well as improve the bargaining power of investors in ex post renegotiations.

In this chapter I examine the governance and financing structure of project finance (PF), which incorporates joint ownership, long-term contracts, and high leverage. I begin by defining project finance, examining how the structure differs from traditional corporate finance or on-balance-sheet investing and how each component performs the role of risk mitigation. I apply my analysis to the Ras Laffan Liquefied Natural Gas company project in Qatar. In the second half of the chapter I analyze a popular project risk assessment model and how credit rating agencies evaluate a PF infrastructure project. Based on my analysis so far, I shift to a prescriptive mode, prescribing the role of government and developing a model that prescribes when investors can use PF profitably. The next section begins by describing a typical PF structure.

PROJECT FINANCE STRUCTURE

Brealey, Cooper, and Habib (1996) and Kim and Yoo (2008) characterize PF by all the following conditions occurring together: separate incorporation, limited or nonrecourse debt, high debt levels, detailed long-term contracts, and the use of the incorporated entity to fund a single-purpose capital asset with finite life whose composition is not altered during the course of the entity's life.[1] Although limited and nonrecourse debt are both found in PF transactions, PF focuses on repayment of loans solely from the assets for which lenders make the loan. I will therefore consider the use of nonrecourse debt in the rest of the chapter.

Exhibit 7.1 shows a typical PF transaction in the oil, gas, and petrochemical industry, Ras Laffan Liquefied Natural Gas Company. The exhibit shows that Ras Laffan is set up as a separate entity from Mobil and Qatar

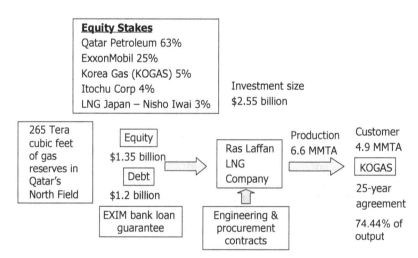

EXHIBIT 7.1   Ras Laffan Liquified Natural Gas Company
Note: MMTA: Millions of Metric Tons per Annum.
Source: R. J. Sawant, "Economics of Large-Scale Infrastructure FDI: The Case of Project Finance, *Journal of International Business Studies* (forthcoming).

Petroleum. Ras Laffan is a large, capital-intensive $2.55 billion project funded with $1.2 billion in debt. Debt holders cannot recover their loan from either Mobil or Qatar Petroleum. Korea Gas is a concentrated customer with equity in the project. We will revisit Ras Laffan and explore PF features after examining their economic functions.

Investors have used project finance to invest in infrastructure assets since ancient times. The Suez Canal was a project-financed transaction as were the North Sea oilfields. The Public Utility Regulatory Policies Act of 1978 heralded the large-scale use of project finance in the electricity generation industry. Independent power producers financed electricity plants with project finance. Power producers sold the generated power contractually through long-term power purchase agreements. A host of contracts also linked fuel suppliers, contractors, and regulatory authorities. A wide range of assets and industries used project finance very successfully during the 1990s, although there were some spectacular failures, too. Investors used the project finance structure very successfully in the development of the North Sea oilfields, the Hopewell Partners Guangzhou Highway in China, and the Petrozuata heavy oil project in Venezuela. Certainly some projects have not been financial successes, such as Motorola's Iridium project, the Channel Tunnel (Eurotunnel), and the Eurodisney theme park in Paris.

PROJECT FINANCE VERSUS CORPORATE FINANCE

A project-financed transaction differs from a corporate-financed transaction because PF requires the creation of an independent rigid structure that is off-balance-sheet and bankruptcy remote from the sponsoring firm. When a firm invests in new assets using its balance sheet, the entire balance sheet is available to repay capital providers. Lenders provide debt capital to the entire firm instead of to individual projects, and debt holders receive debt payments from the combined assets of the firm instead of solely from the newly financed assets. Equity holders share in the equity cash flows from all the assets on the balance sheet.

The equity capital providers to a PF project are called the *sponsors*. Capital providers to a PF project have limited or no recourse to the balance sheet of the investing firm. The assets are their sole source of returns. Lenders to a PF project are repaid only through cash flows generated from these assets. If cash flows are insufficient to repay interest and principal payments, lenders cannot look to the balance sheets of the sponsors to make these payments. Financial distress in the PF asset does not spill over onto the sponsoring firm's balance sheet and, conversely, financial distress from the sponsoring firm does not spill over onto the PF assets. The bankruptcy of Enron, for example, did not affect its project-financed assets, like the Bolivian pipeline company Transredes.[2]

Project finance projects are therefore legally distinct entities structured as special-purpose vehicles (SPVs) for the sole purpose of financing a single-purpose capital asset with a finite life. The composition of the SPV is not altered during the asset's life.

Project finance is also called *contract finance* because of the large number of detailed contracts that pervade every aspect of asset governance and operations. A typical PF project has over 40 contracts between suppliers, buyers, contractors, lenders, managers, employees, and host governments.[3] Project financing is more expensive than corporate financing because of higher returns demanded by lenders and the opportunity cost of time spent in due diligence of projects by sponsors, lenders, lawyers, consultants, engineers, suppliers, buyers, and government agencies. Legal and accounting fees along with greater delays in implementing projects from the many contract negotiations add to the additional costs of structuring an investment as project finance. These transaction costs are distinct from *transaction cost economics*, which refers to the costs from opportunistic holdup.

Klein, So, and Shin (1996) find that total transaction costs for infrastructure projects average 3 to 5 percent of total project cost in well-developed policy environments and 10 to 12 percent in pioneering environments. They note that projects take between two and eight years before lenders approve financing and allot funds. Importantly, the costs of technical studies appear less important than costs of dealing with governments. Klein, So, and Shin also note that there is great variation between costs and that costs show little relationship to the size of the project.[4] However, these additional costs are necessary for the benefits of risk mitigation. I continue the analysis of the risk mitigation functions of these PF features in the next section.

Separate Incorporation

The first feature of PF is the creation of an SPV that is legally distinct, bankruptcy remote, and separate from the sponsoring firm. Joint incorporation implies the use of commingled cash flows from both projects, and the firm sells debt on these combined cash flows. Flannery, Houston, and Venkataraman (1993) analyze the decision to incorporate two projects separately or jointly under a single company and show that project return variances and project return correlation are key variables in the decision to use joint or separate governance structures.[5] Exhibit 7.2 maps the relationship between these variables and agency costs.

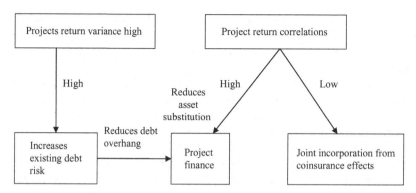

EXHIBIT 7.2 Joint versus Separate Incorporation
Source: M. J. Flannery, J. F. Houston, and S. Venkataraman, "Financing Multiple Investment Projects," *Financial Management*, Vol. 22 (2) 1993: 161–172.

When project returns are not correlated, then joint incorporation offers the benefit of coinsurance, and total cash flows from both projects are stabilized. This makes existing debt safer, reducing the *debt overhang* or underinvestment problem we noted in Chapter 4. This enables the jointly incorporated firm to optimize the debt level so that the firm can maximize the tax advantages of debt. However, joint incorporation exposes new debt holders to the threat of asset substitution (Jensen and Meckling 1976).[6] Asset substitution occurs when equity holders substitute risky assets with high volatility for safe assets with low volatility. We noted in Chapter 4 that equity holders prefer high volatility since their payoffs are akin to the payoffs from call options, which increase in value when volatility of the underlying asset increases. When project returns are correlated, the value of a jointly incorporated firm drops with the increase in correlation. This is because the high correlation of asset returns reduces coinsurance effects while the threat of asset substitution induces new debt holders to pay less for the firm's debt. In this instance, separate incorporation leads to higher firm value because separation eliminates the probability of asset substitution, which induces new debt holders to pay more for the firm's debt and accept a lower yield.

What is the impact of the project return variance? When the variance of project cash flows is high, existing debt becomes risky since the probability of EBITDA falling below required debt payments increases. We have noted that risky debt engenders incentives that lead to the debt overhang problem. In this instance, separate incorporation allows the firm to set the optimal debt level for each project such that the firm can make its debt payments, thereby inducing lenders to accept a lower yield. When project returns are volatile, separate incorporation reduces the debt overhang problem.[7]

Separate incorporation also allows the sponsoring firms to create a joint ownership structure in which sponsors can reconfigure equity stakes among the partners through negotiations. We noted that joint ownership structures are preferred in infrastructure for mitigating political risk because vertical integration is not possible when dealing with sovereign or quasi-sovereign entities. Finnerty (2007) notes that the equity investors in infrastructure projects are usually suppliers to the project or buyers of the project's products or services.[8] Sawant (2009) compares corporate-financed investments to project-financed investments and finds that 86 percent of project-financed investments are joint ventures compared to 50 percent of corporate-financed investments.[9]

Separate incorporation permits sponsoring firms to negotiate equity stakes with the concentrated suppliers or buyers. Concentrated suppliers and/or buyers bear a portion of the up-front costs and put their capital at risk when they take equity stakes in the assets. These equity stakes are sunk costs which suppliers/buyers recover through the successful operation of the project. The sponsors therefore mitigate the risk of ex post holdup by suppliers/buyers because these sunk costs improve the bargaining position of the sponsors in ex post renegotiations by credibly threatening loss of this capital if the supplier/buyer attempts a holdup.[10]

The credible threat of loss of equity capital arises from the strategic use of high leverage. We have noted that high leverage shields wealth from suppliers/buyers and improves the bargaining position of sponsors in ex post renegotiations. When a project's cash flows are precommitted contractually, a holdup results in a shortfall in cash available to repay the project's lenders. This potential threat reduces the probability of holdup when some sunk capital is at risk.

During renegotiations, if the assets halt production the supplier stops supplying to the project and consequently loses revenues. Similarly, a concentrated buyer loses input supplies and loses revenues from production stoppages. This dynamic opens up an interesting methodology for investors in determining their choice of suppliers or buyers. Investors should select suppliers who derive a majority or large proportion of their revenues from sales to the project and who are likely to experience hardships from a loss of those revenues. Similarly, investors should select buyers who source a large proportion of their input needs from the project's output such that a stoppage of production will cause a severe disruption to their business. This strategy is of course industry-specific and would probably not work in all infrastructure industries, for example, road transportation.

In the case of joint ownership with sovereign entities, the equity stake mitigates the risk of sovereign holdup because the probability of a sovereign expropriating itself or its entities is relatively low. Sovereign or quasi-sovereign partners are also likely to be in a better position to influence host government policy and help shift expropriatory inclinations away from the project. A threat of bankruptcy is unlikely to have the same effect there as on a concentrated nonsovereign supplier or buyer, because we noted that host governments can take over infrastructure assets and operate them while vitiating the claims of the lenders, too. Investors need to rely on reputation effects, which I discuss in a later section.

Nonrecourse Debt

The next PF characteristic is the nonrecourse nature of PF debt. A PF investment financed with new capital utilizes cash flows solely from the new assets for returning new capital, unlike a corporate-financed investment which uses commingled cash flows to repay capital providers. If the PF assets do not generate sufficient cash flows for repaying capital providers, lenders cannot look to the sponsoring firm's balance sheet for recouping their capital. The sponsoring firm is therefore insulated from the risk that failure of a large capital-intensive investment will drag down the investing firm.[11] Sawant (2009) shows that the propensity for project finance increases with the size of the investment, implying that firms structure large investments separately as PF.[12]

Nonrecourse debt also plays a strategic role in mitigating holdup. We have noted that a credible threat of bankruptcy mitigates holdup. Nonrecourse makes a threat of default credible because a sovereign or concentrated counterparty cannot look to the balance sheet of the sponsoring firm to meet demands for additional payments. The nonrecourse nature of the debt therefore reinforces the mechanism of high leverage.

Of course, nonrecourse debt also means that debt providers must rely solely on a single stream of cash flows because the complete balance sheet of the borrower is not available to compensate them. Debt providers lose the benefit of coinsurance. While the loss of coinsurance increases the risk for debt providers, debt providers compensate for the risk through due diligence, transparent cash flows, preventing asset substitution, and pricing the debt appropriately. The next section examines the economic function of structuring the SPV with a single-purpose asset whose composition remains unchanged throughout its life.

Single-Purpose Asset

We have seen how separate incorporation permits the sponsoring firm to set an optimal capital structure for the new asset. We also noted that separate incorporation reduces the benefit of coinsurance for lenders while also reducing the threat of asset substitution. Debt providers give up the benefits of coinsurance in exchange for eliminating the threat of asset substitution, which they do by contractually requiring the SPV to maintain a single asset on its balance sheet. Lenders also ensure that the investment generates sufficient cash flows to repay the interest and principal payments by performing due diligence. Due diligence comprises an analysis of the asset's debt service coverage ratios, revenues, capacity utilization, input and output prices, and so on. Later in this chapter I examine the International Project Risk Assessment (IPRA) model, which is one method of performing due diligence. The transparency of cash flows from a single-purpose asset permits sponsors to eliminate the information asymmetries between equity and debt holders that can lead to mispriced debt. By restricting the SPV to a single asset throughout its life, sponsors can reduce the costs from information asymmetry and the need for due diligence.

Lenders then try to isolate the cash flows and ring-fence the assets through contracts. Debt providers also price PF debt in exchange for accepting nonrecourse status. Megginson and Kleimeier (2000) show that PF debt is more expensive than comparable corporate finance debt, at about 44 basis points spread over LIBOR, as demonstrated in Exhibit 7.3. The exhibit shows the pricing of different forms of debt.

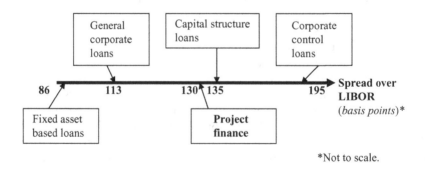

EXHIBIT 7.3   Project Finance versus Other Loans: Spread over LIBOR
Source: S. Kleimeier and W. L. Megginson, "Are Project Finance Loans Different from Other Syndicated Credits?" *Journal of Applied Corporate Finance* 13, no. 1 (2000): 75–87.

Debt and equity providers therefore create a rigid structure that is effectively monitored. The structure fits the characteristics of infrastructure assets since these do not need the flexibility that intangible assets with high growth options require. A corporate firm's managers have the ability to reconfigure the firm's asset portfolio along with the capital structure. The corporate firm is a legal fiction with enduring life. A PF structure remains limited to the finite life of the asset, and interlocking contracts prevent managers from exercising similar flexibility. This is not to say that managers are precluded from exercising operational flexibility. Clearly, the quality of management affects the performance of the assets, as we saw in Chapter 6 the case of Manila Water Company. Managers must work under the constraints of long-term contracts, which are considered in the next section.

Long-Term Contracts

In Chapter 5 I analyzed the holdup problem as a problem of *incomplete contracts*, which means that investors cannot anticipate every future state of the world, yet must make specific investments before they can experience these states. We saw that investors rely on courts to complete the contracts in the sense that the remedies that courts award for breach of contract create different incentives for investors. The remedy of specific performance allows the investing party to force its counterparty to perform as per the terms of the contract and resolve the holdup problem. We also noted that such a legal infrastructure with well-established breach of contract remedies that are speedily administered may be unavailable in developing countries. Additionally, local courts may not be sympathetic to foreign investors in disputes with sovereign entities. In these instances we saw that investors have a variety of hedging and mitigation strategies available to them, including international treaty arbitration. Long-term contracts are therefore a starting and not an end point in the long process of infrastructure investing. They are a necessary but not sufficient condition for preventing and resolving holdup.

In the PF structure, long-term contracts not only fulfill their role of mitigating holdup, they also create a rigid capital structure that significantly reduces managerial discretion. In Chapter 4 we noted that infrastructure asset characteristics imply that discretionary investments in future growth options are not needed. Managers must instead maximize operational effectiveness. Since infrastructure assets generate large amounts of cash flow, investors must create structures that monitor managers and ensure that free cash flows are returned to capital providers.[13] Long-term contracts and high leverage create these incentives. Among the contracts that the PF structure uses, the most important contract is the *cash flow waterfall*.[14] The cash flow

waterfall lays out in great detail cash expenditure as well as cash distribution. The contract specifies capital expenditure as well as maintenance
expenditure and also divvies up the cash flows between lenders and sponsors. The cash flow waterfall precommits future cash flows, removing them
from predatory inclinations. Other contracts include contracts between the
sponsors and contractors, suppliers, customers, and lenders.

High Leverage

Although we have examined high leverage as a solution to holdup, we have
not quantified what constitutes high debt levels or examined whether high
leverage is statistically significant. Esty (2003) notes that project finance
debt levels average around 70 percent.[15] Leverage in Vaaler et al.'s (2008)
sample averages 75.02 percent with a standard deviation of 18.5 percent;[16]
Kim and Yoo (2008) find that average debt level for 2,697 projects from
the Thomson SDC project finance database is 84.8 percent with standard
deviation of 18.9 percent;[17] while in Sawant's (2009) sample, PF debt levels
are 70 percent while corporate debt levels are 39 percent.[18] PF debt is
therefore two standard deviations more than corporate debt levels and is a
statistically significant phenomenon.

We have noted that the strategic use of leverage performs a number of
economic functions: mitigating counterparty holdup, precommitting cash
flows, reducing reported profits, monitoring managers, and increasing the
bargaining power of sponsors in ex post renegotiations. In this section I
examine how high leverage deters creeping expropriation and activates the
reputation effect, which increases the bargaining power of sponsors in ex
post renegotiations with sovereign entities.

High leverage essentially reveals creeping expropriation which, as we
noted in Chapter 6, is mostly hidden. High leverage creates a situation
wherein even a small shortfall in cash flows because of increased host government demand can cause the project to default. A threat of default induces
lenders to join the renegotiations on behalf of the sponsors. Leverage therefore serves as an early warning and monitoring mechanism for the lending
syndicate. The lending syndicate typically comprises major players in the
international financial community, like the multilateral lending institutions,
global lending banks, insurance companies, endowments, and pension
funds. The probability of a favorable outcome for the sponsors and the
lenders increases when these institutions seek to influence host governments.
Woodhouse (2006) demonstrates that the outcome for sponsors is much
better when bilateral and multilateral lending institutions form part of the
lending syndicates.[19] Hainz and Kleimeier (2007) reveal that multilateral
lending institutions like the World Bank's International Finance Corporation,

OPIC, and others, act as political umbrellas and mitigate political risk.[20] The related reputation effect engendered by the syndicate form of lending found in PF is examined in the next section.

Syndicated Lending

Finnerty (2007) finds that only about 10 percent of all PF lending takes place using capital market bond lending,[21] while 90 percent of PF lending takes place using lending syndicates. Moreover, bond lending is a relatively recent phenomenon.[22] I argue in this section that syndicate lending creates incentives for host governments that mitigate sovereign holdup in the form of a reputation effect.

The reputation effect of mitigating sovereign holdup relies on the reputation that host governments need to maintain with major international financial institutions. For example, although the Multilateral Investment Guarantee Agency (MIGA) provides insurance to investors that protects against sovereign holdup, MIGA mediates disputes, thereby preventing insurance claims payout. Since its inception through 2001, MIGA has issued 72 guarantees to 39 electricity investments and has paid just one claim while mediating five disputes with host governments.[23]

In the context of a global economy and relatively free capital flows, government reliance on the international financial markets has increased. In any case, investors are unlikely to venture their capital in countries that are totally cut off from the global economy. When governments resort to expropriatory measures against important players in the international financial markets, they face the risk of penalties for future investments and a demand for increased returns from investors as compensation against the increased risk. Indeed, Woodhouse (2006) notes that government officials regard debt payments as a hard constraint on their ability to restrict payments to a project. The government-owned Tamil Nadu Electricity Board in India continues to make ad-hoc payments to the Pillai Perumal Nallur project (Apollo Infrastructure Projects Finance Co. Ltd. 28 percent, PSEG 20 percent, Marubeni Corporation 26 percent, and El Paso Energy 26 percent owned) for debt payments, despite reneging on contracts to pay for power.[24] Therefore, when host government actions threaten payments to important syndicate lenders, governments forbear from actions that damage their reputations in the international financial markets.

The implication of the reputation effect is that debt syndication is a superior form of lending compared to bond lending because investors can put together a syndicate of lenders who are capable of influencing host governments.[25] Bond lending through the capital markets usually involves diffuse bondholders who lack the ability to influence host governments.

Investors therefore should pay great attention to the quality and type of the lending syndicate. Esty and Megginson (2003) show that syndicates become larger with more participating banks as legal risk increases.[26] Their measure of legal risk is a composite based on five measures: effectiveness of the judiciary, rule of law, risk of contract repudiation, absence of corruption, and risk of expropriation. It is likely, therefore, that the quality of the syndicate is an important variable, particularly in terms of capability for influencing host government behavior.

Leverage also activates the reputation mechanism of the lending syndicate.[27] In the absence of high leverage, governments can expropriate cash flows flowing to equity investors without affecting cash flows to the lending syndicate. As such, the lending syndicate has no inducement to intervene and prevent the creeping expropriation. Additionally, the lending syndicate has no *locus standi* to intervene, since host government actions are not threatening the syndicate's debts. High leverage therefore immediately threatens cash flows flowing to the lending syndicate, inducing it to intervene and giving it the right to do so.

Now that we have examined the economics of each institutional feature of project finance, let us revisit the Ras Laffan project shown in Exhibit 7.1.

RAS LAFFAN REVISITED

Ras Laffan demonstrates typical project finance features. Seventy-five percent of the output LNG is sold to a single buyer, Korea Gas (KOGAS), through a long-term (25-year) take-or-pay contract, with pricing based on a minimum floor price of US $18.60 or higher through a proxy LNG market price based on crude oil, while all the condensate is bought by the sponsors themselves.

The ownership structure shows joint ownership between Qatar government-owned Qatar General Petroleum Corporation (QGPC) and Mobil (later ExxonMobil), with equity stakes held by Korea Gas and LNG marketers Nissho Iwai Corporation and Itochu Corporation for Japanese buyers. The inclusion of QGPC as a state-owned majority local partner is probably required to conduct business in Qatar but it still mitigates sovereign holdup risk. The inclusion of KOGAS and LNG marketers ensures that counterparty risk is mitigated. The financing structure itself shows high leverage. Leverage comprises both capital market bonds and syndicated debt from commercial banks and export credit agencies (ECAs) comprising British Export Credits Guarantee Department (ECGD), French COFACE, Italian SACE, U.S. Export-Import Bank (EXIM), and Export-Import Bank of Japan (JEXIM). The participation of the wide range of ECAs ensures the reputation effect.

Ras Laffan Liquified Natural Gas Co. Ltd. is a bankruptcy-remote special-purpose vehicle organized to exploit the gas reserves from Qatar's North Fields. The asset is a wasting, single-purpose capital asset. Ras Laffan's construction uses debt rather than equity, as we would expect, but completion guarantees from Mobil and QGPC ensure that completion risk is borne by the sponsors. Ras Laffan's investment is sunk and sponsors cannot recover the investment without cash flows from the sale of condensate, sulphur, and gas. KOGAS is responsible for providing, maintaining, repairing, and operating LNG tankers with Ras Laffan approval and exclusively for Ras Laffan LNG. Ras Laffan investments display high asset specificity.

Exhibit 7.4 shows a schematic of the web of contracts between the parties that characterizes a project-financed investment.

Let us begin the discussion with the State of Qatar, which grants the North Fields development and exploitation rights to QGPC under a land

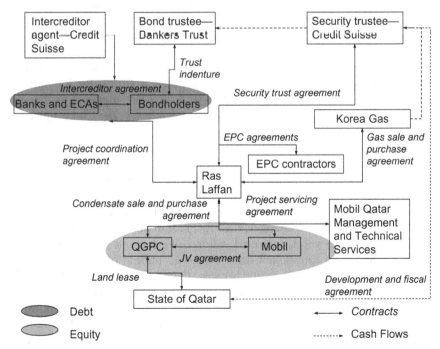

EXHIBIT 7.4 Ras Laffan's Web of Contracts
Source: Author analysis.

lease. QGPC forms Ras Laffan LNG Co. Ltd. with Mobil under a joint venture agreement to exploit these rights. The sponsors, QGPC and Mobil, agree to buy all condensate and sulfur output through the condensate sale and purchase agreement. Korea Gas agrees to purchase gas through the gas sale and purchase agreement. Mobil Qatar Management and Technical Services Inc. agrees to furnish engineering technical expertise and run LNG operations under a project services agreement. Mobil is therefore a contractor and buyer as well as an equity owner in this project. As a contractor running the operations, Mobil's cash flow rights are placed ahead of lenders and the State of Qatar. The State of Qatar gives development and exploitation rights and favorable tax treatment, a 12-year tax holiday, in exchange for royalties at 9 percent of condensate sales indexed to the price of LNG, at a minimum price of US $0.50 per million British thermal units (MMBTU) of gas sold, through the development and fiscal agreement.

Ras Laffan is built through three engineering, procurement, and construction (EPC) contracts which are fixed-price, turnkey, and date-certain, between Ras Laffan and the contractors. LNG contractors are JGC and M.W. Kellogg, while the offshore contractors are Saipem and a joint venture between J. Ray McDermott and ETPM International SA. We noted that although debt is used to fund the construction, the sponsors bear construction risk because sponsors must fund all cost increases with additional equity. The EPC contracts provide for payment approval, performance tests, and warranties. The contractors must pay liquidated damages to Ras Laffan if construction targets are not met. Additionally, Ras Laffan cannot change the scope of the work without lender approval, and must complete work by the specified date or repay lenders as per the completion guarantees.

We noted that PF debt is nonrecourse to the sponsors and that lenders ring-fence the asset. Lenders ring-fence Ras Laffan assets through the project coordination agreement between Ras Laffan, bondholders, ECAs, and the commercial banks. The agreement requires Ras Laffan to seek approval from the ECAs and banks in order to enter into any sale and purchase agreement. If Qatari law changes, then Ras Laffan must allow senior project lenders to obtain a valid, perfected, enforceable security interest in project property. Sponsors cannot sell more than $30 million of assets in a year. The sponsors cannot exit easily because they cannot issue capital stock before completion without consent of the intercreditor agent (I describe the intercreditor agreement shortly), and after completion must maintain a minimum of 21 percent economic interests and voting rights. Ras Laffan can issue additional debt only if the project forecasts a debt service coverage ratio (DSCR) of 1.3 and loan life coverage ratio (LLCR) greater than 1.70. These covenants significantly constrain equity holders as well as managerial discretion, as managers must seek debt holder approval for altering the asset composition and even for selling output to a buyer.

Relations between the lenders, bondholders, ECAs, and commercial banks are defined through the intercreditor agreement. The agreement provides for *pari passu* rights, which means that bondholders, ECAs, and commercial banks have rights, equal to their exposure to the project, on claims on collateral and cash distributions. The intent is to ensure that bondholders, ECAs, and commercial banks have rights equal to their exposure because the exposures change as the loans are amortized. Credit Suisse is the intercreditor agent for Ras Laffan, and the agreement provides it with the authority to establish accounts for bond proceeds, project revenues and proceeds, and denotes the application and priority of those funds. The intercreditor agreement limits the exercise of remedies, including acceleration of payment, subject to the vote of all senior lenders. Bondholders are paid interest and principal through a bond trustee, Bankers Trust Co., under a trust indenture agreement.

The project mitigates currency risk and political risk through a security trust agreement. Korea Gas pays for its gas by depositing dollars in a New York account beyond Qatari shores. Under the security trust agreement, security trustee Credit Suisse ensures that lenders receive interest and principal payments after operations and maintenance expenses have been met. Payment of royalties and taxes takes place next. Distribution to sponsors takes place only after a debt service reserve account is fully funded with at least six months of interest and principal payments. Actual and projected loan life coverage ratios must also exceed 1.40 before cash is distributed to sponsors. This structure removes all free cash flows from management control and returns capital to capital providers.

Finally, the project carries insurance as part of the joint venture (JV) agreement and the project coordination agreement. Insurance covers well control during exploration, construction risk, operating risk, and business interruption risk. Exhibit 7.5 examines the remedies available to lenders in the event of a default.

We noted that in a PF transaction, lenders are repaid solely from cash flows from assets pledged as collateral. In the event of Ras Laffan default the lenders have rights to foreclose on the assets. Qatari law, however, has no provisions for a security interest in the tangible assets of the project. In order to overcome this serious issue Ras Laffan adopted the structure shown in exhibit 7.5. Ras Laffan signs an asset transfer agreement under Qatari law with Ras Laffan Holdings LDC, a Cayman Islands company. The asset transfer agreement assigns absolutely all of Ras Laffan's onshore and off-shore assets, vehicles, and other tangible assets as well as the leasehold interest under the land lease to Ras Laffan Holdings LDC. Ras Laffan

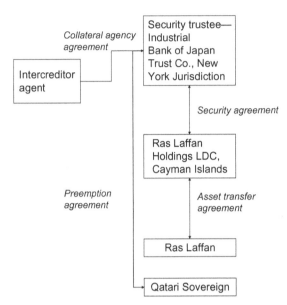

EXHIBIT 7.5 Ras Laffan Lenders' Rights
Source: Author analysis.

Holdings LDC pledges the collateral to the security trustee under a security agreement under New York legal jurisdiction. This method has been ratified by Qatar's Emir under an Emiri decree. The security agreement with the security trustee, the Industrial Bank of Japan Trust Co., in "shared collateral" grants security interest to the lenders, which includes accounts, moneys, personal property, contract rights, assignable government authorizations and approvals, insurance policies, project revenues, produced natural gas, and gas products, except for tangible assets of the project plant.

The collateral agency agreement authorizes the security trustee to administer project collateral, exercise remedies under supervision of the intercreditor agent, and apply the proceeds to the lenders as per their rights specified in the intercreditor agreement. However, under a preemption agreement, the State of Qatar has rights of first refusal if the collateral is foreclosed upon.

This analysis so far demonstrates how project finance handles the risks in infrastructure investing. In the next section I examine how infrastructure investing risks and project finance are analyzed by rating agencies and construction firms. Clearly there is a vast literature and well-developed best practices on the engineering and construction aspects of infrastructure investing. I noted that technical risk, which includes construction, technology, and operations risk, resulted in 1.4 percent of all project debt downgrades in the S&P study of project finance debt from 1994 to 2004.[28] The science of managing construction and operational risk is therefore highly researched and well understood. It is the art of governance and the soft skills of political risk mitigation that are challenging. I briefly examine some of these tools in terms of my analysis.

PROJECT RISK ANALYSIS

I begin with the widely followed International Project Risk Assessment Model (IPRA) from the Construction Industry Institute.[29] The IPRA model follows a reductionist approach to project management, in which project risks are organized into categories and then reduced to subcategories. The risks are organized in a structured form for ease of enumeration and management. The Project Management Institute defines a *risk breakdown structure* (RBS) as "a hierarchically organized depiction of the identified project risks arranged by risk category and subcategory that identifies the various areas and causes of potential risks."[30] The RBS is a qualitative model, and a typical model breaks down project risks into four or more sections—for example, commercial, country, facilities, production, operations. Each section is broken down into further project risks. Exhibit 7.6 shows the IPRA model with its risk components.

We can break down each project into project variables representing the key drivers of the project's performance or cash flows. The decomposition of a project into its key performance drivers is usually industry-specific and is called the *project breakdown structure* (PBS).[31] Similar to the RBS, the PBS further breaks down each key performance driver into subdrivers. Exhibit 7.7 on page 163 shows an example of a PBS.

In the next stage, project planners obtain a clearer picture of how each of the risks is likely to affect each individual performance variable, and consequently the whole project, by combining the risk breakdown structure with the project breakdown structure.[32] Exhibit 7.8 on page 164 shows the risk breakdown structure combined with the project breakdown structure.

Although a thorough analysis of the RBS and PBS models is beyond the scope of this book, let us briefly examine a few aspects of the model. The model ensures that firms gain a comprehensive inventory of project risks and project variables. The model also ensures that the firm understands which risks are likely to affect project variables. For example, in Exhibit 7.8, shaded boxes represent the project variables most affected by risks reflected in the RBS on the left-hand side. Therefore, in this example, country risk on the left-hand side affects the project variables listed at the

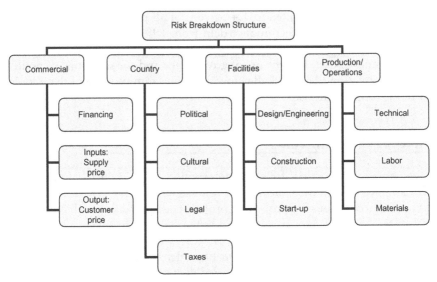

EXHIBIT 7.6   IPRA Model: Risk Breakdown Structure

top through shaded boxes in the country risk row; specifically the construction variable through the licenses and permits subvariable, and the tax variable and revenue variables through the output price and price indexation subvariables.

Since the RBS model is qualitative in nature, investors may use expert opinions to weight the risks. As practiced currently, this model has some shortcomings in the infrastructure context which investors should be aware of. The model combines construction and post-construction risks and project variables together. As we have seen, infrastructure projects face different risks and have different key performance variables during the construction and post-construction phases. Sovereign holdup is less relevant during the construction phase since countries want the new investments. An infrastructure project has no output or input for production and does not generate positive cash flows during the construction phase. Similarly, my analysis of equity as a preferable mode of financing for the construction phase is not revealed by the model since conflicting stakeholder incentives do not show up in the inventory of risks. Simply separating construction and post-construction phases and including stakeholder incentives potentially overcomes these issues.

A more difficult issue relates to the assumption of the hierarchical nature and representation of the risks and project variables. The hierarchical nature

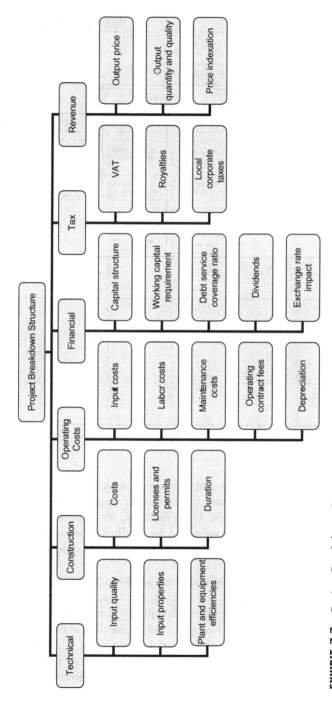

EXHIBIT 7.7   Project Breakdown Structure

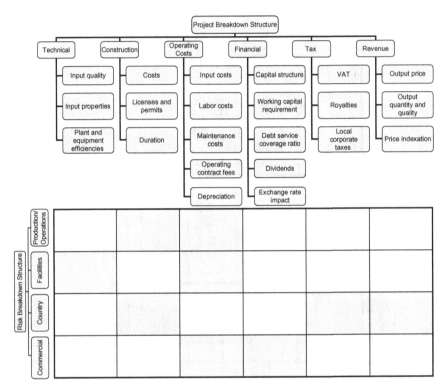

EXHIBIT 7.8 Combination of RBS and PBS

of risks flows from the reductionist approach, which assumes that if we breakdown the multiple risk classes to their individual components we will be able to define the entire system. Unfortunately, this approach does not account for feedback effects that we noted are vitally important in mitigating several risks. The RBS and PBS structures therefore risk ignoring feedback effects *across* variables.

As an example of feedback effect across variables, consider the variable of output prices. Output prices are a key project variable and the project is exposed to the risk that output prices will not rise sufficiently to cover inflation, or devaluation of local currency when the debt is denominated in foreign currency. In order to mitigate this risk, the output sale and purchase contract includes provisions for price increases. We have seen, however, that rising output prices increase the risk of sovereign holdup, the risk of community backlash, and the risk of nonpayment by consumers. The output price variable therefore affects the financial variable.

For example, in 2001, the Philippines began a process of reexamining all 35 independent power producer (IPP) contracts entered into from 1992 through 1993. The process culminated when 6 contracts were cleared and the remaining 29, considered "grossly disadvantageous, or onerous to the government," were renegotiated. These 29 IPPs accepted cost and fee reductions that generated savings with a net present value of almost a $1 billion for the government.[33] The RBS and PBS approach to managing risk in infrastructure project finance is therefore well suited to the construction phase of infrastructure assets but has limitations for the operational phases.

I now examine the process by which rating agencies measure risk in project finance.

CREDIT RATING AGENCIES

Credit rating agencies like Standard & Poors, Moody's, and Fitch primarily rate project finance bonds or capital market securities. We know that although approximately 10 percent of infrastructure assets are funded through capital market instruments like bonds, the trend towards using capital market instruments is increasing. Let us begin by examining Standard & Poor's credit rating framework. Standard & Poor's also uses a hierarchical structure with levels of analysis or categories. Exhibit 7.9 displays the levels of analysis that S&P uses to assign its credit ratings.

Standard & Poor's believes that each project's competitive market position is very important since it drives the project's ability to generate cash flows and therefore to make payments to its creditors. Infrastructure assets, by virtue of their monopoly-like characteristics and provision of basic products and services, must be among the lowest-cost producers to receive high scores. This analysis is critical to the success of any infrastructure investment, and the model addresses the issue very well.

Examining the subcategory of technology, construction, and operations, we have noted that post-construction infrastructure assets are technologically and operationally low-risk assets. Prior to construction, we have noted that intrusive management provided by equity mitigates the risk of cost overruns and delays. Debt is not a good instrument for this task, especially diffuse bondholders who do not possess the supervisory and decision-making authority of owners. Standard & Poor's points to the substantial evidence in project finance when sponsors have not aided SPVs floundering under construction problems and lenders have suffered severe losses.[34] We note that sponsors should have been responsible for construction in the first

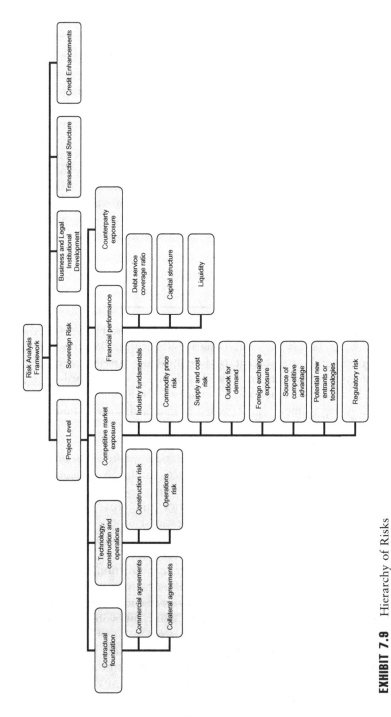

EXHIBIT 7.9 Hierarchy of Risks
Source: Standard and Poor's "Updated Project Finance Summary Debt Rating Criteria," September 18, 2007.

place. Therefore, debt provided for construction must rely on the sponsor's balance sheet, and nonrecourse at this stage is particularly risky.

Standard & Poor's relies on independent engineer's project evaluation if available, and in its absence is likely to grant a speculative rating to a project. We have noted that, first of all, technologically complex assets possess different characteristics, and investors should not consider these as infrastructure assets suitable for project finance. Second, specialized technology introduced in oil and gas or mining, for example, that only the sponsor can control, protects investors from sovereign holdup. An additional complication arises from specialized technology: Sponsors are typically unwilling to share their technology with their JV partners who might be competitors, or to expose their technology to theft by local firms. This implies that the governance structure of project finance is unnecessary since the sponsor protects itself from sovereign holdup using its specialized technology while simultaneously controlling technology leakage through a wholly owned subsidiary.

S&P's subcategory of contractual foundation refers to key commercial agreements like power purchase agreements, concession agreements, oil and gas supply agreements, and so on, which determine the level of protection the assets receive from market and operating conditions. Therefore, hell- or high water, take-or-pay contracts receive the highest rating scores.*

Unfortunately, as we have noted, contracts are subject to renegotiation once assets are in place and capital is sunk. We have also noted the mechanisms through which investors can increase their bargaining power in post-contractual renegotiations, particularly the quality of the lending syndicate, the role of multilateral lending agencies, the role and quality of local partners, the ability of management to influence government policies, relationships with the community and influential opinion leaders, and strategic use of leverage. In fact, host governments may agree to onerous contracts initially that purportedly fully protect investor interests when they need investments, yet the very same ironclad clauses that protected investors can cause renegotiation. Rating agencies must take into account the feedback effect of infrastructure investments for an accurate credit rating. It appears that S&P does not incorporate these factors in its analysis of credit rating. Admittedly some of these factors are so-called soft factors and difficult to measure quantitatively, like management's political management skills, and syndicate quality vis-à-vis the host country.

---

* A hell-or-high-water contract obligates the purchaser of a project's output to make cash payments to the project in all events, even if no product is offered for sale. A take-or-pay contract penalizes the buyer for not purchasing (taking) a minimum quantity of output over some period of time.

Standard & Poor's takes into account the presence of multilateral agencies in its category of credit enhancements only in terms of the insurance coverage they provide. Standard & Poor's does note that insurance may enhance post-default recovery but may not prevent default. We note that the insurance function may in fact be less important than the reputation effect that the multilateral agencies generate. Multilateral agencies mitigate the probability of default through mediation between host governments and investors. Standard & Poor's also ignores the quality of the lending syndicate. For example, investors would benefit by including the Japan Bank of International Cooperation (JBIC) as a syndicate partner when investing in Thailand, and the Asian Development Bank (ADB) when investing in the Philippines.

Standard & Poor's subcategory of financial performance measures debt service coverage ratio (DSCR) and points out that high leverage increases the risk of project default from interest rate volatility, inflation, foreign exchange rate volatility, liquidity, and funding risk.[35] A higher DSCR equates to a better credit rating. We have noted the benefits from strategic use of high debt: precommitting cash flows, thereby removing cash flows from expropriatory attention; serving as an effective monitoring mechanism to expose creeping expropriation; activating the reputation effect; reducing reported profits; reducing agency costs of free cash flow; shielding wealth from counterparties; regulating counterparty behavior; and matching the governance needs of infrastructure assets. These opposing effects indicate that the relationship between leverage and project default is not linear. A high DSCR, indicating low debt, increases the project's ability to service debt obligations but increases the risk from sovereign and counterparty holdup. The precise DSCR that balances the risks of holdup against the risk of liquidity, foreign exchange, and interest rate volatility depends on an individual project's context. Ceteris paribus, higher leverage is better for infrastructure assets, and credit ratings should reflect this fact.

S&P's subcategory of counterparty exposure is assessed primarily on the credit rating of the counterparty and on the nature of the contract with the counterparty.[36] We have noted the joint ownership mode of mitigating counterparty risk and its prevalence in project-financed projects. In conjunction with the specific investments counterparties make with respect to the project, and with the impact of supply or sale disruptions on counterparty business, joint ownership is a powerful incentive to prevent counterparty risk. Including these considerations in the rating methodology rather than relying solely on counterparty credit ratings and contractual obligations likely better reflects the credit risk from counterparty risk.

Finally, S&P's category of business and institutional development, while focusing appropriately on the choice of jurisdiction (New York and

London are preferred), protection of property rights, independent judiciary, legal precedent, and so on, ignores whether investors can take advantage of bilateral investment treaties of the host government and the importance of the international treaty arbitration (ITA) mechanism. The increasing importance of the ITA mechanism as the forum of choice for recovering investments and the deterrence effect this may induce in host governments likely counts towards a project's credit rating.

While I could similarly analyze Moody's and Fitch's rating methodologies, I eschew repeating the analysis in the interests of parsimony. The issues I identified likely apply to these agencies, too. Credit ratings perform the role of credit evaluation for capital market lending similar to the role that banks perform for lending against bank balance sheets. Banks traditionally intermediate between lenders and borrowers, obtaining short-term deposits from depositors, which are bank liabilities, and lending these deposits as long-term loans, which are bank assets. When banks lend against their balance sheet they need to maintain an equity cushion to protect against losses from outstanding loans. The risk capital that banks must maintain increases with the riskiness of the bank's assets or loans. The amount of equity or risk capital that banks must maintain is mandated by government regulations. An increase in risk capital that banks must set aside increases the cost of capital because equity is more expensive than deposits and other sources of bank capital. Banks would much rather be loaning the capital and generating fees and spread income. This requirement of maintaining an equity cushion does not apply to capital market instruments like bonds and, ceteris paribus, leads to a lower cost of capital.

I discuss the differences between capital market securities and bank syndicated debt further in Chapter 8. I also examine the regulations from the Bank for International Settlements, the international organization that serves as a bank for central banks, affecting project finance lending and popularly called Basel II, in Chapter 8. In the following section I describe a simple framework that examines when investors should consider using the project finance structure.

USING THE PROJECT FINANCE STRUCTURE

We can analyze the decision to use project finance as a financing and governance structure for assets in terms of the probability of default and the loss given default. The probability of default rises when an asset is exposed to market risk, technology risk, and exchange rate risk.

Market risk is the risk that the costs of the asset's input increase, or the risk that revenues from sale of the asset's output decrease. Market risk on the revenue side can arise from reduced demand; for example, in an economic recession the number of toll road users may decrease since users prefer to use congested but free alternative roads. Similarly, the economy may see a decreased demand for electricity, in which case electricity generating plants that supply peak load power will see a drop in demand. Utilities demand power from peak load power plants only when the demand for electricity exceeds the electricity supplied by base load power plants. Typically base load power plants produce the cheapest electricity and generate power continuously; a good example is nuclear or hydroelectric plants. Consequently, merchant power plants that supply peak load power will see a drop in their revenues. Market risk on the cost side can arise from rising input prices; for example, rising oil and gas prices increase the costs of inputs for power plants using oil and gas. Market risk therefore relates to uncertainty in demand for output and uncertainty in supply and pricing of inputs.

Technology risk increases the probability of default when projects use new technology and uncertainty about the technology's performance is pervasive. Examples of new technology that used project finance include Iridium, Motorola's satellite telecommunication project, and the Bulong nickel mine in Australia, which used pressure acid leach technology. Bulong nickel mine's problems with the new technology prevented production from reaching full capacity in 2001, five years after the mine commenced operations in 1997.[37] The mine was taken over by Barclays Bank and U.S. bondholders in 2002 after Preston Resources, the equity holders, could not make scheduled debt payments.[38] Motorola's $5 billion Iridium project was even more ambitious and aimed at providing wireless communications to consumers anywhere on the planet through a network of 88 satellites orbiting the earth. The project collapsed when it could not sign up enough customers because the high costs of the service ($3,000 per handset and $3 to $7 a minute) made it impossible to compete with significantly lower-cost cellular tower–based wireless technologies.[39] Private investors bought Iridium for $24 million and, amazingly, a decade later it still exists and is even profitable, providing service to areas of the earth as diverse as the jungles of Amazon and the Arctic regions.

Exhibit 7.10 analyzes the impact of probability of default and loss given default on the decision to use project finance. It shows that a low loss given default is a necessary condition for PF investing. In other words, the asset must retain its value even under conditions of default. We have noted that a default results in significant destruction of the asset's value when the value of the asset depends directly and substantially on the value of embedded growth options and the capability of management to exploit the options. Biotechnology firms, computer software firms, and similar firms possess

EXHIBIT 7.10   Using the PF structure

		Probability of Default	
		High	Low
Loss Given Default	Low	Use either corporate or project finance. Examples: toll roads, theme parks, peak load electricity generating merchant power plants.	Use project finance. Examples: base load electricity generating plants, refineries, mining, pipelines, water and sewer distribution, electricity distribution.
	High	Do not use project finance. Examples: biotechnology firms, computer software and hardware.	Do not use project finance. Examples: intangible asset firms, service businesses, established consumer brands— Procter & Gamble, Coke, Nestlé, Phillip Morris.

Source: Author analysis.

intangible assets with high growth potential but with little value under default. Such assets should not be and are unlikely to be funded with project finance. However, lenders can take possession of the A2 motorway or the Sutton Bridge power project in the United Kingdom, restructure existing management, and relatively easily generate cash flows from the assets. These assets do not lose significant value even when the project company defaults.

The top left-hand box of the exhibit shows the situation of increased probability of default from market risk, exchange rate risk, and technology risk in combination with high value under default. The immediate impact of this combination is that equity holders will lose their investment if default occurs and debt holders foreclose on the asset. Consequently, the debt level in the capital structure probably has to be lower than traditional PF but not low enough that the project loses the advantages of high leverage. If the probability of default due to high leverage is large, then perhaps the project finance structure is simply unsuitable and corporate finance, with its combined cash flows and coinsurance effects, is better suited for these assets. These assets are also likely to benefit from the managerial flexibility that the corporate structure permits. Managerial flexibility is important because managers are able to make optimal decisions as market and technology uncertainty is resolved over time.

I have noted the importance of governments in infrastructure investments throughout the book. In the next section I examine steps that governments can take to encourage investments in infrastructure.

ROLE OF GOVERNMENT

We have reviewed the investments that infrastructure requires to improve and maintain the standard of living—investments which governments must either attract or make themselves. Given the budget constraints that governments increasingly operate under, it's clear that private investments are a necessary component of meeting investment needs. I have also shown that infrastructure asset characteristics make infrastructure investments susceptible to sovereign holdup. Unfortunately, investors will not commit large sums of capital based on government assurances and promises because of the nature of the "obsolescing bargain" in infrastructure investing.[40] We have noted that once capital is sunk, the incentives for reneging on the original bargain are very strong. Governments also change after elections, and the new dispensation may not necessarily choose to honor promises made by the previous incumbents. Governments therefore must credibly commit to their contractual obligations.

The preceding discussion of project finance highlighted PF features that enable governments to demonstrate this commitment. Project finance's high leverage and reputation effect strengthen government accountability. Joint ownership through government capital contribution may also act to strengthen commitment through skin-in-the-game arguments. Other contractual provisions—for example, those which permit arbitration based on a country's bilateral investment treaties—also strengthen government commitment. It is a well-known principle of strategic interaction that by leaving themselves vulnerable to retaliation, players increase the level of cooperation and trust.[41] The logic dictates that a player is unlikely to renege on a promise if it makes itself vulnerable to retaliation. By agreeing to arbitration, governments commit to honoring their contractual obligations because not doing so hurts them. Such a commitment is credible to investors.

It seems reasonable that governments should therefore encourage project finance structures in infrastructure rather than insisting on equity investments. Tiong (1995) analyzes the importance of equity in build-operate-transfer (BOT) infrastructure investments.[42] BOT is defined as the granting of a concession by the government to a private promoter, called a *concessionaire*, who is responsible for the financing, construction, operation, and maintenance of a facility over the concession period before finally transferring the fully operational facility to the government at no cost.[43] Tiong notes that governments specifically require equity as part of the BOT tender in 68 percent of the requests for proposal (RFPs) in his sample. Even so, the largest equity contribution in his sample is only about 30 percent when governments require equity as part of the RFP. My analysis suggests that insisting on equity may be counterproductive and governments should leave financing arrangements to the sponsors and lenders. We have noted that equity capital has an incentive to increase the volatility of the underlying asset's value. Indeed, from a prudential regulatory perspective, such volatility may be desirable for innovative, path-breaking, technological advancement but may be undesirable for infrastructure.

Among the mechanisms that reduce the incidence of government-led renegotiation, Guasch et al. (2007) find the following to be important: existence of a regulator, exclusive private financing, quality of the bureaucracy, and growth.[44] The existence of a regulator is significant in reducing government renegotiations principally because regulators are more effective in weak governance environments and can reduce government opportunistic behavior by separating the regulation function of the government from the political interests of different incumbents. They also create better contracts at the beginning of the concession agreement itself. Woodhouse (2006) reflects this latter feature, too, pointing out that transparent and competitive bidding for infrastructure projects significantly reduces government-led renegotiations in the electricity sector and in fact allows investors to prosper financially.[45]

For example, in 1994 Thailand selected investors for seven independent power producers out of 50 bidders and 88 bids. The winning bidders survived the 1997 Asian financial crisis that hit Thailand hard and depreciated the baht by about half its precrisis value. In Thailand the central regulator played a crucial role in ensuring that the post-crisis renegotiations were successful. By contrast, the Dabhol project in India suffered because of nontransparent contract negotiations and noncompetitive bidding. The newly elected government could credibly claim that the terms of the original contract were too generous to Enron—which, incidentally, they were because there were no competitive bids. Thus, paradoxically, a transparent and competitive bidding process coupled with independent regulators benefits investors because it ensures that the initial contract is fair and possesses public legitimacy that can withstand future challenges. The second obvious benefit remains the reduced scope for corruption.

Unfortunately, it is possible for renegotiations to occur even after a transparent and competitive bidding process because of the monopolistic nature of infrastructure. For example, the government of Argentina awarded the Aguas Argentinas concession after competitive bidding, yet the firm renegotiated after the fact. Just as governments can renegotiate after firms incur sunk costs, firms can deliberately submit low bids and renegotiate tariff increases later. These incentives are destructive for both the government and the firms since a renegotiation demand by the firm is likely to trigger an expropriatory government response.

In the infrastructure space, firms are usually not constrained by a competitive market mechanism. This means that governments must design a bidding and auction process that creates the correct incentives for competing firms. For example, in 1994 Thailand designed a multistage bidding process for private participation in electricity generation.[46] In the first stage the government invited bids for a pool of projects rather than for each individual project. The government then ranked firms for each group of projects by tariff and invited short-listed firms to determine the particulars for each project. After the first firm reached agreement on terms with the government, the next-ranked firms were invited to negotiate for each remaining project. The government set the first set of tariffs as the benchmark, asking the next-ranked firms to match this lower tariff rate. If an agreement could not be reached, there was a large pool of firms waiting in line. By pooling similar projects together, the government obtained a more precise estimate of what firms would bid. The subsequent negotiations allowed rivals to challenge the lowest bid and give the government a clearer picture of market prices. Of course, this is one process, and a huge literature is available for governments to design suitable auctions.[47]

We have noted that infrastructure is a long-duration investment and it is important that contracts remain in alignment over long periods of time. As long as the macroeconomic conditions are beneficial and the economy grows, investments are unlikely to face renegotiations. Guasch and Straub (2006) find that growth is negatively related to renegotiation of contracts.[48] Over long durations, however, conditions change and contracts will face challenges. In these situations governments that ex ante set up a transparent, fair, and independent dispute resolution mechanism will find investors willing to accept lower returns for investments. Independent regulators also fulfill this role in many cases.

Simple bureaucratic processes that are transparent and eliminate delays reduce the costs of dealing with governments. For example, the Dabhol project in India required 50 permits from state and federal authorities.[49] Reengineering the process of obtaining clearances and permits to eliminate delays will pay big dividends for governments. Incidentally, a strategy of encouraging investment by promising above-market high returns to investors is risky because the strategy will engender political opposition, is unlikely to be sustainable over the long duration when governments can change, and implies a lack of competition in the sector. Investors must also beware of such promises because, as we have seen, once investments are sunk, governments can renegotiate and reduce returns.

CONCLUSION

In this chapter I examined the financing and indeed governance structure of project finance. I approached the analysis from a functional perspective rather than describing the unique features that characterize PF. I analyzed how PF mitigates some infrastructure risks by analyzing PF features, their economic functions, and the precise mechanisms by which these features fulfill their functions.

Project finance is a rigid structure that limits managerial discretion and includes separate incorporation, nonrecourse debt, high leverage, long-term contracts, financing of a single purpose, wasting assets, and syndicated lending. Separate incorporation allows sponsors to negotiate equity stakes with concentrated buyers/suppliers and sovereign entities in order to mitigate the risk of holdup. Separate incorporation also permits sponsors to achieve the optimal high leverage and isolate themselves from the risk of project failure through nonrecourse debt. Separate incorporation prevents projects from failing if the sponsors fail.

High leverage shields cash flows from expropriatory attention, precommits cash flows, reduces reported profits, serves as an early-warning mechanism for exposing creeping expropriation, improves the sponsors' bargaining position in ex post renegotiation, and activates the reputation effect. Nonrecourse debt reinforces high leverage since counterparties cannot look to sponsors to meet additional demands. Long-term contracts seek to constrain managerial discretion through a rigid structure, define the parties' obligations, and ring-fence the assets for the lenders. Project finance particularly matches the requirements of financing infrastructure since the assets are single-purpose, wasting assets with limited growth options which lenders can ring-fence and protect from predatory holdup. Syndicated debt gives rise to the reputation effect whereby sovereign governments hesitate appropriating the cash flows of major international players in the financial world. Infrastructure bonds do not possess this feature of syndicated lending. I also examined these features in the context of the Ras Laffan project.

We then examined the IPRA model that investors use to analyze project risks. The model works very well during the construction phase and inventories all the risks very well. However, the model combines construction and operational phases even though different risks influence the phases and separating the phases will improve the output. Another difficult issue relates to the hierarchical nature and reductionist approach of the IPRA model. We have seen that feedback effects occur in infrastructure, particularly in sovereign holdup situations. Feedback effects occur across categories, and a reductionist model has difficulties in incorporating feedback effects. A similar problem also affects the models that credit rating agencies use. I examined S&P's hierarchical model in this chapter and noted that the model does not incorporate feedback effects, principally in its categories of contractual foundation, credit enhancement, and debt service coverage ratio.

I also introduced a simple framework for evaluating infrastructure assets suitable for PF. By interacting the probability of default and loss given default I showed that PF is suitable only for assets that maintain their value under default. Even for such value-maintaining assets, sponsors should be cautious about using PF for assets exposed to market and technology risk. Finally, in light of this study, the chapter examined the policies that governments seeking to attract investment in their infrastructure sectors should encourage.

Chapter 8 examines valuation of existing infrastructure assets. It also examines infrastructure bond returns, risk, and correlation.

Infrastructure Asset Valuation and Bond Returns

Capital must be propelled by self-interest; it cannot be enticed by benevolence.

—Walter Bagehot

Throughout this book I make the case that financing serves a governance function in infrastructure investing. The structural features characterizing project finance—separate incorporation, nonrecourse debt, long-term contracts, high leverage—serve the economic functions of mitigating infrastructure risks and providing the lowest-cost governance. However, these structural features also complicate the valuation of infrastructure assets. Asset valuation is, of course, a fundamental tool of investing since investors must determine that asset returns will likely exceed the cost of capital before investing. The investment decision is contingent on a positive net present value (NPV). This chapter examines the complications in valuing infrastructure assets in the project finance context and the methods available to resolve these complications.

The second half of the chapter examines differences between syndicated bank lending and infrastructure bonds, and the effect of Basel II on bank lending and infrastructure bond returns. Investors seeking to invest directly in infrastructure asset debt can choose syndicated lending with commercial banks or buying infrastructure bonds. I have alluded to the differences between bond funding and syndicated bank lending in infrastructure debt, and I examine these differences here in greater depth. I also examine the effect of Basel II requirements on syndicated bank lending and note the opportunities these requirements present to pension funds, insurance firms, and endowments, which are not subject to Basel II requirements. I close the chapter with an analysis of historical infrastructure bond returns.

AN OVERVIEW OF INFRASTRUCTURE VALUATION THEORY

Although the theory of valuation is well known, I will briefly recap it in order to point out the complexities of infrastructure valuation. Valuation theory teaches us that the value of capital assets equals the present value of future cash flows that the asset generates and returns to capital providers. Investors calculate the present value of future cash flows by discounting cash flows with a discount rate, the cost of capital invested in the asset. The intuition underlying the discounted cash flow method, that a positive present value means asset returns exceed the cost of capital, cloaks the complexities of implementing the method.

$$PV = \frac{\sum_{i=1}^{n} CF_i}{k} \qquad (8.1)$$

where

PV = Present value of cash flows
CF_i = Cash flow in period i
k = Cost of capital

The two methods equity investors use to calculate the value of equity are (1) using a weighted average cost of capital (WACC), with weights equal to the proportional value of debt and equity, as the discount rate to discount free cash flows (FCF) to all capital providers; and (2) using the cost of equity to discount cash flows to equity providers.

$$PV = \frac{\sum_{i=1}^{n} FCF_i}{WACC} \qquad (8.2)$$

where

$WACC$ = Weighted average cost of capital
FCF_i = Free cash flows in period i

$$WACC = \frac{E}{V} \times k_e + \frac{D}{V} \times (k_d \times (1 - \tau)) \qquad (8.3)$$

where

V = Value of the asset
E = Value of equity
D = Value of debt

k_e = Cost of equity
k_d = Pretax cost of debt
τ = Tax rate

$$PV = \frac{\sum_{i=1}^{n} ECF_i}{k_e} \tag{8.4}$$

where
ECF_i = Equity cash flows in period i

Both methods convert accounting data into cash flow data. The FCF method calculates cash flows from net income by adding back noncash deductions and subtracting cash expenses not included in accounting data. Equation 8.5 shows the calculation of FCF where the non–cash flow items of depreciation and amortization are added back while capital expenditure which is not shown on the income statement is deducted.

$$FCF = NI + Depreciation - Capex + \Delta Working\ capital + Amortization \tag{8.5}$$

where
NI = Net income
Capex = Capital expenditure

Since the weights are the proportional value of debt and equity in the capital structure, a circularity problem arises, because we need to simultaneously determine the value of the asset in order to determine the proportional value of the weights for debt and equity.[1] A simple solution to the circularity issue is to use the book values of debt and equity and then calculate the market value of the assets followed by the market value of equity.

There are problems with this approach, however. First, the method assumes that the capital structure of the investment does not change from inception to the time horizon over which we calculate the present value. Second, investors demand returns based on the market value of their investments since the market value correctly captures the opportunity cost of their funds. Finally, the cost of equity itself is a function of the value of the debt as well as the value of the project (see cost of levered equity equation 8.9 below). Therefore, an understated equity value, likely when using the book value of equity, increases the cost of equity (by increasing the levered equity beta), which increases the discount rate and may return a negative NPV, leading to a decision to abandon investment in a project.[2] Conversely, an overstated equity value reduces the discount rate and can return a positive NPV, similarly encouraging faulty investment decisions.

Capital Asset Pricing Model

The cost of equity and debt is calculated using the capital asset pricing model (CAPM), widely used to price capital assets, in both FCF and equity cash flow methods. The CAPM demonstrates that the cost of an asset can be split into two risk components: systematic risk and unsystematic or specific risk.[3] Systematic risk affects the entire market portfolio of securities while specific risk affects an individual asset. Investors can shed specific risk by diversifying but still hold systematic risk for which they must be compensated with the market return, calculated as the excess return over a risk-free security like a U.S. Treasury bill. The return that investors demand for holding specific risk equals the asset's beta, a measure of an individual asset's return correlation with a market portfolio's return, shown in equation 8.6. In other words, if an asset's returns are perfectly correlated with the market portfolio's returns, the specific risk of the asset is equal to the market risk and its asset beta equals one. Therefore, to account for the specific risk of the asset, investors must increase or decrease the risk premium or returns in excess of the risk-free rate that investors require to hold systematic risk as per the asset beta. Equation 8.7 shows the calculation for the capital cost of an asset using the asset beta.

$$\beta_a = \frac{Cov(r_a, r_m)}{Var(r_m)} \tag{8.6}$$

where

$$\beta_a = \text{Asset beta}$$
$$r_a = \text{Asset return}$$
$$Cov(r_a, r_m) = \text{Covariance between the asset return and the market return}$$
$$Var(r_m) = \text{Variance of the market return}$$

$$k_a = r_f + \beta_a (r_m - r_f) \tag{8.7}$$

where

$$k_a = \text{Cost of the asset}$$
$$r_f = \text{Risk-free return}$$
$$r_m = \text{Market return}$$

The cost of equity is also calculated using equation 8.7. However, the cost of equity changes when leverage is introduced in the capital structure.

When debt is risky the debt itself has specific risk, as reflected in the debt beta or the debt's correlation with the market's return. The beta of the asset is a value-weighted average of the equity beta and debt beta, as shown in equation 8.8.[4]

$$\beta_a = \frac{D}{V}\beta_d + \frac{E}{V}\beta_e \qquad (8.8)$$

where

β_d = Debt beta
β_e = Equity beta

Equation 8.3 shows that the cost of debt in the FCF method of valuation is the after-tax cost of debt, because interest payments reduce taxable income, thereby shielding income equal to the interest payments from taxation. The present value of these tax shields is a function of the amount of interest payments and therefore the amount of debt. When the debt is riskless, debt beta equals zero. The FCF method uses a single after-tax cost of debt along with a single value weight for debt. The FCF method therefore assumes constant debt, not only in value but also in risk.

The risk of debt, among other factors, depends on the amount of debt. High leverage increases the debt risk and increases debt betas. Equity holders bear the risk of the asset as well as debt because in the event of bankruptcy, debt holders can seize the assets, wiping out equity in the process. The cost of equity therefore is a function of the asset beta or asset risk as well as debt beta or the risk of leverage. The cost of levered equity is given by the Hamada equation (equation 8.9).[5] Note also that the unlevered equity beta is equal to the asset beta as long as equity funds a single asset, a so called *pure play* firm.

$$\beta_e = \frac{E + D(1 - \tau)}{E}\beta_a \qquad (8.9)$$

Ruback proves that including the value of tax shields along with a fixed amount of riskless debt leads to the standard Hamada equation used to calculate the cost of levered equity, shown in equation 8.9.[6] However, when the amount of debt is fixed and debt beta is not equal to 0 (i.e., the debt is risky), the Hamada equation transforms into equation 8.10. Note that taxes do not appear in equation 8.10; when debt is risky, the value of tax shields is also risky. Equation 8.10 provides a more accurate cost of equity when debt is risky and we can estimate debt betas. Both the Hamada equation and equation 8.10 reveal the linkages between the cost of equity, the value of debt, and the value of equity.

$$\beta_e = \frac{\left(\beta_a - \dfrac{D}{V}\beta_d\right)}{\dfrac{E}{V}} \qquad (8.10)$$

From a practical valuation perspective, the value of debt is usually assumed to be the book value and, except in cases of financial distress, debt betas are assumed to be zero. A problem with this approach arises during valuation of greenfield investments at the investment evaluation stage, when the capital structure is not known with great precision. What value weight should investors assume? The recommendation is that investors should use a target debt to equity ratio to calculate the NPV and make the advance-or-abandon decision.[7] Unfortunately, this can lead to erroneous decisions in infrastructure PF.

The key point in infrastructure and project finance is that the amount of debt is not fixed. The amount of debt varies considerably over the life of the assets, ranging from a high of 70 to 80 percent to a low of 0 percent as the debt is paid down. As the capital structure changes, so does the cost of equity, which must be calculated every year. One way of getting around this problem is to use multiple discount rates for each year based on each period's leverage. However, calculating individual discount rates for each period requires the value of equity in each period, which also changes. A cost of equity calculated using the Hamada equation with a single equity value will therefore be erroneous. Using the book value of equity also introduces errors in the valuation, as noted previously. Equation 8.11 shows the formula for calculating discount rates in each period.[8]

$$k_i = \frac{1}{(1 + k_{e(i-1)})} \times \frac{1}{(1 + k_{ei})} \qquad (8.11)$$

where
$\quad k_i$ = Discount rate for period i
$\quad k_{e(i-1)}$ = Cost of equity in the previous period

Capital Cash Flow Method

Using multiple discount rates does not extract us from the circularity problem of requiring the value of equity even if the value of debt is not a serious issue. A method that does not require the value of equity or of debt is Ruback's capital cash flow (CCF) method. The CCF method notes that asset returns must compensate investors for asset risk. This method assumes that the CAPM works, in which case asset risk decomposes into systematic risk equal to the market return, and specific risk, a function of the asset beta. The CCF method therefore uses equation 8.7 to calculate a single cost of the asset as the discount rate for discounting cash flows to all capital providers, equity as well as debt providers. In order to calculate asset beta we can regress market returns against similar asset returns, as shown in equation 8.12. We then calculate the asset cost by using equation 8.7.

$$r_m = \alpha_a + \beta_a r_a + \varepsilon \tag{8.12}$$

The CCF method gets around the value of debt and equity problem by discounting the after-tax cash flows available to all capital providers, adding interest payments back to net income since debt holders receive interest payments. Equation 8.5, which calculates free cash flows, is therefore modified to include the interest payments made to debt holders. Equation 8.13 shows the cash flow calculation for the CCF method. Note that noncash interest occurs if interest is paid in kind by issuing additional debt. Equation 8.14 shows the calculation of cash flows for the CCF method if we begin with earnings before interest and taxes (EBIT) rather than net income. Note that we need to add the tax shields provided by interest payments plus estimated taxes to EBIT for calculating the CCF.

CCF = NI + Depreciation-Capex + ΔWorking capital + Amortization
+ Cash interest + Noncash interest

$$\tag{8.13}$$

CCF = EBIT + Taxes + Depreciation-Capex + ΔWorking capital
+ Amortization + Interest tax shields $\tag{8.14}$

Ruback proves that the CCF method is algebraically equivalent to the FCF method but is easier to implement and allows for changes in capital structure. The CCF method, however, assumes that asset risk remains constant over the course of the asset's life since we use a single asset beta and a single discount rate over the asset's life. It is possible that asset risk can change over a project's life, but we can relatively easily implement changes in asset risk in the valuation by estimating asset betas for comparable assets by regressing market returns against returns from comparable assets.[9] Investors can therefore implement the CCF method as shown in equation 8.15. We note that the implementation is simple yet equivalent to the FCF and WACC method.

$$PV = \frac{\sum_{i=1}^{n} CCF_i}{k_a} \qquad (8.15)$$

An important term missing from equation 8.15 that is usually found in a corporate valuation is the terminal value of the corporation. Analysts conduct a valuation over a specified time period of 5 or 10 years and assume perpetual cash flows with a constant growth rate to determine the terminal value of the assets, which they add to the present value of cash flows. Infrastructure assets, as we have noted, are wasting assets and have zero terminal value.[10] Consequently it does not make sense to include a terminal value which assumes free cash flows growing at a constant rate in perpetuity. Instead, investors must calculate the life span of the assets and estimate cash flows over the total life span. For example, a greenfield road project indicates that $n = 30$ in equation 8.15.

International Infrastructure Valuation

So far we have not considered international projects. Although international valuation is a topic of sufficient complexity to warrant a separate book by itself, I will briefly sketch the common approaches available to investors. One approach to valuing projects in risky countries simply involves adding a country risk premium to the cost of equity.[11] Many practitioners use the yield spread difference between the risk-free rate, or U.S. Treasury bonds, and U.S. dollar–denominated sovereign bonds of the country in question as the country risk premium.[12] This approach is shown in equation 8.16.

$$k_a = r_f + \beta_a(r_m - r_f) + Sov_f \qquad (8.16)$$

where
Sov_f = Foreign country sovereign spread

Although this approach is simple to implement, especially if the relevant spread data is available, the approach ignores the CAPM principle of evaluating specific and systematic risk. For example, when a country's equity market is negatively correlated with U.S. equity markets, assuming that U.S. investors are considering the investment, then the specific risk of the country as measured by its beta results in a negative risk premium (or risk discount) because the country's contribution to a portfolio of U.S. investments results in lower risk through diversification. However, simply increasing the cost of capital and therefore the required return ignores the beta of the country.

A second approach incorporates country beta in estimating the cost of capital.[13] We can use equation 8.6 to compute the country beta, as shown in equation 8.17.

$$\beta_f = \frac{Cov(r_{mf}, r_{mUS})}{Var(r_{mUS})} \qquad (8.17)$$

where

β_f = Foreign country beta
r_{mf} = Foreign market return
r_{mUS} = U.S. market return

If we have insufficient data we can use the ratio of the standard deviation of the country's equity market to the standard deviation of the U.S. equity market, and multiply by the correlation coefficient of the country, as shown in Equation 8.18.

$$\beta_f = \rho_{f,US} \frac{\sigma_f}{\sigma_{US}} \qquad (8.18)$$

where

$\rho_{f,US}$ = Foreign country and U.S. correlation coefficient
σ_f = Foreign market standard deviation
σ_{US} = U.S. market standard deviation

Now assuming that the relative risk of the assets in the foreign country is the same as that in the United States, we can find the foreign asset beta by multiplying the U.S. asset beta by the foreign country beta, as shown in equation 8.19.

$$\beta_{af} = \beta_{aUS} \times \beta_f \qquad (8.19)$$

where

β_{af} = Foreign asset beta
β_{aUS} = U.S. asset beta

This provides us with the foreign asset beta. In order to compute the cost of capital we also need the relevant risk-free rate and market risk premium, along with the foreign asset beta calculated in equation 8.19. We can compute the risk-free rate for the foreign country by adding the spread between the relevant sovereign bond and U.S. treasuries to the U.S. risk-free rate, as shown in equation 8.20. Although the risk-free rate so calculated likely differs from the risk-free rate available to local investors within the foreign country, it is logical for U.S. investors to require the spread premium over the U.S. risk-free rate.

$$r_{ff} = r_{fUS} + Sov_f \qquad (8.20)$$

where

   r_{ff} = Foreign risk-free rate
   r_{fUS} = U.S. risk-free rate

Finally, we need to compute the market risk premium. We can compute the market risk premium as the excess returns that investors demand over the risk-free rate in order to hold systematic risk. There are two options available to us. We can either use the foreign country risk premium, which is the difference between foreign market returns and the foreign risk-free rate, or we can use the U.S. market risk premium since we assumed that U.S. investors are the decision makers. The U.S. market risk premium has the advantage of being readily available, and we can argue that U.S. investors require this return to hold systematic risk. We now have all the necessary components to calculate the cost of capital for the asset and use the CCF method for an international investment, as shown in equation 8.21.

$$k_{af} = r_{ff} + \beta_{af}(r_{mUS} - r_{fUS}) \qquad (8.21)$$

It is useful to note here that the valuation process involves significant assumptions and is highly error prone. Esty (1999) notes that systematic risk should be included in the discount rate while cash flows should reflect specific risk.[14] Do we incorporate the effect of insurance and exchange rate, interest rate hedges? The presence of hedging instruments should reduce the cost of capital by reducing the uncertainty, but typically risk-reducing benefits are not incorporated in practice.[15]

I have also alluded to the problems arising from including arbitrary risk premiums for country risk. High country risk premiums lead to increased hurdle rates and investors accept projects after higher tariffs are negotiated with governments. Unfortunately, the feedback effect of infrastructure means that the higher tariffs themselves increase the risk, which is not captured in the valuation. One prerequisite to gaining a sense for the true value of an investment is using sensitivity analysis. Monte Carlo simulation provides a complete distribution of scenarios once investors provide input parameters and their distributions. Valuation therefore is a necessary but not sufficient tool and should probably not be treated in exclusion.

The next section examines the impact of Basel II on the costs of financing infrastructure investment for debt providers, specifically the commercial banks.

BASEL II AND INFRASTRUCTURE LENDING

This topic is also large enough to deserve separate treatment, but I will briefly analyze the effects of Basel II on the commercial banks, the cost of their loans, and the opportunities these present to pension funds, insurance firms, and bond investors. The Basel Committee on Banking Supervision, also called Basel II, considers project finance as a form of specialized lending belonging to wholesale lending groups. Basel II (2005) subclassifies specialized lending into project finance, object finance, commodities finance, income-producing real estate, and high-volatility commercial real estate.[16] The Basel Committee requires banks to maintain Tier I and Tier II capital against the assets on its balance sheet; the amount of capital that banks must maintain depends, among other factors, on the credit risk of its assets. A higher credit risk implies that banks must set aside more capital, and the general requirement is that banks must hold total capital equal to at least 8 percent of their assets weighted as per their risk.[17] In the following paragraphs I examine the different methods the Basel Committee outlines for banks to calculate their risk-weighted assets (RWA).

The Basel Committee requires lending institutions to measure credit risk using three criteria: probability of default (PD), loss given default (LGD), and exposure at default (EAD). PD estimates must be the long-run average of one-year default rates for borrowers in the group (i.e., project finance group). The institutions can assess their credit risk through an internal rating–based (IRB) approach, subject to supervisory approval and certain minimum conditions and disclosure requirements, by measuring PD, LGD, EAD, and maturity (M). The IRB approach is subdivided into the foundation IRB approach, wherein banks only provide their own estimate of PD while the other parameters are provided by the supervisory authorities; and the advanced IRB approach, wherein banks use their own estimates of PD, LGD, and EAD.[18]

For banks that meet the requirements for estimating their own PD, Basel II provides four formulae for calculating the capital charge that banks must take based on PD, LGD, and M.

$$\text{Correlation (R)} = 0.12 \times \frac{[1 - \text{EXP}(-50 \times \text{PD})]}{[1 - \text{EXP}(-50)]}$$
$$+ 0.24 \times \left\{ 1 - \frac{[1 - \text{EXP}(-50 \times \text{PD})]}{[1 - \text{EXP}(-50)]} \right\} \qquad (8.22)$$

where

EXP(x) is the exponential function

$$\text{Maturity adjustment (b)} = [0.11852 - 0.05478 \times \ln(\text{PD})]^2 \quad (8.23)$$

where

ln(x) is the lognormal function

$$\text{Capital requirement (K)} = \left[\text{LGD} \times N \left[(1 - R)^{-0.5} \times G(\text{PD}) + \left[\frac{R}{(1 - R)} \right]^{0.5} \right. \right.$$
$$\left. \left. \times\, G(0.999) \right] - \text{PD} \times \text{LGD} \right] \times (1 - 1.5 \times b)^{-1}$$
$$\times (1 + (M - 2.5) \times b) \quad (8.24)$$

where

N(x) represents the cumulative distribution function for a standard normal random variable (i.e., the probability that a random variable with mean 0 and variance 1 is less than or equal to x).

G(z) denotes the inverse cumulative distribution function for a standard normal random variable (i.e., the value of x such that N(x) = z).

$$\text{Risk-weighted assets (RWA)} = K \times 12.5 \times \text{EAD} \quad (8.25)$$

The capital requirement (K) for a defaulted exposure is equal to the greater of zero and the difference between its LGD and the bank's best estimate of expected loss. The risk-weighted asset amount for the defaulted exposure is the product of K, 12.5, and the EAD.

Risk Categories for Banks without Their Own PD Estimates

Basel II specifies that banks that do not meet the requirements to estimate PD must slot their assets into risk categories with laid-down risk weights. This is the *supervisory slotting criteria approach*. Exhibit 8.1 shows the risk categories and their rough equivalence to the ratings provided by S&P.

The risk categories determine the risk weights that banks must use to calculate the RWA. The total capital charge is equal to 8 percent of RWA. Exhibit 8.2 specifies the risk weights based on the risk category for unexpected loss (UL).[19]

The treatment of expected losses (EL) is different. Banks must first calculate the risk-weighted assets and then multiply risk-weighted assets by 0.8 percent to obtain EL. Banks calculate risk-weighted assets by multiplying the risk weights for the appropriate risk category shown in Exhibit 8.3 by the EAD.[20]

EXHIBIT 8.1   Basel II Risk Categories

Risk Category	S&P Equivalence
Strong	BBB– or better
Good	BB+ or BB
Satisfactory	BB– or B+
Weak	B to C–
Default	NA

Source: Basel Committee on Banking Supervision, *International Convergence of Capital Measurement and Capital Standards* (Basel, Switzerland: Bank for International Settlements, 2006); and Jorg Orgeldinger, "Basel II and Project Finance: The Development of a Basel II Confirming Rating Model, *Journal of Structured Finance* 11, no. 4 (2006): 84–95.

EXHIBIT 8.2   Risk Categories and UL Risk Weights

Risk Categories	Strong	Good	Satisfactory	Weak	Default
Risk weights	70%	90%	115%	250%	Per equation 8.25

Source: Basel Committee on Banking Supervision, *International Convergence of Capital Measurement and Capital Standards* (Basel, Switzerland: Bank for International Settlements, 2006).

EXHIBIT 8.3   Risk Categories and EL Risk Weights

Risk Categories	Strong	Good	Satisfactory	Weak	Default
Risk weights	5%	10%	35%	100%	625%

Source: Basel Committee on Banking Supervision, *International Convergence of Capital Measurement and Capital Standards* (Basel, Switzerland: Bank for International Settlements, 2006).

We can imagine that the risk weights specified in Exhibit 8.2 form an upper bound for the capital charge since these are mandated. The risk weights that banks are likely to arrive at using the formulae and their internal estimation of PD will be lower than the mandated risk weights. Basel II (2006) reduced the mandated risk weights from their original weights specified in Basel II (2001) as well as implemented the formula-based standard which allows for a precise continuous rating weight scale

EXHIBIT 8.4 Evolution of Basel II Risk Weights, 2001 to 2006

Risk Category	Risk Weight (2001)	Capital Charge (2001)	Risk Weight (2006)	Capital Charge (2006)
Preferred	50%	4%	NA	NA
Strong	75%	6%	70% (50% with approval)	5.6% (4% with approval)
Good	100%	8%	90% (70% with approval)	7.2% (5.6% with approval)
Satisfactory	150%	12%	115%	9.2%
Weak	350%	28%	250%	20%
Default	625%	50%		Per equation 8.25

Source: Basel Committee on Banking Supervision, *International Convergence of Capital Measurement and Capital Standards* (Basel, Switzerland: Bank for International Settlements, 2006). Also see Jorg Orgeldinger, "Basel II and Project Finance: The Development of a Basel II Confirming Rating Model, *Journal of Structured Finance* 11, no. 4 (2006): 84–95.

instead of rating weight *buckets* and an imprecise capital charge.[21] Exhibit 8.4 compares the two risk weights in 2006 versus 2001.

In addition, the committee recommended that national financial institution supervisory authorities could, at their discretion, permit banks to use preferential risk weights of 50 percent for "strong" and 70 percent for "good" exposures if the remaining maturity of the outstanding exposure was less than 2.5 years, or the supervisory authority determined that the bank's underwriting standards were stronger than those specified by Basel II.[22] The preferential risk weights obviously lower the capital charge that banks have to take. Exhibit 8.5 shows the detailed slotting criteria for project finance loans.[23]

The Basel II recommendations increase the cost of capital for commercial banks that lend using their balance sheet. Pension funds, insurance firms, and endowments without such capital requirements can join with commercial banks in lending syndicates and lend at rates that commercial banks require for their loans. The next subsection examines PF default data.

Default Characteristics of Infrastructure PF Debt

What are the default characteristics of infrastructure asset debt? Beale et al. (2002) report that 10-year cumulative average probability of default is about 7.5 percent, comparable to investment-grade BBB+ rated corporate debt.[24] The default probability over a year is higher, at 1.5 percent, comparable to non-investment-grade corporate debt with BB+ rating. This decrease in probability of default as loan tenor increases matches our

EXHIBIT 8.5 PF Loan Risk Category Slotting Criteria

	Strong	Good	Satisfactory	Weak
Financial Strength				
Market conditions	Few competing suppliers or substantial and durable advantage in location, cost, or technology. Demand is strong and growing.	Few competing suppliers or better than average location, cost, or technology, but this situation may not last. Demand is strong and stable.	Project has no advantage in location, cost, or technology. Demand is adequate and stable.	Project has worse than average location, cost, or technology. Demand is weak and declining.
Financial ratios (e.g., *debt service coverage ratio [DSCR], loan life coverage ratio [LLCR], project life coverage ratio [PLCR], and debt-to-equity ratio)*	Strong financial ratios considering the level of project risk; very robust economic assumptions.	Strong to acceptable financial ratios considering the level of project risk; robust project economic assumptions.	Standard financial ratios considering the level of project risk.	Aggressive financial ratios considering the level of project risk.
Stress analysis	The project can meet its financial obligations under sustained, severely stressed economic or sectoral conditions.	The project can meet its financial obligations under normally stressed economic or sectoral conditions. The project is only likely to default under severe economic conditions.	The project is vulnerable to stresses that are not uncommon through an economic cycle, and may default in a normal downturn.	The project is likely to default unless conditions improve soon.

(Continued)

EXHIBIT 8.5 (*Continued*)

	Strong	Good	Satisfactory	Weak
Financial structure				
Duration of the credit compared to the duration of the project	Useful life of the project significantly exceeds tenor of the loan.	Useful life of the project exceeds tenor of the loan.	Useful life of the project exceeds tenor of the loan.	Useful life of the project may not exceed tenor of the loan.
Amortization schedule	Amortizing debt.	Amortizing debt.	Amortizing debt repayments with limited bullet payment.	Bullet repayment or amortizing debt repayments with high bullet repayment.
Political and Legal Environment				
Political risk, including transfer risk, considering project type and mitigants	Very low exposure; strong mitigation instruments, if needed.	Low exposure; satisfactory mitigation instruments, if needed.	Moderate exposure; fair mitigation instruments.	High exposure; no or weak mitigation instruments.
Force majeure risk (war, civil unrest, etc.)	Low exposure.	Acceptable exposure.	Standard protection.	Significant risks, not fully mitigated.
Government support and project's importance for the country over the long term	Project of strategic importance for the country (preferably export-oriented). Strong support from government.	Project considered important for the country. Good level of support from government.	Project may not be strategic but brings unquestionable benefits for the country. Support from government may not be explicit.	Project not key to the country. No or weak support from government.

	Strong	Satisfactory	Fair	Weak
Stability of legal and regulatory environment (risk of change in law) Acquisition of all necessary supports and approvals for such relief from local content laws	Favorable and stable regulatory environment over the long term.	Favorable and stable regulatory environment over the medium term.	Regulatory changes can be predicted with a fair level of certainty.	Current or future regulatory issues may affect the project.
Enforceability of contracts, collateral, and security	Contracts, collateral, and security are enforceable.	Contracts, collateral, and security are enforceable.	Contracts, collateral, and security are considered enforceable even if certain nonkey issues may exist.	There are unresolved key issues regarding actual enforcement of contracts, collateral, and security.

Transaction characteristics

	Strong	Satisfactory	Fair	Weak
Design and technology risk	Fully proven technology and design.	Fully proven technology and design.	Proven technology and design; start-up issues are mitigated by a strong completion package.	Unproven technology and design; technology issues exist and/or complex design.
Construction risk				
Permitting and siting	All permits have been obtained.	Some permits are still outstanding but their receipt is considered very likely.	Some permits are still outstanding but the permitting process is well defined and they are considered routine.	Key permits still need to be obtained and are not considered routine. Significant conditions may be attached.

(Continued)

EXHIBIT 8.5 (*Continued*)

	Strong	Good	Satisfactory	Weak
Type of construction contract	Fixed-price date-certain turnkey engineering, procurement, and construction (EPC) contract.	Fixed-price date-certain turnkey EPC contract.	Fixed-price date-certain turnkey construction contract with one or several contractors.	No or partial fixed-price turnkey contract and/or interfacing issues with multiple contractors.
Completion guarantees	Substantial liquidated damages supported by financial substance and/or strong completion guarantee from sponsors with excellent financial standing.	Significant liquidated damages supported by financial substance and/or completion guarantee from sponsors with good financial standing.	Adequate liquidated damages supported by financial substance and/or completion guarantee from sponsors with good financial standing.	Inadequate liquidated damages or not supported by financial substance, or weak completion guarantees.
Track record and financial strength of contractor in constructing similar projects	Strong	Good	Satisfactory	Weak
Operating risk Scope and nature of operations and maintenance (O&M) contracts	Strong long-term O&M contract, preferably with contractual performance incentives, and/or O&M reserve accounts.	Long-term O&M contract, and/or O&M reserve accounts.	Limited O&M contract or O&M reserve account.	No O&M contract; risk of high operational cost overruns beyond mitigation.

	Very strong	Strong	Acceptable	Limited/weak
Operator's expertise, track record, and financial strength	Very strong, or committed technical assistance of the sponsors.		Acceptable	Limited/weak, or local operator dependent on local authorities.
Off-take risk				
(a) If there is a take-or-pay or fixed-price off-take contract:	Excellent creditworthiness of off-taker; strong termination clauses; tenor of contract comfortably exceeds the maturity of the debt.	Good creditworthiness of off-taker; strong termination clauses; tenor of contract exceeds the maturity of the debt.	Acceptable financial standing of off-taker; normal termination clauses; tenor of contract generally matches the maturity of the debt.	Weak off-taker; weak termination clauses; tenor of contract does not exceed the maturity of the debt.
(b) If there is no take-or-pay or fixed-price off-take contract:	Project produces essential services or a commodity sold widely on a world market; output can readily be absorbed at projected prices even at lower than historic market growth rates.	Project produces essential services or a commodity sold widely on a regional market that will absorb it at projected prices at historical growth rates.	Commodity is sold on a limited market that may absorb it only at lower than projected prices.	Project output is demanded by only one or a few buyers or is not generally sold on an organized market.
Supply risk				
Price, volume and transportation risk of feedstocks; supplier's track record and financial strength	Long-term supply contract with supplier of excellent financial standing.	Long-term supply contract with supplier of good financial standing.	Long-term supply contract with supplier of good financial standing; a degree of price risk may remain.	Short-term supply contract, or long-term supply contract with financially weak supplier; a degree of price risk definitely remains.

(Continued)

EXHIBIT 8.5 (*Continued*)

	Strong	Good	Satisfactory	Weak
Reserve risks (e.g. natural resource development)	Independently audited, proven, and developed reserves well in excess of requirements over lifetime of the project.	Independently audited, proven, and developed reserves in excess of requirements over lifetime of the project.	Proven reserves can supply the project adequately through the maturity of the debt.	Project relies to some extent on potential and undeveloped reserves.
Strength of Sponsor				
Sponsor's track record, financial strength, and country/sector experience	Strong sponsor with excellent track record and high financial standing.	Good sponsor with satisfactory track record and good financial standing.	Adequate sponsor with adequate track record and good financial standing.	Weak sponsor with no or questionable track record and/or financial weaknesses.
Sponsor support, as evidenced by equity, ownership clause and incentive to inject additional cash if necessary	Strong. Project is highly strategic for the sponsor (core business, long-term strategy).	Good. Project is strategic for the sponsor (core business, long-term strategy).	Acceptable. Project is considered important for the sponsor (core business).	Limited. Project is not key to sponsor's long-term strategy or core business.
Security Package				
Assignment of contracts and accounts	Fully comprehensive	Comprehensive	Acceptable	Weak

	Strong	Satisfactory	Fair	Weak
Pledge of assets, taking into account quality, value, and liquidity of assets	First perfected security interest in all project assets, contracts, permits, and accounts necessary to run the project.	Perfected security interest in all project assets, contracts, permits, and accounts necessary to run the project.	Acceptable security interest in all project assets, contracts, permits, and accounts necessary to run the project.	Little security or collateral for lenders; weak negative pledge clause.
Lender's control over cash flow (e.g., cash sweeps, independent escrow accounts)	Strong	Satisfactory	Fair	Weak
Strength of the covenant package (mandatory prepayments, payment deferrals, payment cascade, dividend restrictions, etc.)	Covenant package is strong for this type of project. Project may issue no additional debt.	Covenant package is satisfactory for this type of project. Project may issue extremely limited additional debt.	Covenant package is fair for this type of project. Project may issue limited additional debt.	Covenant package is insufficient for this type of project. Project may issue unlimited additional debt.
Reserve funds (debt service, O&M, renewal and replacement, unforeseen events, etc.)	Longer than average coverage period, all reserve funds fully funded in cash or letters of credit from highly rated bank.	Average coverage period, all reserve funds fully funded.	Average coverage period, all reserve funds fully funded.	Shorter than average coverage period, reserve funds funded from operating cash flows.

Source: Basel Committee on Banking Supervision, *International Convergence of Capital Measurement and Capital Standards* (Basel, Switzerland: Bank for International Settlements, 2006).

intuition that asset risk decreases as loans mature over time. Comparable default rates for infrastructure PF bonds are 8.8 percent, 6.6 percent for investment-grade bonds, and 12.5 percent for non-investment-grade bonds. Default rate for investment-grade corporate bonds is 3.8 percent and 31 percent for non-investment-grade corporate bonds. Of course, bondholders are not required to set aside capital and Basel II does not apply to them.

Infrastructure Bonds versus Syndicated Debt

Clearly the capital charge that banks must set aside increases the cost of funds for loans. Capital market instruments like bonds do not face this cost, and projects can access lower cost capital depending on their credit ratings. Unfortunately, capital market PF infrastructure bonds have other drawbacks.

It is difficult for bondholders to create the same reputation effect for mitigating sovereign holdup that syndicated lending creates. Syndicated lending also permits lenders to monitor the assets relatively easily as compared to diffuse bondholders. The bond trustee is typically responsible for holding and dealing with the security, enforcing the covenants set forth in the indenture, and enforcing the remedial provisions of the indenture if the issuer defaults.[25] Bond trustees do not monitor assets or take actions to prevent default. Bondholders cannot act preemptively in the same manner as lending syndicates in preventing default or renegotiating with sponsors, governments, or contractors once default occurs. Furthermore, it is easier for commercial banks to conduct the deep and systematic due diligence required of infrastructure assets. Of course, this diligence is performed for bondholders by the credit rating agencies.

It is difficult for PF infrastructure bonds to obtain the highest credit ratings because of nonrecourse debt and single-asset source of cash flows without the benefits of coinsurance and the parent's credit rating. Political risk guarantees are very expensive, and a guarantee covering 70 percent of the entire issue will only move the credit rating for a bond from borderline to strong investment-grade (Baa3 to Baa1 on Moody's scale).[26] Between 2002 and 2005, S&P rated about 40 percent of all project debt at BBB, the lowest investment-grade rating, and another 15 percent at BB, the highest non-investment-grade rating.[27] Most PF infrastructure bonds are therefore rated at or just below investment grade, where the costs and benefits of issuing the bond converge.[28]

It is also easier for bank syndicates to restructure syndicated debt than bonds because resolution is cheaper and quicker when there are fewer classes of creditors.[29] Finally, if lenders take over the asset, it is easier for banks to hire managers and operate the assets as compared to diffuse bondholders. Infrastructure investments financed with 100 percent debt are operated by lenders. For example, the BOT projects Dartford, Second Severn, and Skye Bridge crossings in the United Kingdom are 100 percent debt-financed by Bank of America.[30] This aspect is particularly important in infrastructure because these assets retain their value and can produce cash flows after default.

These drawbacks suggest that bond financing is unsuitable for new greenfield projects but may work better in projects with low construction risk or for assets with long proven operating history. In the next section I examine the returns from portfolios of PF infrastructure bonds in light of their drawbacks.

INFRASTRUCTURE BOND RETURNS

It is difficult to analyze the historical return performance of PF bonds issued for infrastructure assets because a relevant bond index does not exist. Bonds are not classified as infrastructure bonds, and no prior studies exist to the best of the author's knowledge. Moreover, bonds issued for PF are a relatively recent phenomenon.

In order to collect a sample of PF infrastructure bonds for analysis, I use a sample examined by Dailami and Hauswald (2003) in their study of covenant provisions and at-issue spread determinants of PF bonds.[31] Their sample comprises 105 bonds issued between 1993 and March 2002. I utilize this sample and obtain monthly price data for each bond from Bloomberg. Of the 105 initial bonds, pricing data is available for 59 bonds. Exhibit 8.6 displays a table of the resulting sample. Exhibit 8.6 shows that the sample comprises bonds issued by 15 countries, in five sectors, with maturities ranging from 3 to 100 years and issue sizes ranging from $100 million to $1 billion. Of the 59 bonds, 4 bonds defaulted and were restructured while 2 were called. Sample bonds are dollar-denominated fixed coupon bonds and, except for the 2 bonds that were called, do not have embedded options.

Portfolio Construction

In order to analyze historical returns from the sample of PF infrastructure bonds, I construct portfolios by investing $1/n$ of the portfolio in each of n bonds, following Fabozzi (1996), which implies equal value weights for each constituent bond of the portfolio.[32] The investing strategy is a naive buy-and-hold strategy without short-selling or optimization. The beginning of period wealth is invested in $(n + 1)$ bonds when a new bond is added to the portfolio and in $(n - 1)$ bonds when a bond reaches maturity. In order to compare the risk and return characteristics with those of the equity infrastructure indexes examined in Chapter 2, I evaluate monthly returns

EXHIBIT 8.6 Sample Infrastructure Bond Description

Country	Project	Sector	Issue Date	Maturity	Amount $ millions	Coupon	Maturity Date	Status
Czech Republic	Aero Vodochody	Other	11/17/1998	7	200	7.5	11/17/2005	
Venezuela	Cerro Negro Finance Ltd.	Energy	6/18/1998	11.46	200	7.33	12/1/2009	
Venezuela	Cerro Negro Finance Ltd.	Energy	6/18/1998	22.47	350	7.9	12/1/2020	
Czech Republic	CEZ Finance BV	Power	7/22/1997	10	200	7.125	7/22/2007	
Chile	Chilgener S.A.	Power	1/26/1996	10	200	6.5	1/15/2006	
China	China Mobile (Hong Kong) Ltd.	Telecom	11/2/1999	5	600	7.875	11/2/2004	
Mexico	Conproca S.A. De C.V	Other	6/30/1998	12	370.3	12	6/16/2010	
Chile	Empresa Electrica Pehuenche S.A.	Power	5/2/1996	7	170	7.3	5/1/2003	
Chile	Enersis S.A.	Power	11/26/1996	10	300	6.9	12/1/2006	
Philippines	Globe Telecom	Telecom	8/6/1999	10	220	13	8/1/2004	Called
Philippines	Globe Telecom	Telecom	3/27/2002	10	200	9.75	4/15/2007	Called
Korea	Korea Electric Power Corp.	Power	3/31/2000	5	300	8.25	3/31/2005	
Hong Kong	Kowloon Canton Railway Corp.	Transport	3/16/2000	10	1000	8	3/15/2010	
Mexico	Monterrey Power, S.A. de C.V.	Power	4/24/1998	11.57	235.54	9.625	11/15/2009	
Russia	Mosenergo Finance, AO	Power	10/9/1997	5	200	8.375	10/9/2002	
Philippines	National Power Corp.	Power	12/13/1996	10	200	7.875	12/15/2006	

Philippines	National Power Corp.	Power	12/13/1996	20	160	8.4	12/15/2016
Philippines	National Power Corp.	Power	5/6/1998	30	300	9.625	5/15/2028
Hong Kong	New World Infrastructure Limited	Other	3/24/1998	5	300	1	4/15/2003
Mexico	Pemex Finance	Energy	2/25/1999	11.73	200	8.875	11/15/2010
Mexico	Pemex Finance	Energy	12/14/1998	20	250	9.15	11/15/2018
Mexico	Pemex Finance	Energy	7/27/1999	10	600	9.69	8/15/2009
Mexico	Pemex Finance	Energy	7/27/1999	18	200	10.61	8/15/2017
Mexico	Pemex Finance	Energy	12/12/2002	7	1000	7.875	2/1/2009
Mexico	Pemex Finance	Energy	2/10/2000	11	800	9.03	2/15/2011
Mexico	Petacalco Trust	Power	4/23/1997	13	308.9	10.16	12/23/2009
Malaysia	Petroliam Nasional Berhard	Energy	8/12/1999	5	650	8.875	8/1/2004
Malaysia	Petroliam Nasional Berhard	Energy	7/1/1993	10	500	6.875	6/22/2003
Malaysia	Petroliam Nasional Berhard	Energy	8/17/1995	10	375	7.125	8/17/2005
Malaysia	Petroliam Nasional Berhard	Energy	10/18/1996	10	800	7.125	10/18/2006
Malaysia	Petroliam Nasional Berhard	Energy	8/17/1995	20	625	7.75	8/15/2015
Venezuela	Petrozuata Finance or Petrolera Zuata	Energy	6/27/1997	20	625	8.22	4/1/2017
Venezuela	Petrozuata Finance or Petrolera Zuata	Energy	6/27/1997	12	300	7.63	4/1/2009
Mexico	Proyectos de Energia, S.A. de C.V.	Power	5/14/1998	15	100	9.75	7/15/2013

(*Continued*)

EXHIBIT 8.6 *(Continued)*

Country	Project	Sector	Issue Date	Maturity	Amount $ millions	Coupon	Maturity Date	Status
Philippines	Quezon Power (Philippines) Ltd.	Power	7/3/1997	20	215	8.86	6/15/2017	
Qatar	Ras Laffan Liquefied Natural Gas Co. Ltd.	Energy	12/12/1996	18	800	8.294	3/15/2014	
India	Tata Electric Companies (The)	Power	8/12/1997	10	150	7.875	8/19/2007	
Malaysia	Telekom Malaysia	Telecom	8/10/1995	10	200	7.125	8/1/2005	
Malaysia	Telekom Malaysia	Telecom	8/3/1995	20	300	7.875	8/1/2025	
Malaysia	Tenaga Nasional Berhad	Power	6/22/1994	10	600	7.875	6/15/2004	
Malaysia	Tenaga Nasional Berhad	Power	4/29/1997	10	300	7.2	4/29/2007	
Malaysia	Tenaga Nasional Berhad	Power	4/29/1997	10	500	7.625	4/29/2007	
Malaysia	Tenaga Nasional Berhad	Power	4/4/2001	10	600	7.625	4/1/2011	
Malaysia	Tenaga Nasional Berhad	Power	10/31/1995	30	350	7.5	11/1/2025	
Malaysia	Tenaga Nasional Berhad	Power	1/16/1996	100	150	7.5	1/15/2096	
Thailand	Total Access Communications	Telecom	11/4/1996	10	300	8.375	11/4/2006	
Chile	Cia de Telecom de Chile	Telecom	1/8/1999	7	200	8.375	1/1/2006	
Chile	Cia de Telecom de Chile	Telecom	7/25/96	10	200	7.625	7/15/2006	

Country	Company	Sector						
Brazil	Companhia Petrolifera Marlim	Energy	12/17/1999	5	200	13.125	12/17/2004	
Brazil	Companhia Petrolifera Marlim	Energy	9/26/2000	8	200	12.25	9/26/2008	
Thailand	Electricity Generating Authority of Thailand	Power	10/6/1998	10	300	7	10/14/1998	
Brazil	Eletrobras Centrais Eletricas Brasileiras S.A.	Power	6/9/2000	5	300	12	6/9/2005	
Brazil	Eletrobras Centrais Eletricas Brasileiras S.A.	Power	6/27/1996	8	250	10	7/6/2004	
Brazil	Espirito Santo Centrais Eletricas S.A.	Power	7/28/1997	10	500	10	7/15/2007	
China	Huaneng Power International Inc.	Energy	11/21/1997	6.5	230	1.75	5/21/2004	
Argentina	Inversora Electrica de Buenos Aires S.A.	Power	9/24/1997	5	100	8.65		Default
Argentina	Inversora Electrica de Buenos Aires S.A.	Power	9/24/1997	7	130	9		Default
Argentina	Metrogas S.A.	Power	3/27/2000	3	100	9.875	4/1/2003	Default
Argentina	Transportadora de Gas del Sur S.A. (TGS)	Energy	4/25/2000	3	150	10.375	4/15/2003	Default

Source: M. Dailami and R. Hauswald, "The Emerging Project Bond Market: Covenant Provisions and Credit Spreads," World Bank Policy Research Working Paper 3095, 2003. Author analysis.

for the period June 2000 to March 2009. Following Bessembinder, Kahle, Maxwell, and Xu (2009), I calculate the return from each bond as follows:[33]

$$\text{Return} = \frac{(\text{End of period price} - \text{Beginning of period price} + \text{coupon})}{\text{Beginning of period price}}$$

Compared to equities, pricing information for infrastructure bonds is not available for every period, and the data has missing price data. We handle missing price data following Venkatesh (2003) and assume an unchanged price from the previous period.[34] This results in a zero return for the period in which bond prices are unavailable. From an economic perspective, the assumption that investors get zero returns when bonds trade infrequently does not seem unreasonable. However, the assumption also likely reduces the variance of the bond returns.

It is harder to predict the impact on portfolio variance since portfolio variance is a function of the variance of individual constituent bonds as well as the covariance of those bonds. We measure the portfolio return as the value-weighted average of each constituent bond return, using equation 2.3 from Chapter 2. We measure the portfolio risk or standard deviation using equation 2.6 from Chapter 2. Exhibit 8.7 shows the returns from infrastructure bonds from June 2000 to March 2009.

Infrastructure Bond Portfolio Returns

Exhibit 8.7 shows that infrastructure bonds provide relatively stable returns as compared to the S&P 500 over the period June 2000 to March 2009. The period over which we consider the analysis does matter, since extending the period beyond 1997 when the Asian financial crisis and then the Russian financial crisis occurred increases the volatility of infrastructure bond returns. However, our returns include the Argentinean crisis of 2000, reflected in the defaults of four bonds by Argentinean firms in our sample.

The mean monthly return provided by infrastructure bonds in this sample is quite low at 0.0983 percent, and the Sharpe ratio is negative at −0.14. Infrastructure bonds in this sample therefore do not compensate investors adequately for risk. The distribution of bond returns shown in Exhibit 8.8 supports this analysis: return distribution from −3.33 to 2.29 percent, skew −1.137, kurtosis 8.17, standard deviation 1.02 percent, Sharpe ratio −0.14.

The infrastructure bond return distribution's skew of −1.137 implies a higher likelihood of negative returns. The high kurtosis of 8.17 shows that a larger proportion of returns comes from outliers as compared to a normal distribution.

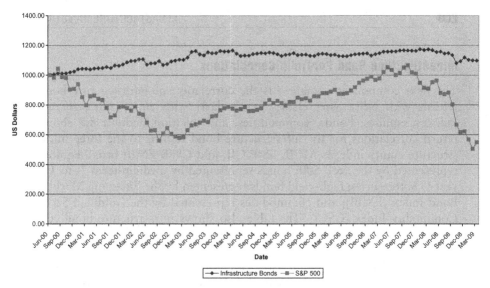

EXHIBIT 8.7   Value of $1,000 Invested in S&P 500 and PF Infrastructure Bonds

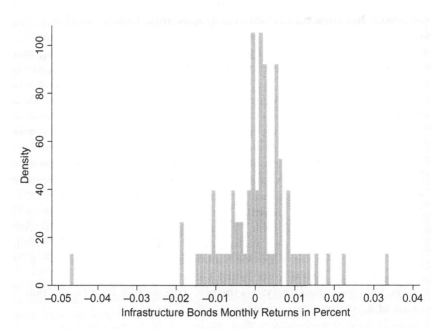

EXHIBIT 8.8   Infrastructure Monthly Bond Return Distribution
Source: Author analysis.

Infrastructure Bond Portfolio Correlations

The next component I analyze is the correlation of infrastructure bond returns with other asset classes, particularly with equity infrastructure indexes, equities, bonds, commodities, and inflation. Exhibit 8.9 shows return correlations for the infrastructure bond returns to the three infrastructure equity indexes MGII, S&P GII, and CSFB EMII; broad equities represented by the S&P 500; bonds represented by medium-term 7- to 10-year U.S. treasuries; high-yield bonds represented by the Emerging Markets Bond Index (EMBI); and commodities represented by the Goldman Sachs Commodity Index (GSCI). The table also shows infrastructure bond correlation to the monthly consumer price index (CPI) representing the U.S. inflation rate.

Exhibit 8.9 shows that infrastructure bonds are not strongly correlated with equities at 0.35. They are correlated with bonds with a correlation of 0.80 with the EMBI index, which makes sense since the index also tracks bonds from emerging markets. Interestingly, the returns show a higher correlation to the equity infrastructure indexes at about 0.5 than to equities themselves. Infrastructure return correlations are even less correlated with commodities at 0.21. Finally, infrastructure bond returns are negatively correlated to inflation, which implies that they are a very poor hedge against inflation. The negative correlation implies that as inflation increases, infrastructure bond returns decline. The decline in returns is likely because the bonds pay fixed dollar-denominated coupons whose value decreases when inflation increases.

The analysis so far shows that infrastructure bonds provide relatively stable returns with low correlation with equities. Infrastructure bonds therefore match the underlying economics of infrastructure assets and provide the type of returns that investors seek from infrastructure assets, namely stable, low-volatility, long-tenor returns. Unfortunately they also provide very low returns with a negative Sharpe ratio, indicating that the risk/reward calculus is not favorable. It may of course be possible to improve the returns through active management and portfolio optimization. Moreover, the analysis is a historical analysis and, as the truism says, past performance is no guarantee of future performance.

The final question I analyze is the performance of infrastructure bonds as part of a portfolio comprising equities and treasuries.

Efficient Frontier with Infrastructure Bonds

Exhibit 8.10 on page 208 shows the efficient frontiers for two portfolios: a portfolio comprising stocks and Treasuries and a portfolio with stocks,

EXHIBIT 8.9 Infrastructure Bond Monthly Return Correlations with Other Asset Classes

	S&P 500	Infrastructure Bonds	MGII	S&P GII	CSFB EMII	EMBI	GSCI	10-Year Treasury	CPI
S&P 500	1								
Infrastructure Bonds	0.3508	1							
MGII	0.7682	0.5804	1						
S&P GII	0.8175	0.5546	0.9455	1					
CSFB EMII	0.7991	0.4794	0.8389	0.888	1				
EMBI	0.5548	0.7999	0.6995	0.6868	0.6458	1			
GSCI	0.2837	0.2089	0.3827	0.4303	0.5069	0.2483	1		
10-Year Treasury	−0.0125	0.6501	0.2261	0.1868	0.0318	0.5013	−0.042	1	
CPI	0.0551	−0.0897	0.0908	0.107	0.1134	−0.0106	0.4263	−0.3779	1

Source: Author analysis.

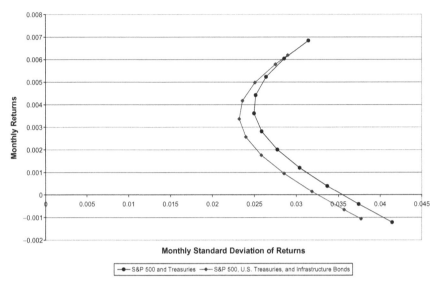

EXHIBIT 8.10 Efficient Frontier: S&P 500, Infrastructure Bonds, and U.S. Treasuries

Treasuries, and infrastructure bonds. The efficient frontier for the first portfolio is constructed by varying the proportion of stocks and Treasuries and plotting the resulting portfolio returns against portfolio risk, measured by portfolio standard deviation. The efficient frontier for the latter portfolio is constructed by varying the proportion of stocks and bonds while holding the proportion of infrastructure bonds constant at 10 percent of the portfolio. We can see that the efficient frontier shifts outward when infrastructure bonds are added to a portfolio of stocks and bonds, resulting in higher returns for the same level of risk or the same returns with lower risk. However, as the proportion of Treasuries in the portfolio increases, the returns for the portfolio drop and the efficient frontier shifts inward.

CONCLUSION

This chapter highlighted the pitfalls of using the traditional DCF method for valuing infrastructure assets that use high leverage with rapid changes in capital structure. Since valuation is the bedrock for making advance-or-abandon decisions, an erroneous valuation can lead to incorrect decisions and poor returns. In the infrastructure investing context, investors need to be particularly careful because the investments are irreversible and if planned revenues do not materialize, it is difficult to create new revenue streams. Ruback's CCF method circumvents issues created by the changing capital structure and the circularity problem of valuing equity accurately.

We also saw that the cost of bank lending is affected by the requirement of setting aside bank equity capital, mandated by Basel II. Although capital market instruments do not suffer from this capital charge, bank lending does possess certain advantages vis-à-vis capital market bonds. Among the advantages that syndicated bank lending possesses, of those likely to impact investment returns, the following are particularly important: ability to conduct quality due diligence, effective monitoring, ability to intervene and renegotiate early, and the reputation effect. It is possible that the disadvantages of capital market bonds are reflected in their returns.

We saw that PF infrastructure bond returns actually mimic infrastructure asset characteristics fairly well, displaying stable returns over long durations. However, the returns are very low and display a negative Sharpe ratio, which means that investors are not compensated for the risk. The returns have low correlations with equities and the equity infrastructure indexes, and high correlation with bond indexes like the EMBI and U.S. Treasuries, as expected. Nevertheless, infrastructure bonds improve the efficient frontier as part of a portfolio of stocks and bonds. We have of course used historical data for the analysis, and the risk always exists that the future will be unlike the past. At least in the infrastructure context, the future is more likely to be like the past than perhaps in most other investment contexts. The problem is that we do not know how the covariances are likely to evolve. We can use only very recent data, in which case we risk making estimation errors.[35]

I have not been able to analyze returns to direct syndicated bank lending in this book. Unfortunately, there is not sufficient data to analyze the returns from syndicated debt lending. These are likely to reflect infrastructure characteristics far more closely than capital market bonds and offer higher returns. I have made the case that debt matches infrastructure governance needs better than equities do. Pension funds should therefore be well advised to consider investing directly as part of lending syndicates instead of taking equity positions.

CHAPTER 9

Case Studies

Give just weight and full measure.

—The Koran

This chapter takes the analytical strands of the previous chapters and weaves them into two case studies. I examine two investments: Aguas Argentinas S.A. (AASA), a water and sanitation company providing service to the capital of Argentina, Buenos Aires; and Dabhol power company (DPC), generating electricity in the state of Maharashtra in India.

Both case studies highlight the paradox of infrastructure investing explored in the earlier chapters of this book. Sponsors considered AASA and DPC as shining jewels in their portfolios, but both became millstones instead. AASA investors were hurt as much by management's decisions as by the Argentine economic crisis of 2002. DPC investors were similarly hurt as much by the economics of the project as by sovereign holdup.

CASE STUDY 1: AGUAS ARGENTINAS S.A.

In May 1993, Aguas Argentinas S.A. (AASA) won its bid to supply water and sanitation services to Buenos Aires, the capital of Argentina, and its surrounding areas for the next 30 years. Within 13 years, in March 2006, the government of Argentina rescinded the concession and repossessed its assets, after three years of often acrimonious negotiations. Some months later, lenders sued AASA's main sponsor and one of the world's largest water companies, the French multinational Suez, for $135 million.[1] On July 17, 2003, Suez itself had already filed arbitration proceedings claiming $1.7 billion against the government of Argentina in the World Bank's International

Centre for Settlement of Investments Disputes (ICSID) court under the bilateral investment treaty (BIT) between Argentina and France.[2] Was AASA a victim of the economic and political turmoil that consumed Argentina during the 2002 crisis? What could AASA have done differently in order to fulfill its obligations to its different stakeholders—its shareholders, lenders, customers, government, and society at large?

The city of Buenos Aires, Argentina's capital city, and 17 suburban districts covers an area of 2,800 square kilometers and is home to some 10 million inhabitants. Rapid growth of the city in the 1990s outstripped the capacity of Obras Sanitarias de la Nación, the government-owned water and sewerage utility, to provide service. In May 1993 only 67 percent of the population had access to drinking water, and only 53 percent were connected to the sewer system. Moreover, 30 percent of the population lived below the poverty line and significant investments were required to enlarge the water and sewerage networks.[3]

The government of Carlos Menem believed that privatization was the solution and chose the concession model in which the assets would remain under public ownership and the concessionaire would have the rights to operate the assets. The privatization was carried out by competitive bidding and the government selected the winner on the basis of two criteria: the bidder with the lowest tariff and commitment to investing in increasing the distribution network. The concession contract required that tariffs were to remain unchanged for 10 years and anticipated an investment of $4.1 billion, mostly in the early years of the concession, thereby connecting 100 percent of the population to water and 95 percent of the population to sewerage services.

Ordinary tariff revisions would take place every five years. The first revision would lower the tariff. Extraordinary tariff revisions were allowed if costs increased by more than 7 percent. This clause transferred the risk of cost increases onto customers who would pay more for higher costs when AASA was the party that could control costs. AASA would subsequently use this contract clause to negotiate multiple tariff increases. Exhibit 9.1 shows Aguas Argentinas performance targets required by its contract.

Naturally the contract also required the concessionaire to guarantee water quality. In 1992 the government also created an independent regulator called Ente Tripartito de Obras y Servicios Sanitarios (ETOSS), responsible for enforcing the contract, imposing fines, and making tariff revisions. Therefore tariffs and investments were the centerpiece of the concession contract.[4] Curiously, 90 percent of all tariffs in the contract were flat-rate tariffs based on property characteristics like the size of the lot, quality of the dwelling, and so on, which meant that the concessionaire did not need to invest in meters. Lack of meters also meant that customers could not

EXHIBIT 9.1 Aguas Argentinas Performance Targets

Year of Contract	Percent Population Serviced by Water	Percent Population Serviced by Sewerage	Percent Collected Sewerage that is treated		Network Renovation (Cumulative)		Percent of Unaccounted-for Water
			Primary	Secondary	Water	Sewerage	
0	70	58	4	4	0	0	45
5	81	64	64	7	9	2	37
10	90	73	73	14	12	3	34
20	97	82	82	88	28	4	28
30	100	90	90	93	45	5	25

Source: Alexander J. Loftus and David A. McDonald, "Of Liquid Dreams: A Political Ecology of Water Privatization in Buenos Aires," in Somsook Boonyabancha, Diana Mitlin, and International Institute for Environment and Development, eds., *Civil Society in Action: Transforming Opportunities for the Urban Poor* (IIED, 2001), 189.

control their bills by consuming less water, so they had little incentive to save water.

The privatization plan's opponents included the labor unions and customers who feared tariff increases from profit-seeking private investors. In order to lower customer opposition for the upcoming privatization, the government increased water tariffs in 1991, by 25 percent in February and then another 29 percent in April. In 1992, it added an 18 percent sales tax and raised the rates another 8 percent. The concessionaire could therefore reduce tariffs on taking over the concession and earn public goodwill. The unions were offered an employee stock option plan with 10 percent of the shares and one seat on the board.

AASA was a consortium comprising Suez, 25.30 percent; Sociedad General Aguas de Barcelona S.A. (Agbar), 12.60 percent (Suez owned 25 percent of Agbar); Vivendi, 8 percent; Anglian Water Plc., 4.50 percent; Soldati group, 20.70 percent; Meller family, 10.80 percent; Banco de Galicia, 8.10 percent; and employees, 10 percent. The Soldati group and the Meller family were local partners with strong political connections to President Carlos Menem, while Banco de Galicia was the largest local bank.[5] AASA won the bid with a tariff reduction of 26.9 percent over the current tariff, beating the closest competing bid by Aguas de Buenos Aires, a consortium led by British Thames Water which offered a 26.1 percent discount. The contract included a clause that permitted Suez a fee as the concession's operator for providing technical know-how and so on, equal to 6 percent of gross margin.

The Early Years

AASA took over the concession in May 1993 and reduced tariffs by 26.9 percent. It also improved bill collection from 55 percent in 1993 to 95 percent by mid-1995. AASA reduced the workforce by 48 percent[6] and the firm was profitable right from the get-go. The feeling within Suez in France was that AASA was one of its most successful subsidiaries. How did it serve its other stakeholders, its customers? AASA improved the water pressure and there were no interruptions in the summer.

How did AASA fulfill its contractual obligation of increasing the population connected to water and sewerage services? The very next year of the contract, in 1994 AASA petitioned ETOSS for an increase in tariffs to generate funds for investments. ETOSS agreed to a 13.5 percent increase in exchange for advancing the dates for the investment and for connecting the shanty towns. The original contract did not require AASA to connect residents without proper title to their land, which included most of the shanty towns. In addition, the contract stipulated connection fees of $450 for water supply and $670 for sewerage. In 1994 AASA obtained $172.5 million from the World Bank's International Finance Corporation for undertaking the planned expansions. In 1996, as the expansion continued into the poorer neighborhoods of Buenos Aires, where customers earned $200 to $245 a month, customers could not pay the connection fees. Protests erupted in the town of Lomas de Zamora and spread to the capital. AASA and ETOSS agreed to reduce the connection fees to $200 but added an additional universal service fee for old customers, thereby subsidizing the new connections. A 1996 World Bank report noted that AASA delayed construction of a sewage treatment plant in Berazategui, thereby increasing concentration of nitrates in the water. Apparently the delay saved AASA $100,000 a day.[7]

AASA certainly achieved water coverage targets, making impressive gains in the number of people connected by water. But even by the year 1999, primary sewage treatment, which involved settling out undissolved solids from suspension in the form of sludge, increased from 5 percent to a mere 7 percent instead of the required 74 percent. AASA essentially dumped most of the raw sewage into the Rio de la Plata (the silver river), separating Buenos Aires from Montevideo, the capital of Uruguay.

Tariffs and Renegotiations

On February 14, 1997, President Carlos Menem signed Decree N149/97 granting Maria Julia Alsogaray, the secretary of environment, authority over the fulfillment of the contract and authorizing her to renegotiate the contract with Aguas Argentinas. This surprising action allowed AASA to bypass ETOSS, whose authority and credibility was seriously damaged. AASA asked for a contract renegotiation based on its inability to collect connection fees for expanding the network, and the negotiations with Alsogaray resulted in two new and important clauses. The first clause granted AASA the "right to economic equilibrium," which meant that AASA had the right to recover all operating costs and expenses, including financial costs. The second clause granted revenue protection against currency devaluation and inflation. Revenues were denominated in U.S. dollars and tariffs were automatically adjusted monthly based on the US$-AR$ exchange rate. Revenues were protected from inflation through annual tariff adjustments. Unfortunately, revenues were protected from *U.S. inflation* since the tariff adjustments were based on the average U.S. producer price index and U.S. consumer price index. These clauses removed entrepreneurial incentives for AASA to lower costs since it was a monopoly and competitive market forces were absent. Alsogaray was a controversial and reputedly corrupt politician, accused and convicted later of enriching herself to the tune of millions of U.S. dollars.[8]

During the next four years, from 1998 to 2001, AASA got three upward tariff revisions. Argentina's exchange rate pegged to the U.S. dollar remained unchanged while inflation within Argentina remained well below the tariff increases. In fact Argentina experienced deflation in 1998, 1999, and 2001 when the tariffs increased based on U.S. inflation. Exhibit 9.2 displays tariff increases, inflation, and the exchange rate. From 1993 when AASA took

EXHIBIT 9.2   AASA Tariffs, Argentine Inflation, and Exchange Rates

Year	Tariffs in AR$	Tariff Index	Exchange Rate AR$ per US$	Inflation, Wholesale Price Index
1993	14.56	100	1	
1994	16.53	114	1	−0.20%
1995	16.53		1	6.50%
1996	16.53		1	3.20%
1997	20.55		1	0.10%
1998	21.65	149	1	−3.20%
1999	23.73	163	1	−3.80%
2000	23.73		1	4%
2001	26.25	180	1	−2.30%

Source: Louis T. Wells and Alexandra De Royere, *Aguas Argentinas, Case Study # 9-705-019* (Cambridge, MA: Harvard Business School, 2003).

over the concession to 2001, tariffs increased by 80 percent while inflation in Argentina remained near 0 percent and the exchange rate remained unchanged.

Some of these increases were not authorized by ETOSS. In May 1998 AASA asked ETOSS for an 11.7 percent increase but ETOSS granted only 1.61 percent. AASA approached the Secretary, Ms. Alsogaray, and got a 17 percent increase. Although the increase was frozen because of a legal challenge, the government appealed and the hike went through. In July 1998 Suez offered to buy out the Soldati group's 20.70 percent stake, worth $24.8 million in 1993, for $90 million. On October 9, 1998, Suez bought the Soldati group stake for 150 million after the 17 percent rate hike was approved by the government,[9] a premium of 248 percent over Soldati's book value of equity and representing a compound annual return of 43.28 percent to the group. In 1999, based on the U.S. inflation rate, AASA received another tariff hike days before the Menem government relinquished power, having lost the elections earlier. In 2001, during the second five-year revision of tariffs, ETOSS agreed to increase tariffs by 3.9 percent per year until 2003 in order to finance a five-year $1.1 billion investment plan.

The 2002 Argentine Crisis

Argentina was in a recession in 1998 and by November 2001 there were delays in the country's debt restructuring. By giving up monetary independence with its currency peg to the U.S. dollar, Argentina had no monetary tools to fight the recession.[10] Bank deposits dropped as capital fled the country. In 2002, Argentina finally abolished the U.S. dollar peg and allowed the currency to float. The Central Bank immediately extended liquidity to the banks and the government to bridge its deficit, thereby increasing money supply. The Argentine currency rapidly devalued by 350 percent to reach AR $3.50 per US $1, from the earlier exchange rate of AR $1 per US $1. Wholesale prices increased 110 percent, 2002 inflation reached 43 percent, imports fell by 54 percent, Argentines living below the poverty line increased from 35 percent to 57 percent, and GDP decreased by 12 percent. The government declared that all utility tariffs would be calculated in Argentinean dollars, tariff increases would be frozen, and all contracts would be renegotiated.

By 2002 AASA had taken a total of $884.8 million in U.S. dollar–denominated loans and found itself with $706.12 million in loans at the end of December 2001. Exhibit 9.3 shows AASA loans and their tenors. The World Bank's International Finance Corporation (IFC), Inter-American Development Bank (IDB), European Investment Bank (EIB), and a banking syndicate led by ING Barings were AASA's lenders.

EXHIBIT 9.3 Aguas Argentinas Debt

Date	Lender	Amount	Interest Rate	Maturity
1989	IDB	$97.5 million	5.88%	12 years
1994	IFC Loan A	$25 million	LIBOR + 3%	10 years
1994	IFC Loan B	$134.5 million	LIBOR + 2.75%	8 years
1994	IFC Loan C	$13 million	LIBOR + 4.5%	12 years
1996	IFC Loan A	$40 million	LIBOR + 3.5%	12 years
1996	IFC Loan B (21 bank syndicate)	$173 million	LIBOR + 3.0%	8 years
1997	EIB	Euro 70 million	LIBOR + 0.15%	10 years
1999	IDB Tranche A	$75 million	LIBOR + 3.42%	12 years
1999	IDB Tranche B	$140 million	10.5%	12 years
2000	8-bank syndicate	$108 million	LIBOR + 2% (first 2 years) LIBOR + 2.5% (next 2 years) LIBOR + 2.375% (year 5)	5 years

Source: Louis T. Wells and Alexandra De Royere, *Aguas Argentinas, Case Study #9-705-019* (Cambridge, MA: Harvard Business School, 2003).

On April 11, 2002, AASA suspended debt payments and tried to restructure its debt of $706 million. It also suspended the operating fee of 6 percent that it paid its owner-operator, Suez. In March 2003, the government created UNIREN and charged it with renegotiating the contracts by determining which utilities had complied with original contract terms and made the investments envisaged in the original contracts. In September 2003 ETOSS completed a review of AASA investments and concluded that of the promised $2,202 million, AASA had invested $1,266 million. ETOSS criticized AASA's high debt level.

Critics alleged that AASA had made inordinate profits with return on assets (ROA) of 20 percent and net income/revenues of 13 percent.[11] AASA correctly claimed that ROA was a misleading figure since assets existing at the beginning of the concession were not reflected on its balance sheet. Critics also alleged that the net income to revenue ratio of 13 percent was almost twice that of comparable water utilities in the United States (6 percent to 12.5 percent) and the United Kingdom (6 percent to 7 percent). Exhibit 9.4 displays revenues, net profit margin, operating profits, net profits, fees paid to Suez, dividends, and return over equity. In addition to $125.46 million that Suez received from AASA, it also received its share of

EXHIBIT 9.4 AASA Financials and Fees to Suez

Year	Revenues, (AR $000s)	Revenues (US $000s)	Net Profit Margin	Gross Operating Profits (AR $000s)	Net Profits (AR $000s)	Fees to Suez (US $000s)	Dividends (AR $000s)	Return over Equity
1994	304,980	304,980	8.7%	121,410	26,454	7,285	0	20.10%
1995	360,779	360,779	14.8%	208,863	53,557	12,532	0	28.90%
1996	377,157	377,157	15.4%	221,650	58,252	13,299	14,000	25.40%
1997	419,998	419,998	13.7%	264,098	57,736	15,846	14,000	21.10%
1998	436,722	436,722	8.4%	267,225	36,545	16,034	18,000	12.50%
1999	510,958	510,958	12.2%	331,110	62,119	19,867	20,000	18.60%
2000	514,246	514,246	16.5%	325,586	85,061	19,535	21,000	21.40%
2001	566,037	566,037	13.1%	351,049	73,879	21,063	22,000	16.60%
2002	735,833	240,468	(113.2%)	374,094	(832,726)		0	(601.80%)
2003	593,994	199,998	24.9%	265,651	148,122		0	56.60%
					Total	125,459	109,000	

Source: AASA annual reports; author analysis.

$109 million of dividends, equal to $45.37 million, between 1996 and 2000.*

With devaluation hitting U.S. dollar revenues hard and no tariff increases, AASA filed arbitration against Argentina in the ICSID under the bilateral investment treaty between France and Argentina in July 2003. ETOSS imposed a fine of 3 million pesos for a cut in service that affected 6 million people in September 2003, and weeks later imposed another fine of 8.6 million pesos for nonfulfillment of contract clauses.[12] Diplomatic efforts by the French foreign minister and others led to a transitional agreement in May 2004 in which AASA agreed to invest $242 million and suspend its ICSID arbitration for a year, while the government suspended AASA fines but did not agree to tariff increases. In the meantime, Suez had also changed its corporate strategy, withdrawing from emerging markets to concentrate on Europe and North America. With the government refusing to budge on its position of granting tariff increases, Suez attempted to sell its stake to a number of contenders—the Chilean Grupo Solari, investment funds Fintech and Latam Assets, and a consortium led by investor Eduardo Eurnekian—but ultimately failed to get its asking price of $350 to $375 million.[13] On March 21, 2006, the government of Argentina rescinded the AASA concession, citing breach of contract due to high nitrate levels in the water supply, and handed over the assets to new state group Agua y Saneamientos Argentinos (AySA). Suez left AASA with $660 million in debt and a $1.7 billion arbitration claim in the ICSID.

AASA had virtually no support from Buenos Aires residents. A public opinion poll conducted by Publica Servicios y Mercados (OPSM) of people in and around Buenos Aires showed that 83.4 percent of those interviewed said they "agreed" or "agreed very much" with the decision to rescind the concession, while 14.2 percent disagreed. A larger percentage of 25 percent opposed nationalization.[14]

Lessons from AASA

The AASA case clearly demonstrates the characteristics and pitfalls of infrastructure investing. AASA demonstrates the economic characteristics of the asset's monopoly status, inelastic demand, the social nature of goods, significant government oversight, high operating margins, and stable cash flows. Exhibit 9.4 shows that even in 2002 when the Argentine GDP contracted by 12 percent and the economy was reeling, AASA's operating profits grew 40.57 percent and operating profit margin remained 49.16

*Calculated assuming that AASA disbursed dividends on the basis of shareholding.

percent. The drastic currency devaluation, however, caused AASA to default on its dollar-denominated debt. Although AASA did not suffer a sovereign holdup, it was severely affected by political *force majeure* in the form of the Argentine crisis and devaluation. Its financial structure, lack of competitive returns to equity, involvement with specific local partners, and management's poor community involvement reduced the firm's bargaining power in the post-devaluation renegotiations. I evaluate each in the following paragraphs.

Financial Structure From 1994 to 2001, AASA's long-term debt to capital ratio was about 55.88 percent, which is about 36 to 45 percent less than the typical PF and infrastructure project leverage of 75 to 80 percent. Exhibit 9.5 shows equity, debt, and debt to capital ratio for AASA from 1994 to 2001.

The net income shown in Exhibit 9.4 suggests that the firm could have supported a much higher leverage level. Doing so would have allowed the firm to make the investments it had promised and reduced the reported net profits which proved to be such a lightning rod for critics. More importantly, it would have lowered the cost of capital for AASA, boosted the returns to equity, likely mitigated the incentives that drove equity owners to seek growth through tariff increases, and forced management to run operations as efficiently as possible by lowering costs.

One problem with the concession model which could have restricted lenders' ability to lend to AASA is the problem of collateral. Since the Argentine state and not AASA had legal title to the assets, lenders could

EXHIBIT 9.5 Equity, Debt, and Debt to Capital Ratio for AASA, 1994–2001

Year	Equity (AR $000s)	Debt(AR $000s)	Debt to Capital
1993	120,000	136,272	50.82%
1994	131,880	155,229	45.57%
1995	185,437	337,574	59.51%
1996	229,689	337,136	55.22%
1997	273,425	424,146	59.23%
1998	291,970	586,266	63.70%
1999	334,089	561,779	58.52%
2000	398,150	532,948	54.49%
2001	445,029	136,272	50.82%

Source: Louis T. Wells and Alexandra De Royere, *Aguas Argentinas, Case Study #9-705-019* (Cambridge, MA: Harvard Business School, 2003); author analysis.

probably not have been guaranteed a security interest in the assets and likely could not have foreclosed on the assets in the event of default. This appears to be a serious drawback of the concession model, although creative solutions can be found. Of course, the increased leverage that the reported net income could support includes the effect of the increased tariffs, which I argue did not serve the company well during renegotiations.

Competitive Rate of Return   The high equity stakes in AASA required high rates of return. We have noted that it is important in infrastructure investing to maintain competitive rates of return and not to be seen to make too much money. The operator and main shareholder, Suez, invested $34.14 million in 1993, $30.36 million directly and an additional 25 percent through its ownership of Agbar. Its share of dividends plus fees from 1993 to 2001 was $170.83 million (see Exhibit 9.4). Excluding the Soldati stake investment, these provided a compounded annual return for the investment of 22.30 percent while the fees themselves provided a compounded annual return of 17.67 percent. Clearly these were excellent returns for investing in a water and sewage company. As it turned out, the buyout of the Soldati stake for $150 million seriously damaged returns to Suez shareholders. Suez could not have foreseen the 2002 crisis and probably believed it could continue growing its revenues and net profits. Unfortunately, it did not help itself by increasing tariffs and not making the promised investments.

Local Partners   AASA was highly tied into the Perónist presidency of Carlos Menem through its equity partners. Although AASA benefited from these ties with tariff increases and its ability to bypass the legitimate regulator ETOSS, it was perceived to be a part of corrupt practices. As has happened in Bolivia, Indonesia, and many other countries, a firm with a tarnished reputation finds it difficult to navigate the altered landscape from a change in political power.

Community Involvement   AASA had a real opportunity to cement relations with the community of Buenos Aires and its surrounding areas, which would have provided it with the wherewithal to withstand challenges to its business over the long run and increased its bargaining power in renegotiations. Even though the firm invested $1.7 billion to connect poor communities to a reliable water supply, it alienated its customers by its inability or unwillingness to explain the rationale for the tariff increases and connection fees, and to convince people that their payments would improve services to less fortunate neighbors. Moreover, the focus of investment in water and neglect of the sewerage investments required by the concession provided ammunition to critics who alleged that water was more profitable than sewerage. In comparison, as we saw in Chapter 6, Manila Water did not dump sewage into the sea even when its contract expressly allowed it to do so, and its employee and community relations have allowed it to obtain tariff increases without rancor.

What about the devaluation of the Argentinean dollar and the reduction in dollar-denominated revenues? There is no evidence that AASA considered the possibilities of a pesification of Argentina and the value of the Argentine dollar, or that it took any actions to mitigate the threat of devaluation. It is possible that AASA could have hedged its AR$ exposure through financial instruments like currency swaps, forwards, or options and thereby avoided tariff increases. Alternatively, it could have borrowed in AR$. which was probably more expensive on a hedged basis as compared to dollar-denominated debt in the absence of the crisis. It is not clear whether these solutions were considered and abandoned as unworkable or too expensive.

Role of Government   Clearly, we must also consider the government of Argentina's role in the case. From the start the government insisted on equity, and ETOSS criticized AASA's debt. We know that equity holders prefer to increase the volatility of revenues and require growth. Equity is also more expensive and increases required rates of return. It appears that the government expected AASA to fund investments through internal accruals. Internal accruals require higher rates of return because they are equity capital and have a higher cost of capital than debt. Moreover, the government itself acted in ways that damaged the independence of the regulator and permitted AASA to obtain unsustainable and ultimately temporary gains.

Suez, Agbar, and Vivendi continue their $1.7 billion ICSID arbitration case against Argentina. The three-member tribunal was constituted on February 17, 2004, and comprised Dr. Jeswald W. Salacuse, professor and former dean of the Fletcher School at Tufts University, as the tribunal's president; Dr. Pedro Nikken, professor of law at Universidad Central de Venezuela, representing Argentina; and Dr. Gabrielle Kaufmann-Kohler, professor at Geneva University Law School, representing Suez, Sociedad General de Aguas de Barcelona S.A., and Vivendi Universal S.A.[15] The outcome of the arbitration is pending.

In conclusion, critics characterize the AASA case as private capital's inability to provide infrastructure investment, and state that the profit motive is inconsistent with provision of infrastructure services. Unfortunately, the ability of public capital to provide cost-efficient and quality services and make the best use of taxpayer capital is also open to question. In this case, note that the form of capital is important, as are firm characteristics related to mitigating political and currency risks. In the Dabhol case next, we once again revisit firm-specific and government behavior, as well as management capabilities that can develop or doom a project.

CASE STUDY 2: DABHOL POWER COMPANY

Dabhol Power Company (DPC), an Enron-promoted 2,450-megawatt, $2.9 billion project-financed power generation project in India's western state of Maharashtra, became a poster child for sovereign holdup, renegotiation, and lawsuits, spawning numerous case studies, legal articles,[16] and a book. Rather than chronologically recounting the decade-long saga of the project, I will link the case study to the infrastructure risks presented in this book. Exhibit 9.6 shows the major events of the DPC saga.

DPC came into existence after the government of India decided to encourage private investment in India's chronically underinvested power sector in 1992 and approved eight fast-track projects.[17] As the world's largest gas-fired power plant, DPC was twice the size of the second largest and four times the average size. It was also one of three gas-based generators and the only project to use imported fuel, requiring the construction of a shipping berth, pipeline, ocean breakwater, and liquefied natural gas (LNG) terminal. Exhibit 9.7 on page 225 lists the project sponsor and name, project size in megawatts, construction cost per megawatt, output costs, fuel type, and effect of exchange rate on output costs in May 1999 when DPC began generating electricity. Assuming that the price of foreign gas, which was indexed to the US$ price of oil, did not change and other costs remained constant, the cost of DPC power increased by 42.92 percent as the rupee depreciated. Exhibit 9.7 also shows that DPC displayed no economies of scale in plant costs and was the most expensive gas fuel plant because of the requirement for constructing additional infrastructure.

Although locally available coal and naphtha were cheaper than imported gas and neither was exposed to exchange rate risk, Enron proposed an expensive mega-project because it was looking to sell LNG obtained from its Qatargas project in Qatar.[18] Each LNG train is about 2,000 megawatts, and an electricity plant of this size is necessary for economically transporting LNG by ship. Enron's margin on the sale of gas from Qatargas ensured a 15 percent ROE for its proposed investments in Qatar with the economies of scale provided by DPC's size.[19] The provision of gas from Qatar also determined the location of the plant on India's western coast in Maharashtra, although other states were far more power starved and the infrastructure to sell excess power to power-deficit states was rudimentary at best.

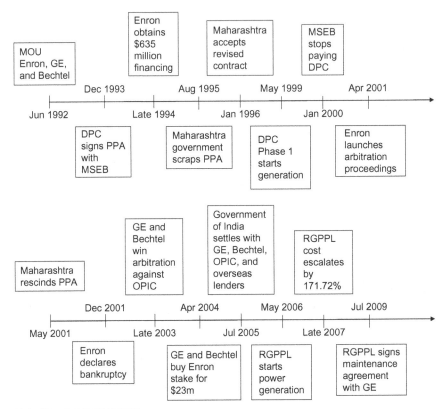

Note: Time line is not to scale.

EXHIBIT 9.6   Dabhol Power Company Major Events
Note: PPA: Power Purchase Agreement.

Risk Management by DPC Sponsors

DPC was organized as a project-financed transaction with debt to capital ratio of approximately 73.88 percent.[20] Enron's contract with the sole state-owned buyer, Maharashtra State Electricity Board (MSEB), denominated revenues in U.S. dollars increasing at the U.S. rate of inflation, guaranteed revenues through a 20-year take-or-pay contract, and included capital recovery costs that increased by 4 percent per year. By including the two contractors GE and Bechtel as equity partners, each contributing 10 percent of equity, the project ensured that construction risk was eliminated. Enron hedged political risk by purchasing insurance from OPIC, through arbitration clauses in the power purchase agreement, and by partnering with

EXHIBIT 9.7 Fast-Track Project Cost Comparison

Project Sponsor Name	Megawatts	Rupees (Million) per Megawatt	Rupees per Kw (US $1 = Rs.32 in 1995)	Fuel	Exchange Rate May 1999 (US$1 = Rs.42.86)
GVK-Jegurupada	648	35.30	–	Coal	–
Spectrum-Godavari	208	36.00	1.87	Gas	1.87
Torrent-Gandhar	654	42.70	2.17	Gas	2.17
Enron-Dabhol	2,450	44.91	2.4 ($.08)	Gas	3.43 ($.08)
Cogentrix-Mangalore	1,000	50.80	2.59	Coal	2.59
AES-Ib Valley	420	48.20	2.39	Coal	2.39
Ashok Leyland-Vizag	1,000	58.10	–	Coal	–
CMS-Neyveli	250	45.00	3.1	Coal	3.1

Source: Krishna G. Palepu and V. Kasturi Rangan, "Enron Development Corporation: The Dabhol Power Project in Maharashtra, India (B)," Harvard Business School, Case #9-797-086, 1997.

Indian state-owned and private banks (IDBI, ICICI, SBI, IFCI, and Canara Bank) as lenders to the project, as well as having MSEB, the sole customer, as an equity stakeholder.

In 1993 the World Bank refused to support the project because more expensive DPC power would replace cheaper coal-based power for base loads and would place an unsustainable burden on the MSEB.[21] To protect against default by MSEB, Enron secured counterguarantees from the state of Maharashtra and the federal government in New Delhi. Enron therefore bore no risks except for sovereign holdup and yet negotiated a return of 25.52 percent which resulted in even higher tariffs.[22] DPC therefore satisfied the promoters', particularly Enron's, wider objectives of earnings management and making satisfactory cash flow numbers, but did so at the cost of MSEB's viability and the consumers of the state of Maharashtra.

Why did the government of Maharashtra agree to such a one-sided deal? Undoubtedly India faced a crippling shortage of generating capacity, and lack of electricity was holding back its economic development. Perhaps the government also wanted to demonstrate its commitment to private capital and encourage further investments. Perhaps the government relied on the sponsors' sunk investments to create the leverage necessary for renegotiation. In practical terms the irreversible nature of the investments always made the investors vulnerable to holdup by the state, a fact the government of Maharashtra exploited. Additionally, critics also alleged corruption because the deal was negotiated privately in a matter of days without competing proposals or a bidding process.[23] The process by which the deal was negotiated provided ammunition to opposing politicians, who won the elections in 1995 and promptly cancelled the DPC contract. In subsequent renegotiations Enron agreed to lower the capital cost by $300 million from a new turbine design and offered a 30 percent stake to MSEB, and the project was back on track. However, MSEB could not meet its equity capital requirements, and subsequently its stake was reduced to 15 percent.

DPC began producing power in May 1999 from its Phase 1 plant, but within a month MSEB could not pay its monthly $20 million bill, equal to the entire state's budget for education. In December 2000 the bill had increased to $22 million because of dollar appreciation. However, MSEB was only buying 10 percent to 20 percent of DPC Phase I output while its contract required it to pay for 95 percent of the output, which of course increased the price per unit to five times that available from other generating sources. In February 2001 DPC invoked the state government's counter-guarantee to ensure payment, and in May 2001 the MSEB rescinded the contract, claiming that DPC had misrepresented the plant's ramp-up capability. In April 2001, DPC initiated arbitration proceedings in London and declared political *force majeure*. In June 2001, construction on Phase 2, which was 90 percent complete, was halted. In December 2001, Enron went into bankruptcy in one of the biggest financial and accounting frauds in corporate history.

Before Enron imploded, its DPC investment received considerable attention from the highest echelons of the U.S. government.[24] During the first renegotiation in 1995, U.S. officials including then Energy Secretary Hazel O'Leary warned India that its actions would discourage future investments. In April 2001, after MSEB had stopped payments to DPC, Secretary of State Colin Powell raised Enron's problems with India's foreign minister. In June 2001, Vice President Dick Cheney raised the Dabhol issue with Sonia Gandhi, the president of India's Congress Party. In July 2001, the National Security Council formed a "Dabhol working group" that included officials from Treasury, State, the Export-Import Bank, and OPIC. In July 2001, Assistant Secretary of State Christina B. Rocca met with Indian officials to discuss the Dabhol project. In October 2001, Alan Larson, undersecretary of state for economics, business and agricultural affairs, raised

Dabhol with India's foreign minister and India's national security adviser. In November 2001, Dabhol was included as part of President Bush's talking points with India's Prime Minister A. B. Vajpayee but was removed once Enron's travails became known.

Post-Default Negotiations

The main sponsor's bankruptcy was a highly unusual event that altered the negotiating environment. However, DPC was project-financed and therefore its assets were shielded from Enron's bankruptcy. Nevertheless, the Indian lenders approached the local Mumbai courts to place DPC assets into receivership to prevent Enron's bankruptcy proceedings from including DPC assets. This violated the Indian lenders' intercreditor agreement with the offshore lenders, who filed for arbitration against the violation.

Enron's creditors claimed $142 million in political insurance from OPIC. OPIC brokered a deal in which Enron creditors gave up their insurance claims against OPIC and sold their equity stakes to GE and Bechtel. In April 2004, OPIC returned the premiums with interest that it had received from Enron, and GE and Bechtel paid $23 million for the equity. In 2003 GE and Bechtel themselves won an arbitral award that required OPIC to pay their insurance claims. OPIC attempted to recover its payments from the government of India by launching arbitration proceedings through the government of the United States against India.

In March 2004, the government of India took over the DPC assets. GE and Bechtel separately launched arbitration proceedings against the government of India using the bilateral investment treaty between Mauritius and India since they had invested in DPC through Mauritian subsidiaries. The 2004 elections in India brought a new federal government to power. DPC could not be restarted without Bechtel and GE's technical assistance in restarting the turbines and completing Phase 2 of the project. On July 11 and 12, 2005, Indian lenders agreed to settle with offshore lenders for $230 million and with OPIC for $220 million.[25] They also settled with Bechtel for $160 million and GE for $145 million.[26] Offshore lenders agreed to take a 20 percent haircut on their outstanding debt. The government of India was DPC's sole owner after four years of litigation and a web of suits and countersuits.

Government Ownership

The government of India rechristened DPC as Ratnagiri Gas and Power Private Ltd. (RGPPL), which resumed generating electricity in May 2006 after a gap of almost six years. RGPPL took over DPC assets for Rs.71.23 billion.[27] The local bank consortium lent Rs.53.57 billion as debt. RGPPL's equity capital was Rs.17.65 billion, of which the banking consortium owned 28.33 percent (Rs.5 billion). The remaining Rs.12.65 billion of equity was split up between three entities: state-owned power generating company National Thermal Power Corporation (NTPC), which would operate the assets; Gas Authority of India Ltd. (GAIL), which would supply the gas for the plant; and MSEB, which was the main customer. NTPC and GAIL contributed Rs.5 billion each for a 28.33 percent stake and MSEB contributed Rs.2.65 billion for a 15 percent stake. The funds would be needed to complete Phase 2 of the project, which required the completion of Block 1 of the power plant and the construction of the LNG terminal.

Rather than using imported LNG, recently discovered local gas deposits from the Krishna Godavari river basins were earmarked for the project, although there were doubts whether sufficient gas existed for attaining the maximum plant load factor. The estimated expense for Block 1 of the power plant was Rs.2.14 billion and for the LNG terminal was Rs.6.56 billion, for a total expense of Rs.8.7 billion. Within three years the price tag for the power plant had increased fivefold to Rs.10.20 billion and the LNG terminal doubled to Rs.13.44 billion. Instead of Rs.8.7 billion the costs escalated to Rs.23.64 billion.

The equity holders are to fund the cost escalation by investing an additional Rs.4.75 billion from NTPC and GAIL, each increasing their equity stake to 32.88 percent. MSEB invests Rs.2.50 billion, increasing its equity stake to 17.37 percent. The bank consortium's stake drops to 16.86 percent from 28.33 percent.[28] The cost escalation is putting upward pressure on tariffs. Presently the cost of electricity is Rs.3.01 per kWh and the lenders are concerned that RGPPL will be unable to generate sufficient cash flow to service its debt.[29] In February 2009, they were demanding a tariff increase to Rs.8 per kWh.[30] In July 2009 the plant was also producing only 950 megawatts of power, and of the six turbines only three were working.[31] In July 2009 RGPPL signed an eight-year, $130 million comprehensive service agreement and rehabilitation agreement with GE Energy for maintenance and spare parts supply for the turbines. GE therefore reentered the project as a contractor.

The low capacity utilization and tariffs have already caused one debt restructuring. RGPPL was to pay Rs.11.04 billion as interest and principal to the banking consortium by 2008–2009 and the consortium agreed to extend the tenor to two more years.[32] The Central Electricity Regulatory Commission (CERC), India's independent federal electricity regulatory authority, denied RGPPL's proposed tariff increase to Rs.4.44 per kWh.[33] RGPPL is not yet out of the woods.

Lessons from DPC

The DPC case presents a number of remarkable lessons. The DPC invest-ment included almost every risk hedging and mitigating mechanism: a project finance structure; high leverage; take-or-pay long-duration con-tracts; international treaty arbitration clauses; influential local partners; political lobbying on behalf of the sponsors by the highest levels of the U.S. government; U.S. inflation-adjusted dollar-denominated revenues; equity stakes to suppliers, contractors, and customer; counterguarantees from host state and federal governments; and syndicated lending by major inter-national banks with OPIC, U.S., and Japan EXIM bank support; yet the investment failed to provide the expected returns.

The first lesson is that investors must focus on the capacity of the concentrated buyer to pay for the output and if possible find alternative buyers. Yet it is inadequate as an explanation for the project's problems. After all, state and federal government counterguarantees promised payment if MSEB could not pay. One can argue that MSEB was forced to take on risks it could not bear, chiefly exchange rate risk and U.S. inflation risk. Although US$-rupee forward or futures contracts or options were not available for the duration of the power purchase agreement, MSEB could have fashioned hedges against rupee depreciation. But foreign exchange hedging contracts are not costless and would have added to the cost of DPC power.

Possibly the most important lesson pertains to the feedback effect of infrastructure investing. The DPC case shows that risk hedging and miti-gating mechanisms fail when a transaction is fundamentally one-sided and the economics do not justify the investment. The returns that Enron obtained for its equity participation and from supplying the gas for the project created high tariffs that ultimately caused the project to fail. The enormous project generated electricity that MSEB did not need as a base load plant and which it could not afford. Indeed, the project also did not have the support of the community who were the ultimate consumers of electricity from DPC. Federal legislation introduced in 2003 in India now allows electricity producers to sell power directly to consumers by paying a fee to the local distributors.[34] Even though this provision came into existence within two years of default and was available during the rene-gotiations, it's unclear that DPC would have found other customers for its power.

Investors in DPC found themselves between Scylla and Charybdis because the government entered into a contract that was detrimental to its own interests and ultimately the investors' interests. The DPC investment was not negotiated in full public view, and it lacked competitors during the first negotiation between Enron and the government of Maharashtra led by the Congress party, as well as in the second negotiation between Rebecca Mark, Enron International's CEO, and Bal Thackeray, the leader of the Shiv Sena, the then current ruling party. The power purchase agreement in both instances lacked legitimacy among consumers. Politicians exploited this lack of legitimacy for their electoral interests and further alienated the consumers from the company. Transparent, open, and competitive contracting protects investors as well as governments from making bad deals and bestows legitimacy on contracts. Legitimate contracts are far more likely to stay aligned over their duration and to withstand the challenges that changing circumstances create. The DPC case also shows that, in addition to the ethical and moral problems with corruption, contracts tainted by even the suspicion of corruption are unlikely to persist over the long duration typical of infrastructure investments.

The DPC case also demonstrates that infrastructure assets retain their value under conditions of default, and recovery rates tend to be high. The foreign lenders to the project took a 20 percent haircut on their debt while the government of India made whole all the other parties including the equity holders, except Enron, which sold its stake to GE and Bechtel. The case also demonstrates the importance of technology that only investing firms can control. GE and Bechtel were required to ensure that DPC produced electricity. This requirement certainly improved their bargaining position during the renegotiations. In fact, GE was able to reap the benefits of its position as a technology contractor and continue its profitable relationship with DPC reborn as RGPPL after the acrimonious suits and countersuits.

The issues that haunted DPC have not escaped RGPPL. RGPPL displays the perils of public funding and the value that private capital brings to infrastructure investing. DPC did not suffer from a single cost overrun and construction was completed on time. RGPPL has struggled to control cost overruns, which increased an astonishing 171.72 percent. Cost overruns are affecting the tariffs that RGPPL must charge to pay its investors. With one default already forcing the banks to restructure debt and extend its tenor, whether returns on invested capital will exceed the cost of capital remains an unresolved question.

CONCLUSION

Analysis of AASA and DPC shows the importance of managing the tension between maximizing returns to investors and minimizing the cost of service. Critics of private capital argue that investor goals are incompatible with the public good. Yet governments cannot fulfill the demands placed on infrastructure to improve living standards without the skills and participation of private investors. AASA squandered the opportunity to provide safe, reliable water and sewerage services to millions of people and generate returns for its investors, while DPC could not fulfill the promise of India's electricity sector. Investors who can resolve the paradox of infrastructure investing stand to reap the benefits of this asset class.

Conclusion

Forewarned, forearmed; to be prepared is half the battle won.
—Cervantes

This book has focused on infrastructure's economic characteristics and laid out the implications for investors. Worldwide infrastructure demand is huge, likely to grow, and possesses the potential to satisfy pension fund and insurance companies' liability matching requirements. Investors can simultaneously get diversification benefits, long tenor, and stable cash flows, and create economic growth while improving the quality of life for people starved of infrastructure. Unfortunately, one message of this book is that there is no magic bullet for quickly realizing this beguiling vision.

Infrastructure's economic characteristics, like asset specificity, large up-front sunk costs, and ease of managing operations, engender the principle problem of counterparty and sovereign holdup which investors must manage before their investments deliver on infrastructure's promise. It is unlikely that investors can entirely avoid this risk by investing only in the developed economies. Governments will not ignore politically sensitive concerns. Moreover, competition from investors for these assets will likely depress returns.

Investors seeking infrastructure-like returns from equity infrastructure indexes have not found them so far, since these investments have similar and sometimes higher risk and high correlations with equities. Although the indexes have indeed outperformed the S&P 500, they do not reflect the economic characteristics that make infrastructure attractive in the first place. Infrastructure bond portfolios have low correlations with equities and low risk; their returns are correlated with bonds yet do not match bond returns over the investing period. Remaining investment options available to investors are to invest in private equity–style infrastructure funds or invest directly.

It is not clear that infrastructure can deliver private equity–like returns, principally because infrastructure's economic characteristics militate against achieving such returns, even though some infrastructure funds have reduced the fees that traditional private equity funds charge.[1] In the infrastructure space, counterparty and sovereign holdup tends to squeeze equity returns, leaving debt returns relatively untouched. Equity's strengths—intrusive management, control rights, and management of high growth options—do not match infrastructure governance needs during the operational phase. Equity's strengths suit greenfield infrastructure assets during the construction phase when time and cost overrun risks must be managed. During the operational phase, some observers have argued that equity owners can achieve high returns through operational improvements and efficiencies. While this is certainly possible, debt offers a lower cost of governance that can incentivize managers to make operational improvements and disgorge free cash flow to capital providers, while offering protection from counterparty and sovereign holdup. Ironically, high leverage at the individual investment level matches private equity practices but leverage at the fund level in infrastructure is fraught with risk. Infrastructure assets are also wasting assets that are illiquid, which can prevent profitable exits and detract from private equity returns.

However, important sovereign holdup mitigation strategies rely on managers whose selection, motivation, and monitoring is a function of equity holders. Equity therefore exposes itself to risk of creeping expropriation but can manage it better in emerging economies. Investors with skilled managers who can handle political risk can protect their investments and gain returns from growth in emerging markets. In order to deliver long-term, low-volatility cash flows that have low correlations with other asset classes, infrastructure funds need to broaden their existing skill sets to include political management skills, including government and community relationship building, navigating government interests, and balancing the competing objectives of earning returns while providing infrastructure services in the most cost-efficient manner.

The challenge for governments is to harness private capital's skills at providing the most cost-effective service while ensuring that capital providers are compensated for their investments. Equity holders seek growth, and increased volatility of returns increases the value of equity. Debt seeks stable interest and principal payments, so lower volatility increases the value of debt. Governments and investors must therefore consider the form of investment.

Investors can exploit the project finance (PF) form of financial engineering which mitigates the twin risks of counterparty and sovereign holdup. The project finance structure traditionally protected equity holders with economic interests in the assets by providing cash flow seniority through management and operation fees and engineering, procurement, and construction (EPC) contracts, and by selling to or buying from the project. Purely financial equity investors are unlikely to obtain cash flow seniority in this manner. In fact, PF sponsors rely on nonrecourse debt, high leverage, and powerful debt syndicates to prevent creeping expropriation. This suggests that investors should consider joining a debt syndicate and should form syndicates that maximize their bargaining power in the event of renegotiations. Pension funds, insurance companies, and endowments possess a natural reputational advantage in this aspect of investing, which they can exploit.

Unfortunately, relying only on financial structuring in infrastructure investing is insufficient. Investors must also gain deep understanding of local political and social contexts, improve service, create community buy-in, partner locally with care, and eschew contextually exorbitant returns. Contracts that are fair and appear to be fair because they are created through transparent and competitive mechanisms withstand the inevitable challenges that long periods of time and changing circumstances throw up. Investors and governments should not underestimate the importance of independent regulators for this process.

The preceding discussion implies that investors should begin with an analysis of the geographical and sectoral demand for infrastructure and develop expertise in the promising areas. Investors must then decide the infrastructure phase that suits their needs and accordingly choose the right form of investment. Investors choosing to invest during the construction phase can use equity, build equity partnerships with EPC contractors, and switch to debt during the operational phase of the project. For example, equity sponsors provided twice the amount of equity capital as subordinated debt in the Equate project in Kuwait.[2] If investors team up with a lending syndicate and use debt during the construction phase itself, construction risk should belong to the equity holders. Equate's lenders—Chase Manhattan, JP Morgan, and Chemical Bank—required completion guarantees from the sponsors, Union Carbide Corporation, Petrochemical Industries Company, and Buobyan Petrochemical Company.[3]

Direct debt investors in infrastructure assets usually use a floating interest rate like LIBOR to hedge against interest rate risk. Similarly, investors can consider using money market hedges to protect against devaluation risk when foreign exchange markets are underdeveloped, rather than transferring devaluation risk to the project's buyers, because experience shows that such an action actually triggers sovereign holdup after a devaluation. Typically, exchange rate hedges using forward, futures, options, and currency swap contracts are not available for the long duration of infrastructure cash flows. Long-duration, stable cash flows are susceptible to inflation, and investors seeking to hedge inflation with infrastructure cash flows could index tariffs to inflation.

Should investors consider indexing local tariffs to inflation in the investor's country? For example, Aguas Argentinas indexed Argentine cash flows to U.S. inflation. The theory of relative purchasing power parity (PPP) states that percentage change in exchange rates between two countries equals the inflation rate differential between them.[4] As such, if local country cash flows are indexed to local inflation, high inflation will cause the local currency to devalue. If foreign investors have hedged local currency devaluation they will receive larger cash flows, and tariffs indexed to local inflation will serve their purpose. If local inflation is lower than inflation in the investor's country, then tariffs indexed to local inflation will be lower, resulting in lower local cash flows. The local currency is, however, likely to appreciate and foreign investors will therefore receive higher cash flows. Assuming that relative PPP holds and investors can hedge currency devaluation, investors should index local tariffs to local inflation. Indexing local cash flows to foreign inflation increases sovereign holdup risk.

Finally, investors seeking infrastructure exposure must differentiate between infrastructure-like assets that are economically distinct from the infrastructure assets analyzed in this book. In closing, the book highlights the rewards and perils that infrastructure investors face and focuses investor attention on the strategic threats they must mitigate. In doing so I hope that the book bridges the gulf separating investors with capital that must generate returns and consumers of infrastructure services who thirst for good roads, reliable electricity, and clean water.

Notes

Preface

1. J. Walters et al., *Connecting East Asia: A New Framework for Infrastructure* (ADB, JBIC, and the World Bank, 2005).
2. J. Worenklein, "The Global Crises in Power and Infrastructure: Lessons Learned and New Directions," *Journal of Structured and Project Finance* 9: 7–11.
3. Ibid.
4. L. S. Dodds, "However You Define It, Infrastructure Appeals," *Global Investor*, February 2007.
5. R. J. Orr, "The Rise of Infra Funds," *Project Finance International, Global Infrastructure Report 2007*, Supplement, 2–12.
6. Henry A. Davis, ed., *Infrastructure Finance: Trends and Techniques* (London: Euromoney Books, 2008), 538.
7. M. J. Anson, *Handbook of Alternative Assets* (New York: John Wiley & Sons, 2006).
8. J. Finnerty, *Project Financing: Asset Based Financial Engineering* (New York: John Wiley & Sons, 2007).
9. R. Orr and J. Kennedy, "Highlights of Recent Trends in Global Infrastructure: New Players and Revised Game Rules," *Transnational Corporations* 17 (1) (2008): 95–130.
10. Orr, "The Rise of Infra Funds."

CHAPTER 1   Infrastructure Demand and Investment Funds

1. "Roads and Highways," *Encyclopædia Britannica*, Encyclopædia Britannica Online, www.britannica.com/EBchecked/topic/505109/road/71891/Ancient-roads-of-South-and-East-Asia (accessed August 3, 2009).
2. David Rickards, "Global Infrastructure: A Growth Story," in *Infrastructure Finance: Trends and Techniques*, ed. Henry A. Davis (London: Euromoney Books, 2008).
3. The Millennium Project, World Federation of UN Associations, www.millennium-project.org/millennium/scenarios/energy-scenarios.html (accessed January 25, 2009).

4. World Bank, *The World Development Report: Infrastructure for Development* (Washington, DC: World Bank, 1994).

5. Marianne Fay and Tito Yepes, "Investing in Infrastructure: What Is Needed from 2000 to 2010?" World Bank Policy Research Working Paper 3102 (July 2003).

6. OECD Report, *Infrastructure to 2030: Telecom, Land Transport, Water and Electricity* (OECD Publishing, 2006).

7. International Energy Agency, *World Energy Outlook 2008* (OECD Publishing, 2008).

8. Adapted from Fay and Yepes, "Investing in Infrastructure."

9. Indralal De Silva, "Demographic and Social Trends Affecting Families in the South and Central Asian Region," in *Major Trends Affecting Families: A Background Document*, report for United Nations, Department of Economic and Social Affairs, Division for Social Policy and Development, Program on the Family (2003), 4; www.un.org/esa/socdev/family/Publications/mtdesilva.pdf.

10. B. M. Popkin et al., Russia Longitudinal Monitoring Survey, Carolina Population Center, University of North Carolina (2008), www.cpc.unc.edu/rlms (accessed January 1, 2009).

11. *United Nations Demographic Yearbook* (United Nations, 1995), http://unstats. un.org/unsd/demographic/products/dyb/dybsets/1995%20DYB.pdf (accessed January 5, 2009).

12. N. Keilman, "Biodiversity: The Threat of Small Households," *Nature* 421 (2003): 489–490.

13. "Why Wait for WiMax?" *Economist*, August 18, 2005.

14. J. Finnerty, *Project Financing: Asset-based Financial Engineering* (New York: John Wiley & Sons, 2007), 219–220.

15. C. Ervin and S. Schich, "Asset Allocation Challenges for Pension Funds," *OECD Financial Market Trends* 1, no. 92 (2007): 129–147.

16. OECD Insurance and Private Pensions Committee and Working Party on Private Pensions, "Guidelines on Pension Fund Asset Management" (OECD, 2006).

17. P. Antolin, "Longevity Risk and Private Pensions," *OECD Financial Market Trends* 1, no. 92 (2007): 107–122.

18. Ervin and Schich, "Asset Allocation Challenges."

19. J. K. Thompson, "Pension Reform and Financial Markets: The Impact of the Post-2000 Downturn," *OECD Financial Market Trends* 1, no. 84 (2003): 75–94.

20. Ervin and Schich, "Asset Allocation Challenges."

CHAPTER 2 Infrastructure Asset Characteristics

1. Robert Greer, "What Is an Asset Class Anyway?" *Journal of Portfolio Management* 23 (1997): 83–91.

2. Ibid.

3. B. C. Esty, "The Economic Motivations for Using Project Finance," working paper, Harvard Business School, 2003.

4. From Forbes Digital Company's Investopedia.com, www.investopedia.com/terms/a/assetclasses.asp.
5. Harry Markowitz, *Portfolio Selection* (New Haven, CT: Yale University Press, 1959).
6. Sharpe, William F. *Macro-Investment Analysis*, www.stanford.edu/~wfsharpe/mia/mia.htm (accessed June 1, 2009).
7. Ibid.
8. Raphael Edinger, *Distributed Electricity Generation with Renewable Resources: Assessing the Economics of Photovoltaic Technologies in Vertically Integrated and in Restructured Energy Markets* (Marburg, Germany: Tectum Verlag, 1999), 98.
9. B. Ambrose and D. Winters, "Does an Industry Effect Exist for Leveraged Buyouts?" *Financial Management* 21 (1992): 89–101.
10. Paul Lund and Jonathan Manley, "Securitisation Financing of Infrastructure from a Credit Perspective," in *Infrastructure Finance: Trends and Techniques*, ed. Henry A. Davis (London: Euromoney Books, 2008).
11. Ryan J. Orr, "The Rise of Infra Funds," *Project Finance International, Global Infrastructure Report 2007*, Supplement, 2–12.
12. M. Schnitzer, "Debt v. Foreign Direct Investment: The Impact of Sovereign Risk on the Structure of International Capital Flows," *Economica* 69 (2002): 41–67; R. J. Sawant, "The Economics of Large-scale Infrastructure FDI: The Case of Project Finance," *Journal of International Business Studies*, forthcoming.
13. R. J. Sawant, "The Economics of Large scale Infrastructure FDI: The Case of Project Finance," *Journal of International Business Studies*, forthcoming.
14. S. C. Myers, "Determinants of Corporate Borrowing," *Journal of Financial Economics* 5 (1977): 147–175.
15. N. Kulatilaka and Enrico Perotti, "Strategic Growth Options," *Management Science* 44 (1998): 1021–1031.
16. M. C. Jensen and William Meckling, "Theory of the Firm: Managerial Behavior, Agency Costs and Capital Structure," *Journal of Financial Economics* 2 (1976): 305–360.
17. W. Henisz and B. Zelner, "Managing Policy Risk," IFC/FT first annual essay competition (2006), 66.
18. C. Beale, M. Chatain, N. Fox, S. Bell, J. Berner, R. Perminger, and J. Prins, "Credit Attributes of Project Finance," *Journal of Structured and Project Finance* 8 (2002): 5–9.
19. Christopher Dymond, "Value Recovery after a Default: The Project Finance Perspective," *Journal of Structured and Project Finance* 9 (2003): 14–18.
20. Beale et. al., "Credit Attributes."

CHAPTER 3 Equity Infrastructure Indexes

1. "Shell Is Selling Intergen Unit to Investor Duo for $1.75 Billion," *Wall Street Journal*, April 20, 2005.
2. Ontario Teachers Pension Plan, Annual Report 2008, http://70.35.24.107/otpp/ar_08/ar08_index.htm.

3. S. Michael Giliberto, "Measuring Real Estate Returns: The Hedged REIT Index," *Journal of Portfolio Management* Spring 1993: 94–99.
4. Standard & Poor's, "Listed Infrastructure Assets—A Primer," April 14, 2008, www2.standardandpoors.com/spf/pdf/index/Gbl_Infrastructure_Primer_April.pdf.
5. FTSE, "Ground Rules for the Management of the Macquarie Global Infrastructure Index Series," FTSE, October 2008, www.ftse.com/Indices/Macquarie_Global_Infrastructure_Index_Series/Downloads/Macquarie_Global_Infrastructure_Index_Rules.pdf.
6. Ryan J. Orr, "The Rise of Infra Funds," *Project Finance International, Global Infrastructure Report 2007*, Supplement, 2–12.
7. David Rickards, "Global Infrastructure: A Growth Story," in *Infrastructure Finance: Trends and Techniques*, ed. Henry A. Davis (London: Euromoney Books, 2008).
8. Probitas Partners, "Investing in Infrastructure Funds," September 2007, www.probitaspartners.com/pdfs/infrastructure.pdf (accessed April 29, 2009).
9. F. K. Reilly, *Investment Analysis and Portfolio Management* (Dryden Press, 1989), 272.

CHAPTER 4   Debt versus Equity Mode of Investment

1. F. Modigliani and M. H. Miller, "The Cost of Capital, Corporation Finance and the Theory of Investment," *American Economic Review* 48 (1958): 267–297.
2. J. C. Stiglitz, "A Re-examination of the Modigliani-Miller Theorem," *American Economic Review* 59 (1969): 784–793; and "On the Irrelevance of Corporate Financial Policy," *American Economic Review* 64 (1974): 851–866.
3. E. F. Fama and M. H. Miller, *The Theory of Finance* (New York: Holt, Reinhart, and Wilson, 1972).
4. E. Fama, "The Effects of a Firm's Investment and Financing Decisions," *American Economic Review* 68 (1978): 272–284.
5. S. C. Myers, "Capital Structure," *Journal of Economic Perspectives* 15 (2001): 81–102.
6. Fama, "The Effects."
7. S. C. Myers, "Determinants of Corporate Borrowing," *Journal of Financial Economics* 5 (1977): 147–175.
8. M. J. Barclay, C. W. Smith Jr., and R. L. Watts, "The Determinants of Corporate Leverage and Dividend Policies," *Journal of Applied Corporate Finance* 7 (1995): 4–19; C. W. Smith Jr. and R. L. Watts, "The Investment Opportunity Set and Corporate Financing, Dividend, and Compensation Policies," *Journal of Financial Economics* 32 (1992): 263–292.
9. M. Bradley, G. Jarrell, and E. H. Kim, "On the Existence of an Optimal Capital Structure: Theory and Evidence," *Journal of Finance* 39 (1984): 857–878.
10. J. K. Wald, "How Firm Characteristics Affect Capital Structure: An International Comparison," *Journal of Financial Research* 22 (1999): 161–187.

11. J. R. Graham, "How Big Are the Tax Benefits of Debt?" *Journal of Finance* 55 (2000): 1901–1941.
12. S. C. Myers and N. S. Majluf, "Corporate Financing and Investment Decisions When Firms Have Information That Investors Do Not Have," *Journal of Financial and Quantitative Analysis* 23 (1984): 39–51.
13. M. C. Jensen and W. H. Meckling, "Theory of the Firm: Managerial Behavior, Agency Costs and Capital Structure," *Journal of Financial Economics* 2 (1976): 305–360.
14. A. Shleifer and R. Vishny, "Management Entrenchment: The Case of Manager-specific Investments," *Journal of Financial Economics* 25 (1989): 123–139; P. Berger, E. Ofek, and D. Yermack, "Managerial Entrenchment and Capital Structure Decisions," *Journal of Finance* 52 (1997): 1411–1438.
15. S. Kaplan, "Management Buyouts: Evidence of Taxes as a Source of Value," *Journal of Finance* 44 (1989): 611–632.
16. Sheridan Titman, "The Effect of Capital Structure on a Firm's Liquidation Decision," *Journal of Financial Economics* 13 (1984): 137–151.
17. M. C. Jensen and W. H. Meckling, "Theory of the Firm: Managerial Behavior, Agency Costs and Capital Structure," *Journal of Financial Economics* 2 (1976): 305–360.
18. S. C. Myers, "Determinants of Corporate Borrowing," *Journal of Financial Economics* 5 (1977): 147–175.
19. T. C. Opler, and Sheridan Titman, "Financial Distress and Corporate Performance," *Journal of Finance* 49 (1994): 1015–1040.
20. O. E. Williamson, "Corporate Finance and Corporate Governance," *Journal of Finance* 43 (1988): 567–591.
21. S. Grossman and O. Hart, "The Costs and Benefits of Ownership: A Theory of Vertical and Lateral Integration," *Journal of Political Economy* 94 (1986): 691–719.
22. D. Grey and S. Malone, *Macrofinancial Risk Analysis* (New York: John Wiley & Sons 2008), 63.
23. R. N. Palter, J. Walder, and S. Westlake, "How Investors Can Get More Out of Infrastructure," *McKinsey Quarterly*, February 2008.
24. J. Finnerty, *Project Financing: Asset-based Financial Engineering* (New York: John Wiley & Sons, 2007).
25. Ibid., 210.
26. R. J. Sawant, "The Economics of Large-scale Infrastructure FDI: The Case of Project Finance," *Journal of International Business Studies,* forthcoming.
27. Ryan J. Orr, "The Rise of Infra Funds," *Project Finance International, Global Infrastructure Report 2007,* Supplement, 2–12.
28. W. L. Megginson, "Toward a Global Model of Venture Capital?" *Journal of Applied Corporate Finance* 16, no. 1 (2004): 89–107.
29. M. Anson, *Handbook of Alternative Assets* (New York: John Wiley & Sons, 2006).
30. Ibid., 512.
31. T. Opler and Sheridan Titman, "The Determinants of Leveraged Buyout Activity: Free Cash Flow vs. Financial Distress Costs," *Journal of Finance* 48 (1993): 1985–1999.

32. M. C. Jensen, "Agency Costs of Free Cash Flow, Corporate Finance and Takeovers," *American Economic Review* 76 (1986): 323–329.

33. Anson, *Handbook of Alternative Assets*, 514.

34. Ibid., 515.

35. Ibid., 516.

36. L. T. Wells and E. Gleason, "Is Foreign Infrastructure Investment Still Risky?" *Harvard Business Review* 73 (1995): 4–12.

37. L. T. Wells and A. De Royere, *Aguas Argentinas*, Case no. 9-705-019 (Cambridge, MA: Harvard Business School, 2003), 3.

38. R. E. Kennedy and B. P. Irwin, *Intergen and the Quezon Power Project: Building Infrastructure in Emerging Markets*, Case no. 5-799-102. Cambridge, MA: Harvard Business School, 2000).

39. "Shell Is Selling Intergen Unit to Investor Duo for $1.75 Billion," *Wall Street Journal*, April 20, 2005.

40. "Indian Infrastructure Company Lands Intergen Stake," *Power, Finance and Risk*, June 30, 2008.

41. J. Wilkinson, "Refinancing Risk: Local Funds Strive to Keep their Momentum," *Money Management (Australia)*, Oct 16, 2008.

42. J. Hutton and M. Smith "Hard Sell for BBI's Diminishing Assets," *Australasian Business Intelligence*, August 12, 2009.

43. M. F. Guillen and E. Garcia-Canal, "The American Model of the Multinational Firm and the 'New' Multinationals from Emerging Economies," *Academy of Management Perspectives* 23 (2009): 23–35.

44. "Gravis Capital Launches First Infra Debt Fund," *Project Finance Magazine*, June 5, 2009.

45. City of Chicago, Office of Budget and Management, "City Closes Parking Meter Transaction, Provides $1.15 Billion to Bolster City Reserves, Balance the Budget, and Help People Most in Need," February 13, 2009, http://egov. cityofchicago.org/city/webportal/portalContentItemAction.do?contentOID= 537031875&contenTypeName=COC_EDITORIAL&topChannelName=Dept &blockName=Budget+%26+Management%2FI+Want+To&context=dept &channelId=0&programId=0&entityName=Budget+%26+Management& deptMainCategoryOID= (accessed Aug 12, 2009).

46. V. Tenorio and C. Idzelis, "Can Private Equity Play the Infrastructure Game?" *The Deal*, April 3, 2009.

CHAPTER 5   Infrastructure and the Threat of Holdup

1. Ronald H. Coase, "The Nature of the Firm," *Economica* 4, no. 16 (1937): 386–405.

2. O. E. Williamson, *Markets and Hierarchies: Analysis and Anti-trust Implications* (New York: The Free Press, 1975).

3. Ibid.

4. S. Ghoshal and P. Moran, "Bad for Practice: A Critique of the Transaction Cost Theory," *Academy of Management Review* 21, no. 1 (1996): 13–47.

5. B. Klein, V. Crawford, and A. Alchian, "Vertical Integration, Appropriable Rents, and the Competitive Contracting Process, *Journal of Law and Economics* 21 (1978): 297–326.
6. Oliver Williamson, *The Economic Institutions of Capitalism*, (New York: Free Press, 1985), 66–67.
7. Oliver Hart and John Moore, "Foundations of Incomplete Contracts, National Bureau of Economic Research Working Paper no. 6726, 1998.
8. M. B. Lieberman, "Determinants of Vertical Integration: An Empirical Test," *Journal of Industrial Economics* 39 (1991): 451–466.
9. P. L. Joskow, "Vertical Integration and Long-term Contracts: The Case of Coal-burning Electric Generating Plants. *Journal of Law, Economics & Organization* 1 (1985): 33–80.
10. A. S. Edlin, and S. Reichelstein, "Holdups, Standard Breach Remedies and Optimal Investment," *American Economic Review* 86 (1996): 478–501.
11. Ibid.
12. Ibid.
13. J. Tirole, *The Theory of Industrial Organization* (Cambridge: MIT Press, 1990), 30.
14. Klein, Crawford, and Alchian, "Vertical Integration."
15. P. G. Berger and E. Ofek, "Diversification's Effect on Firm Value," *Journal of Financial Economics* 37 (1995): 39–65.
16. S. J. Grossman and O. D. Hart, "The Costs and Benefits of Ownership: A Theory of Vertical and Lateral Integration," *Journal of Political Economy* 94, no. 4 (1986): 691–719.
17. S. N. Wiggins, "The Comparative Advantage of Long-Term Contracts and Firms," *Journal of Law, Economics and Organization* 6 (1990): 155–170.
18. M. Riordan, "What Is Vertical Integration?" in *The Firm as a Nexus of Treaties*, ed. M. Aoki, B. Gustafsson, and O. Williamson (London: Sage, 1989).
19. J. M. MacDonald, "Market Exchange or Vertical Integration: An Empirical Analysis," *Review of Economics and Statistics* 67 (1985): 327–331.
20. D. T. Levy, "The Transactions Cost Approach to Vertical Integration: An Empirical Examination," *Review of Economics and Statistics* 67 (1985): 438–445.
21. S. G. Bronars and D. R. Deere, "The Threat of Unionization, The Use of Debt, and The Preservation of Shareholder Wealth," *The Quarterly Journal of Economics* 106 (1991): 231–254.
22. C. Y. Baldwin, "Productivity and Labor Unions: An Application of the Theory of Self-enforcing Contracts," *Journal of Business* 56 (1983): 155–185.
23. V. Subramaniam, "Underinvestment, Debt Financing, and Long-term Supplier Relations," *Journal of Law, Economics and Organization* 12 (1996): 461–479.
24. E. C. Perotti and K. E. Spier, "Capital Structure as a Bargaining Tool: The Role of Leverage in Contract Renegotiation," *American Economic Review* 83 (1993): 1131–1141.
25. R. J. Sawant, "The Economics of Large-scale Infrastructure FDI: The Case of Project Finance," *Journal of International Business Studies*, forthcoming.

CHAPTER 6 Infrastructure Assets and Political Risk

1. D. R. Lessard, "Country Risk and the Structure of International Financial Intermediation," in *Financial risk: Theory, Evidence, and Implications*, ed. Courtenay Stone (Boston: Kluwer, 1989); reprinted in *International Finance: Contemporary Issues*, ed. Dilip Das (Florence, KY: Routledge, 1993).
2. L. D. Howell and B. Chaddick, "Models of Political Risk for Foreign Investment and Trade: An Assessment of Three Approaches," *Columbia Journal of World Business* 29, no. 3 (1994): 70–91.
3. P. Rigby, "Project Finance Debt Risk Analysis," in *Infrastructure Finance: Trends and Techniques*, ed. Henry A. Davis (London: Euromoney Books, 2008), 551.
4. J. L. Guasch, *Granting and Renegotiating Infrastructure Concessions: Doing It Right* (Washington D.C.: World Bank Institute of Development Studies, 2004).
5. J. L. Guasch, Jean-Jacques Laffont, and S. Straub, "Concessions of Infrastructure in Latin America: Government-led Renegotiation," *Journal of Applied Econometrics* 27 (2007): 1267–1294.
6. P. M. Vaaler, "How Do MNCs Vote in Developing Country Elections?" *Academy of Management Journal* 51 (2008): 21–43.
7. P. M. Vaaler, B. Schrage, and S. A. Block, "Elections, Opportunism, Partisanship and Sovereign Ratings in Developing Countries," *Review of Development Economics* 10, no. 1 (2006): 154–170.
8. "Hedging," *Encyclopædia Britannica*, Encyclopædia Britannica Online, www .britannica.com/EBchecked/topic/259286/hedging (accessed August 31, 2009).
9. "Two Energy Bills, Including Windfall Tax, Stall in Senate," *New York Times*, June 11, 2008.
10. "CPUC Seeks Abrogation of Long-term Deals," *Natural Gas Week*, March 4, 2002, 10; J. L. Sweeney, *The California Electricity Crisis* (Stanford, CA: Hoover Institution Press, 2002).
11. M. Schnitzer, "Debt v. Foreign Direct Investment: The Impact of Sovereign Risk on the Structure of International Capital Flows," *Economica* 69 (2002): 41–67.
12. Felton Johnston, "Finding Common Ground: An Independent Consultant's Perspective," in *International Political Risk Management: The Brave New World*, ed. Thomas Moran (Washington D.C.: World Bank, 2004).
13. D. S. Meyers, "In Defense of the International Treaty Arbitration System," *Houston Journal of International Law*, Fall 2008.
14. S. J. Kobrin, "Foreign Enterprise and Forced Divestment in LDCs," *International Organization* 34 (1980): 65–88.
15. M. Schnitzer, "Debt v. Foreign Direct Investment: The Impact of Sovereign Risk on the Structure of International Capital Flows," *Economica* 69 (2002): 41–67.
16. B. D. Oseghale, *Political Instability, Interstate Conflict, Adverse Changes in Host Government Policies and Foreign Direct Investment: A Sensitivity Analysis* (New York: Garland, 1993).

17. Meyers, "In Defense of the International Treaty Arbitration System"; G. Van Harten, *International Treaty Arbitration and Public Law* (Oxford, UK: Oxford University Press, 2007).
18. News report, *Power, Finance and Risk,* September 29, 2003, 6.
19. K. Hansen, "PRI and the Rise (and Fall?) of Private Investment in Public Infrastructure," in *International Political Risk Management: The Brave New World,* ed. Thomas Moran (Washington D.C.: World Bank, 2004).
20. L. E. Peterson, "Ecuador Will Denounce at Least Nine Bilateral Investment Treaties," *International Institute for Sustainable Development,* February 5, 2008, www.iisd.org/pdf/2008/itn_feb5_2008.pdf (accessed May 31, 2009).
21. S. J. Shackelford, "Investment Treaty Arbitration and Public Law (Book Review)," *Stanford Journal of International Law* 44, no. 2 (2008): 215.
22. G. Van Harten, *International Treaty Arbitration and Public Law* (Oxford, UK: Oxford University Press, 2007).
23. ICSID Case No. ARB/02/1, *LG & E Energy Corp. LG&E Capital Corp. LG&E International Inc. v. Argentine Republic,* award of October 3, 2006, http://icsid.worldbank.org/ICSID/FrontServlet?requestType=CasesRH&action Val=showDoc&docId=DC627_En&caseId=C208 (accessed May 31, 2009).
24. ICSID Case No. ARB/01/8, *CMS Gas Transmission Company v. Argentine Republic,* award of May 12, 2005, http://icsid.worldbank.org/ICSID/FrontServ let?requestType=CasesRH&actionVal=showDoc&docId=DC687_En&caseId= C4.
25. United Nations Commission on International Trade Law (UNCITRAL) status report on the New York Convention, www.uncitral.org/uncitral/en/uncitral_texts/arbitration/NYConvention_status.html (accessed Aug 14, 2009).
26. L. L. Jacque, *Management and Control of Foreign Exchange Risk* (Boston: Kluwer Academic Publishers 1996), 239.
27. C. Berry, "Shall the Twain Meet? Finding Common Ground or Uncommon Solutions: A Broker's Perspective," in *International Political Risk Management: The Brave New World,* ed. Thomas Moran (Washington D.C.: World Bank, 2004).
28. Comments from Felton M. Johnston.
29. E. P. Quintrell, "Commentary on Finding Common Ground or Uncommon Solutions: A Public Provider's View," in *International Political Risk Management: The Brave New World,* ed. Thomas Moran (Washington D.C.: World Bank, 2004).
30. Hansen, "PRI and the Rise (and Fall?)."
31. Berry, "Shall the Twain Meet?"
32. Comments from Felton M. Johnston.
33. S. Ghoshal and P. Moran, "Bad for Practice: A Critique of the Transaction Cost Theory," *Academy of Management Review* 21, no.1 (1996): 13–47.
34. W. J. Henisz and B. A. Zelner, *AES Telasi: Power Trip or Power Play? (A)* (Philadelphia, PA: Wharton School, University of Pennsylvania, 2006).
35. J. A. Lampietti, H. Gonzalez, and M. Wilson, *Revisiting Reform in the Energy Sector: Lessons from Georgia* (Washington D.C.: World Bank, 2004), 20.

36. W. J. Henisz and B. A. Zelner, "Political Risk Management: A Strategic Perspective," in *International Political Risk Management: The Brave New World*, ed. Thomas Moran (Washington D.C.: World Bank, 2004).
37. L. T. Wells and E. Gleason, "Is Foreign Infrastructure Investment Still Risky?" *Harvard Business Review* 73 (1995): 4–12.
38. Ibid., 10.
39. E. Weldon and M. Beer, *Manila Water Company (A)*, Case no. 9-401-014 (Cambridge, MA: Harvard Business School, 2000).
40. M. Alipalo, "Country Water Action: Philippines Manila Water's Neo-Way with Sanitation—Desludge and Dilute, Connect and Treat, Put Waste to Use," Asian Development Bank Report, August 2007, www.adb.org/water/actions/phi/manila-water-sanitation.asp (accessed June 6, 2009).

CHAPTER 7   Project Finance and Infrastructure

1. R. A. Brealey, I. A. Cooper, and M. A. Habib, "Using Project Finance to Fund Infrastructure Investments," *Journal of Applied Corporate Finance* 9, no.3 (1996): 25–38; J. Kim and S. S. Yoo, "Project Finance and Determinants of Its Leverage," working paper, San Diego State University, College of Business Administration, 2008.
2. "Beg, Borrow and Deal: Enron-led Consortium Applies for a Loan." *Fortune*, August 12, 2002; "Transredes, Bolivia's Largest Oil and Gas Pipeline Company," *Latin Trade*, May 2004.
3. J. Finnerty, *Project Financing: Asset-based Financial Engineering* (New York: John Wiley & Sons, 2007).
4. M. Klein, J. So, and B. Shin, "Transaction Costs in Private Infrastructure Projects: Are They Too High? *Viewpoint*, note no. 95 (1996), World Bank Group.
5. M. J. Flannery, J. F. Houston, and S. Venkataraman, "Financing Multiple Investment Projects," *Financial Management* 1993, Vol. 22, No. 2: 161–172.
6. M. C. Jensen and W. H. Meckling, "Theory of the Firm: Managerial Behavior, Agency Costs and Capital Structure," *Journal of Financial Economics* 2 (1976): 305–360.
7. E. Berkovitch and E. H. Kim, "Financial Contracting and Leverage Induced Over- and Underinvestment Incentives," *Journal of Finance* 45 (1990): 765–794.
8. Finnerty, *Project Financing*.
9. R. J. Sawant, "Economics of Large-scale Infrastructure FDI: The Case of Project Finance," *Journal of International Business Studies* (forthcoming).
10. Ibid.
11. B. C. Esty, "The Economic Motivations for Using Project Finance," working paper, Harvard Business School, 2003.
12. Sawant, "Economics of Large-scale Infrastructure."
13. J. Finnerty, *Project Financing*; J. W. Kensinger, and J. D. Martin, "Project Finance: Raising Money the Old-fashioned Way," *Journal of Applied Corporate Finance* 1988, volume 9: 69–81.

14. Esty, "The Economic Motivations."
15. Ibid.
16. P. M. Vaaler, R. V. Aguilera, and B. E. James, "Risk and Capital Structure in Asian Project Finance," *Asia Pacific Journal of Management,* 25(1): 25–50 (2008).
17. Kim and Yoo, "Project Finance and Determinants of Its Leverage."
18. Sawant, "Economics of Large-scale Infrastructure."
19. E. J. Woodhouse, "The Obsolescing Bargain Redux? Foreign Investment in the Electric Power Sector in Developing Countries," *N.Y.U. Journal of International Law and Politics* 38 (2005–2006): 121–219, 179–180.
20. C. Hainz and S. Kleimeier, "Project Finance as a Risk Management Tool in International Syndicated Lending. Discussion Paper No. 183, GESY, University of Mannheim, Germany, 2006).
21. Finnerty, *Project Financing.*
22. R. J. Orr and J. R. Kennedy, "Highlights of Recent Trends in Global Infrastructure: New Players and Revised Game Rules," *Transnational Corporations* 17 (2008): 99–133.
23. World Bank, *Private Sector Development in the Electric Power Sector: A Joint OED/OEG/OEU Review of the World Bank Group's Assistance in the 1990s,* Report no. 26427 (2003), 23, 26, and 54.
24. Woodhouse, "The Obsolescing Bargain Redux?" 160.
25. D. Diamond, "Financial Intermediation and Delegated Monitoring," *Review of Economic Studies* 1984: 393–414.
26. B. C. Esty and W. L. Megginson, "Creditor Rights, Enforcement, and Debt Ownership Structure: Evidence from the Global Syndicated Loan Market," *Journal of Financial and Quantitative Analysis* 38 (2003): 37–59.
27. Sawant, "Economics of Large-scale Infrastructure."
28. P. Rigby, "Project Finance Debt Risk Analysis," in *Infrastructure Finance: Trends and Techniques,* ed. Henry A. Davis (London: Euromoney Books, 2008), 551.
29. International Project Risk Assessment. Construction Industry Institute, 2003. https://www.construction-institute.org/scriptcontent/more/ir181_2_more.cfm
30. Project Management Institute, *A Guide to the Project Management Body of Knowledge* (PMBoK® Guide), 3rd ed. (Newtown Square, PA: Project Management Institute, 2004), 373.
31. R. D. Archibald, *Managing High-Technology Programs and Projects,* 3rd ed. (New York, NY: John Wiley & Sons, 2003); J. R. Schuyler, *Risk and Decision Analysis in Projects* (Newtown, PA: Project Management Institute, 2001).
32. S. Gatti, A. Rigamonti, F. Saita, and M. Senati, "Measuring Value-at-Risk in Project Finance Transactions," *European Financial Management* 13 (2007): 135–158.
33. Woodhouse, "The Obsolescing Bargain Redux?"
34. Rigby, "Project Finance Debt Risk Analysis."
35. Ribgy, "Project Finance Debt Risk Analysis," 547.
36. Ibid., 558.
37. "Bulong Output, *Mining Journal,* June 8, 2001, 443.

38. "Directors Pour Acid on Bulong Nickel Mine," *Australasian Business Intelligence*, May 27, 2003.

39. Scott Woolley, "Iridium Rising (Iridium LLC)," *Forbes*, April 13, 2009.

40. R. Vernon, *Sovereignty at Bay: The Multinational Spread of U.S. Enterprises* (New York: Basic Books, 1971).

41. A. Dixit and S. Skeath, "Strategic Moves," in *Games of Strategy*, 2nd ed. (New York: W. W. Norton & Co., 2004).

42. R. L. K. Tiong, "Competitive Advantage of Equity in BOT Tender," *Journal of Construction Engineering and Management* 121 (1995): 282–289.

43. Ibid., 282.

44. J. L. Guasch, Jean-Jacques Laffont, and S. Straub, "Concessions of Infrastructure in Latin America: Government-led Renegotiation," *Journal of Applied Econometrics* 27 (2007): 1267–1294.

45. Woodhouse, "The Obsolescing Bargain Redux?" 149.

46. Ibid., 189.

47. R. B. Myerson, "Optimal Auction Design," *Mathematics of Operations Research* 6 (1981): 58–73.

48. J. L. Guasch and S. Straub, "Renegotiation of Infrastructure Concessions: An Overview," *Annals of Public and Cooperative Economics* 77, no. 4 (2006): 479–493.

49. C. W. L. Hill, "Enron International in India," additional case in *International Business: Competition in the Global Marketplace* 5th ed. (New York: Pearson Addison Wesley, 2005).

CHAPTER 8 Infrastructure Asset Valuation and Bond Returns

1. R. S. Ruback, "Capital Cash Flows: A Simple Approach to Valuing Risky Cash Flows," *Financial Management* 31 (2002): 85–103, page 86.

2. B. C. Esty, "Improved Techniques for Valuing Large-scale Projects," *Journal of Project Finance* 5 (1999): 9–25.

3. E. F. Brigham, L. C. Gapenski, and M. C. Ehrhardt, *Financial Management: Theory and Practice*, 9th ed. (The Dryden Press, 1999), 178.

4. Ruback, "Capital Cash Flows," 89.

5. R. S. Hamada, "The Effect of the Firm's Capital Structure on the Systematic Risk of Common Stocks," *Journal of Finance* 26 (1972): 435–452.

6. Ruback, "Capital Cash Flows."

7. Brigham, Gapenski, and Ehrhardt, *Financial Management*.

8. A. Damodaran, *Damodaran on Valuation: Security Analysis for Investment and Corporate Finance* (New York: John Wiley & Sons, 1994).

9. Brigham, Gapenski, and Ehrhardt, *Financial Management*, 392.

10. Esty, "Improved Techniques."

11. D. R. Lessard, "Incorporating Country Risk in the Valuation of Offshore Projects," *Journal of Applied Corporate Finance* 9, no. 3 (1996): 52–63.

12. Ibid.

13. D. Eiteman, A. Stonehill, and M. Moffett, *Multinational Business Finance*, 11th ed. (New York: Pearson Addison Wesley, 2007), 610.
14. Esty, "Improved Techniques," 13.
15. Felton Johnston, "Finding Common Ground: An Independent Consultant's Perspective," in *International Political Risk Management: The Brave New World*, ed. Thomas Moran (Washington D.C.: World Bank, 2004) 133.
16. Basel Committee on Banking Supervision, *International Convergence of Capital Measurement and Capital Standards* (Bank for International Settlements, 2006), 49; www.bis.org/publ/bcbs128.pdf.
17. Ibid., 2.
18. Ibid., 56.
19. Ibid., 61.
20. Ibid., 83.
21. H. Orgeldinger, "Basel II and Project Finance: The Development of a Basel II Confirming Rating Model," *Journal of Structured Finance* 11, no. 4 (2006): 84–95, page 86.
22. Basel Committee, *International Convergence*, 61.
23. Ibid., 231.
24. C. Beale M. Chatain, N. Fox, S. Bell, J. Berner, R. Perminger, and J. Prins. "Credit Attributes of Project Finance," *Journal of Structured and Project Finance* 8 (2002): 5–9.
25. P. Hall, "Bond Trustees Reexamine Role," *ABA Banking Journal* 81 (1989): 42–47.
26. A. Predieri and A. Zuck, "Political Risk Insurance as Penicillin? A Lender's Perspective," in *International Political Risk Management: The Brave New World*, ed. Thomas Moran (Washington D.C.: World Bank, 2004), 110.
27. J. Finnerty, *Project Financing: Asset-based Financial Engineering* (New York: John Wiley & Sons, 2007), 59.
28. M. Dailami and R. Hauswald, "The Emerging Project Bond Market: Covenant Provisions and Credit Spreads," World Bank Policy Research Working Paper 3095, 2003.
29. R. Gertner and D. Scharfstein, "A Theory of Workouts and the Effects of Reorganization Law," *Journal of Finance* 46 (1991): 1189–1222.
30. R. L. K. Tiong, "Competitive Advantage of Equity in BOT Tender," *Journal of Construction Engineering and Management* 121 (1995): 282–289, page 286.
31. Dailami and Hauswald, "The Emerging Project Bond Market."
32. F. J. Fabozzi, *Bond Markets, Analysis and Strategies*, 3rd ed. (Upper Saddle River, NJ: Prentice-Hall, 1996), 418–419.
33. H. Bessembinder, K. Kahle, W. F. Maxwell, and D. Xu, "Measuring Abnormal Bond Performance," *Review of Financial Studies*, 2009, 22(10): 4219–4258.
34. P. C. Venkatesh, "Value at Risk for Corporate Bond Portfolios," *Journal of Fixed Income* 13, no. 2 (2003): 19–32.
35. William F. Sharpe, *Macro-Investment Analysis*, www.stanford.edu/~wfsharpe/mia/mia.htm (accessed June 29, 2009).

CHAPTER 9   Case Studies

1. *America's Intelligence Wire*, October 3, 2006.
2. *America's Intelligence Wire*, March 24, 2006.
3. http://mepriv.mecon.gov.ar/Obras_Sanitarias/CapitalSocial.htm (accessed July 22, 2009).
4. L. T. Wells and A. De Royere, *Aguas Argentinas*, Case no. 9-705-019 (Cambridge, MA: Harvard Business School, 2003).
5. D. Santoro, "The 'Aguas' Tango: Cashing In on Buenos Aires Privatization," *Center for Public Integrity*, February 6, 2003, www.globalpolicy.org/socecon/tncs/2003/0206argentinewater.htm (accessed July 25, 2009).
6. C. Crampes and A. Estache, "Regulating Water Concessions: Lessons from the Buenos Aires Concession," World Bank, Note no. 91, September 1996.
7. D. Rivera, *Private Sector Participation in the Water Supply and Wastewater Sector: Lessons from Six Developing Countries.* Washington, D.C.: World Bank, 1996).
8. "Ex-aide to Former President Carlos Menem Convicted in Corruption Case," *America's Intelligence Wire*, May 22, 2004.
9. Santoro, "The 'Aguas' Tango."
10. L. L. Jacque and A. Gribe, "Is the Euro Doomed?" *Le Monde*, January 15, 2004.
11. Carlos Vilas, "Water Privatization in Buenos Aires," *NACLA Report on the Americas* 38, no. 1 (July/August 2004), 34–42.
12. S. Hacer, "Argentina Water Privatization Scheme Runs Dry," *CorpWatch*, February 26, 2004, www.corpwatch.org/article.php?id=10088 (accessed July 25, 2009).
13. "Argentina: Chilean Interest in Aguas Argentinas," *America's Intelligence Wire*, October 6, 2005; "Two Investment Funds Eye Up 70% of BA Water Concession—Argentina," *America's Intelligence Wire*, October 17, 2005; "Argentina: Eurnekian-led Consortium Preparing Bid for Aguas Argentinas," *America's Intelligence Wire*, March 16, 2006.
14. "Argentina: Government Rescinds Contract with Aguas Argentinas, Renationalizes Water Service," *NotiSur—South American Political and Economic Affairs,* April 7, 2006.
15. ICSID Case no. ARB/03/19, http://icsid.worldbank.org/ICSID/FrontServlet?requestType=CasesRH&actionVal=showDoc&docId=DC517_En&caseId=C19.
16. J. W. Salacuse, "Renegotiating International Project Agreements," *Fordham International Law Journal* 24 (2001): 1319–1370.
17. S. Rekhi, "Fast Track to Darkness," *India Today,* May 4, 1998.
18. "Gas Turns a Minnow into a Major," *MEED Middle East Economic Digest* 41, no. 35 (August 29, 1997).
19. C. W. L. Hill, "Enron International in India," additional case in *International Business: Competition in the Global Marketplace*, 5th ed. (New York: Pearson Addison Wesley, 2005).
20. P. Lejot and F. Pretorius, *Politics Institutions and Project Finance: The Dabhol Power Project* (University of Hong Kong, Asia Case Research Center, 2007);

K. Hansen, R. C. O'Sullivan, and G. W. Anderson, "The Dabhol Power Project Settlement: What Happened? And How?" *Infrastructure Journal* 2005, www .chadbourne.com/files/publication/a5aa1e52-4285-4bb5-87e6-7201123895a0/ presentation/publicationattachment/352f8f09-ae96-40fc-a293-720d0b8f0ca8/ Dabhol_InfrastructureJournal12_2005.pdf (accessed August 1, 2009).

21. Human Rights Watch, "The Enron Corporation: Corporate Complicity in Human Rights Violations," January 1, 1999, www.hrw.org/en/node/24491/ section/1 (accessed August 2, 2009).

22. K. G. Palepu and V. Kasturi Rangan, *Enron Development Corporation: The Dabhol Power Project in Maharashtra, India (A).* Case no. 9-797-086 (Cambridge, MA: Harvard Business School, 1997).

23. "The Biggest Fraud in India's History," *Guardian*, November 30, 2001.

24. U.S. House of Representatives *Background on Enron's Dabhol Power Project, Minority Staff Committee on Government Reform*, February 22, 2002, 1–3.

25. "GE, OPIC Sign Dabhol Deal (Deal with OPIC Estimated at $220 Million)," *Asia Africa Intelligence Wire,* July 13, 2005.

26. "DPC: Settlement Complete with Bechtel (Bechtel Agrees to Pay Tax on Settlement Amount)," *Asia Africa Intelligence Wire,* August 5, 2005.

27. Central Electricity Regulatory Commission in New Delhi, Petition no. 96/2007, 9.

28. "NTPC, GAIL, MSEB to Infuse Additional Equity in Dabhol," *The Press Trust of India*, September 11, 2007.

29. Central Electricity Regulatory Commission Petition, 3.

30. "Lenders Insist Hike in Dabhol Power Tariff to Rs. 8 per Unit," *Financial Express,* February 12, 2009.

31. "GE Energy Inks Pact for Equipment Supply with Ratnagiri Gas," *AsiaPulse News,* July 9, 2009.

32. "Lenders Agree to Chalk Out Dabhol Rescue Plan (Power)," *The Economic Times,* April 11, 2009.

33. "RGPPL to Consider CERC's Tariff Recommendations Tomorrow," *The Press Trust of India,* June 15, 2009.

34. Government of India, Electricity Reform Act of 2003.

Conclusion

1. V. Tenorio and C. Idzelis, "Can Private Equity Play the Infrastructure Game?" *The Deal*, April 3, 2009.

2. B. C. Esty, *The International Investor: Islamic Finance and the Equate Project*, Case no. 9-200-012, (Cambridge, MA: Harvard Business School, 2003).

3. Ibid., 4.

4. Paul R. Krugman and Maurice Obstfeld, *International Economics: Theory and Policy*, 8th ed. (New York: Pearson Addison Wesley, 2009), 388.

About the Author

Rajeev J. Sawant (Boston, MA) is a financial markets Research Fellow at the Fletcher School at Tufts University and lecturer at Northeastern University. His research on infrastructure has been published in the peer-reviewed *Journal of International Business Studies* and *Journal of Structured Finance*. He is a member of the Academy of Management and the Financial Management Association. He has consulted for JSA Partners (an AT Kearney spin-off) in international strategic alliances in aerospace and defense, and has extensive public and private sector experience in emerging markets. He was the Aide-de-Camp to the President of India and has traveled extensively in Africa, Latin America, and Europe. He has worked with state government officials in India's remote Northeastern state of Tripura (which borders Bangladesh and Burma), helping to improve infrastructure services. His PhD on the economics of large-scale infrastructure project finance and emerging market field experience led to many insights for this book.

Sawant graduated summa cum laude from Jawaharlal Nehru University, New Delhi, India, and received a Master's degree in International Business from the Fletcher School at Tufts University. He is the recipient of the prestigious Inlaks Foundation scholarship for graduate studies.

Index

A

Act of God (force majeure), 116
Advertising
  investment, 41
  level, 73
AES, Telasi purchase, 135–136
AES-Telasi debt, 136
AES-Telasi focus, 138
Agency costs, concept (usage), 76
Agency problem, 76
Aguas Argentinas, 139
  cash flows, 90
  equity holders, 89
Aguas Argentinas S.A. (AASA), 211
  case study, 211–223
  community involvement, 221–222
  competitive rate of return, 221
  consortium, 213
  debt, 217e
  equity/debt/debt to capital ratio, 220e
  exchange rates, 215e
  financials/fees, 218e
  financial structure, 220–221
  government, role, 222–223
  history, 214
  lessons, 219–223
  local partners, 221
  performance targets, 213e
  return on assets (ROA), 217, 219
  tariffs/renegotiations, 214–216
    list, 215e
Aguas del Tunari
  aim, 121
  Bolivian law, relationship, 121–122
  concession, 120–122
  interaction, 136
AIG Highstar, Intergen exit, 91
AIG Highstar Capital, purchase, 91

All-World Developed Index (FTSE),
  correlation, 64
Alternative energy, investment
  attractiveness, 27
Ampère, André-Marie, 1
Annual infrastructure demand, estimation,
  7e, 9e
Apollo Infrastructure Projects Finance Co.,
  Ltd., 155
Aquino, Antonino, 140
Arbitral award default (AAD) coverage,
  133
Arbitral awards, enforcement mechanisms,
  129
Argentina
  crisis (2002), 216–219
  inflation, 215e
  LG&E claim, filing, 128–129
Asea Brown Boveri (ABB), equity stakes, 89
Asian Development Bank (ADB), 131, 168
Asian financial crisis, impact, 46, 127
Asset classes
  boundaries, 29
  defining, 28–29
  division, 28–29
  return characteristics, 55e
  term, usage, 27
Assets
  book value, 118
  cash flow, separation, 78
  cash generating capacity, measure, 34
  characteristics, classifying criteria, 2
  classification, portfolio perspective, 29–31
  covariance matrix, 31
  expected return, 30
  governance, cash flow stability (impact),
    36
  growth options, example, 42e

Assets (*Continued*)
  management, 19e
  operating margin, measure, 34
  present value, consideration, 40
  price
    increase, buyer benefit, 84
    percentage change, 30
    volatility, 83–84
  purchase, option buyer right, 40
  replacement value, 118
  returns, 183
    measurement, 30
    standard deviation, 31
  specificity, 97–99
  substitution, 79
    occurrence, 149
  utility rates, increase, 116
Asset-specific transaction, 97
Assets under management (AUM),
    comparison, 21, 23
Asymmetric payoff, 83
Australia
  AUM comparison, 23
  infrastructure investment development, 23
  North West Shelf (NWS) project, 32–33
  pension fund assets, GDP comparison, 20
Available cash, shortfall, 150
Ayala group, 139–140

B
Babcock and Brown Infrastructure (BBI),
    asset support, 92
Back taxes, imposition, 123
Backward vertical integration, 107e
Balance sheet, usage, 147
Bankruptcies
  costs, 80
  occurrence, 56
  risk (increase), debt (impact), 78
  threat, 103
Barclays Bank, takeover, 170
Bargaining costs, 96
Basel Committee on Banking Supervision,
    187
Basel II
  infrastructure lending, relationship,
    187–199
  risk categories, 189e
  risk weights, evolution, 190e
Base load power plants, 170

Bechtel
  arbitration, 128
  equity stakes, 89
BHP Petroleum, NWS domestic phase
    shareholder, 32
Bilateral investment treaty (BIT), 212
  execution, 127–128
  provisions, 128–129
Bilateral monopolists, impact, 103
Bona fide actions, 133
Bonds
  correlations, 64e
  efficient frontier, example, 66e
  lending, 155–156
  returns, infrastructure asset valuation
    (contrast), 177
Bougainville Copper, 134
Brand building investments, 41
Brazil, cumulative investments, 17e
Brazil Russia India China (BRIC)
  growth, 56
  MNE growth, 93
Breach of contract, 127–129, 132–133
  risk, 127
Breach-of-contract remedies, 106
Breach subsidy, 105–106
British Petroleum (BP), NWS domestic
    phase shareholder, 32
British Thames Water, 213
Build-Operate-transfer (BOT) infrastructure
    investments, 172–173
Bureaucratic processes, transparency,
    174–175
Business development, S&P subcategory,
    168–169
Buy-and-hold strategy, 199, 204

C
California contract abrogation, example,
    119–120
California Department of Water Resources
    (CDWR), 119
California Public Utilities Commission
    (CPUC), complaint filing, 119–120
Call option
  asset present value, relationship, 40
  payoff, 40e
Canada
  AUM comparison, 23
  infrastructure investment development, 23

Capacity utilization, 152
Capital
  assets, 28
  expenditures, meeting, 32
  gains, 89
  intrusive form, 81
  investments
    example, 32–33
    necessity, 110
  outlays, irreversible investments
    (combination), 39
  recovery, enhancement, 44–45
  requirement, 188
  usage, 80
Capital asset pricing model (CAPM),
  180–182
  principle, 184–185
Capital cash flow (CCF) method, 182–184,
  186
Capital structure
  change, 112
  form, 77
  governance, relationship, 81–82
  Irrelevance, Miller/Modigliani theorem,
    71–72
  observation, 72–73
  role, importance, 43
  theories, 71–74
  trade-off theory, 78–80
  usage, 103, 110–113
Case studies, 211, 223
Cash expenses, subtraction, 179
Cash flows
  assets, separation, 78
  CV, measure, 36
  debt rights, 81
  distribution ranking, 87e
  duration, 38
  generation, 38
  infrastructure provider generation, 36
  mean, example, 37e
  precommitment, 134
  reduction, 103
  rights, 90
  stability, 36, 61, 82
  strength, 34–36
  volatility, reduction, 82
  waterfall, 153–154
Cash generating capacity, measure, 34
Cash outflows, probability, 85

Cellular communications, investment
  attractiveness, 27
Central Electricity Regulatory Commission
  (CERC), 228
Ceteris paribus, 168
Cheney, Dick, 226
Chevron, NWS domestic phase shareholder,
  32
Chicago Skyway Toll Bridge, concession
  period, 93–94
China, cumulative investments, 17e
Civil war, impact, 116
Cochabamba
  case, 136
  user income, 138
  water shortages, 120–121
Coefficient of Variation (CV), 36
  example, 37e
COFACE Italian SACE, 156–157
Cognitive capabilities, limitation, 99–100
Collateral agency agreement, 160
Commitment fees, 139
Commodities
  correlations, 64e
  GSCI representation, 63
  prices, increase, 10
Competitive bidding process, 173–174
Competitive returns, 137–138
Complementarities, 3
Compound annual growth rate (CAGR),
  20
Concessionaire, 173
Construction phases, 162
Consumable assets, 28
Consumer Price Index (CPI)
  correlations, 64e
  indexes, correlations, 63
  U.S. inflation rate representation, 206
  usage, 53
Contract breach, 124, 127–129, 132–133
  creeping expropriation, contrast, 126–127
  expectation damages remedy, 105e
  expropriatory consequences, 125
  risk, 127
Contract finance, 148
Contracts, incompleteness, 99–101, 104e
  problem, 153
Control rights
  exercise, 81
  sale, 107

Convention on the Recognition and
   Enforcement of Foreign Arbitral
   Awards, 129
Corporate finance, project finance
   (contrast), 147–156
Corporate-financed investments,
   comparison, 150
Corporate-financed transaction, 147
Cost overruns, prevention, 88–89
Counterparty
   exposure, S&P subcategory, 168
   holdup, sovereign holdup (contrast),
      100
   replacement, 102
Countries
   correlation coefficient, 185
   cumulative investments, 17e
   risk, arbitrary risk premiums, 186
   withdrawal, 128
   World Bank classification, 13–14
Country beta, computation, 185
Credit rating agencies, 165–169
Credit rating performance, 169
Credit Suisse First Boston (CSFB),
   intercreditor agent, 159
Credit Suisse First Boston Emerging
   Markets Infrastructure Index (CSFB
   EMII), 51, 206
   average monthly return, 53–54
   efficient frontier
      example, 68e
      impact, 67
   equity price performance sensitivity,
      60–61
   infrastructure definition, usage, 60–61
   investment value, example, 53e
   leptokurtic return distribution, 61
   limitation, 56
   monthly returns, distribution, 63e
   performance, comparison, 52–53
   sectors, 62e
   Sharpe ratio, comparison, 61
   stocks, geographic distribution, 61e
   themes, 60–61
   usage, 59–63
Creeping expropriation, 125–127
   contract breach, contract, 126–127
   difficulty, 132
   revelation, 154–155
Cumulative distribution function, 188

Currency
   conversion, 129
   devaluations, 116
   fluctuation exclusion, 133
   purchasing power, 28–29

D
Dabhol Power Company (DPC), 211
   case study, 223–230
   events, 224e
   fast-track project cost comparison, 225e
   government ownership, 227–228
   investment, attention, 226
   lessons, 229–230
   post-default negotiations, 227
   power, increase, 223
   power production, 226
   sponsors, risk management, 224–227
   support, World Bank refusal, 225
Dabhol project, 173
   purchasing project, 130
Date-certain contracts, 158
Debt
   after-tax cost, 181
   amount, variation, 182
   betas, increase, 181
   capital, inexpensiveness, 82
   costs, imposition, 112–113
   forms, pricing, 152–153
   fund level, individual asset level
      (contrast), 92e
   holders
      disinterest, 111
      liquidation preference, 81
   mode, equity mode (contrast), 71
   overhang, 79
   payments, increase, 149–150
   proportional value, 179
   provision, 87–88
   ratios, level, 74
   repayments, 138
   rights, 81
   risk, 181
   syndication, lending form, 155–156
   usage, 91–92, 103, 113
      impact, 111
      model, 111
   value, 182
Debt service coverage ratio (DSCR), 158–
   159, 168

Debt to capital ratios, 73e
Default, exposure, 187
Default, probability, 44, 187
    impact, 170–172
    increase, 79
Defined benefit pensions, 20–21
    plans, total pension fund asset percentage,
        21e
Defined contribution pensions, 20–21
Demand
    analysis, 2
    destruction, inflation, 109
    impact, factors, 3
    uniformity, absence, 3
Denmark, AUM comparison, 23
Devaluation risk, 129–130
    transfer, 130
Diplomatic protection, 123–124
Discounted cash flow (DCF)
    usage, 178
    valuation, usage, 28
Discriminatory taxation, 125–126
Diseconomies of scale/scope, 107
Distressed debt, private equity (usage), 88
Dividends, forms, 91–92
Dot-com bubble, 23–24
Due diligence, performing, 152

E
Earnings before interest, taxes, depreciation,
        and amortization (EBITDA), 140
    measure, 34
    probability, 149–150
Earnings before interest and taxes (EBIT),
        183
Economies of scale
    implication, 35
    importance, 33–34
Edison, Thomas, 1
Efficient frontier, 65–68
    CSFB EMII impact, 67
    examples, 66e, 67e, 68e
    relationship, 208e
    usage, 206, 208
Election effect, 117
Electricity
    annual investments, 13e
    concessions, data set, 117
    demand, IEA estimate, 7–8
    generation/transmission/distribution

annual investment demand estimate, 9e
    investments, 12
    plants, holdup susceptibility, 100
El Paso Energy, 155
Emerging Markets Bond Index (EMBI) (JP
        Morgan), 52–53
    high-yield bonds representation, 206
    yield bond representation, 63
Emerging market stocks, S&P GII selection,
        59
Energy
    infrastructure, investment estimate
        factors, 8, 10
    prices
        energy infrastructure factor, 8
        increase, 10
    term, usage, 1
Engineering, procurement, and construction
        (EPC), 89
    contractors, 92
    Ras Laffan contracts, 158
Enron, implosion, 226–227
Ente Tripartitio de Obras y Servicios
        Sanitarios (ETOSS), 212–215
Entrenching investments, 76
Entrepreneur, employee hiring, 96
Equity
    cost, usage, 178
    holders
        bargaining position, 112
        incentives, 81
    investors, cash flow rights, 90
    issue, implication, 75
    mode, debt mode (contrast), 71
    proportional value, 179
    replacement, 112–113
    retirement, 111–112
    stakes, 150
    values, destruction, 24, 52
Equity-based infrastructure indexes,
        purchase, 50–51
Equity capital
    intrusiveness, 81
    loss, threat, 150
    providers, usage, 147–148
Equity cash flow (ECF), 178–179
Equity infrastructure indexes, 49
    risk-return relationship, 52–53
    usage, 51–54
    value, 64

Equity REIT index, S&P500 (correlation), 50–51
ETPM International SA, joint venture, 158
European Bank for Reconstruction and Development (EBRD), 131
European call option, Black-Scholes value change, 82
  volatility level, 83
European Investment Bank (EIB), 219
Eurotunnel project, construction phase, 85
Eventualities, occurrence, 99
Ex ante investment, efficiency, 112
Excess return, calculation, 180
Exchange rate policy, 123
Expectation damages
  breach remedy, 105–106
  remedy, 104
    contract breach example, 105e
Expected loss (EL), 44
  risk weights, risk categories (relationship), 189e
  treatment, 188–189
Export credit agencies (ECAs), 156–157
  coordination agreement, 158–159
  relationship, 159
Export Credits Guarantee Department (ECGD), 156–157
Export-Import Bank of Japan (JEXIM), 156–157
Export phase shareholders, 32
Exposure at default (EAD), 187
Expropriation, 125, 131–132
  coverage, 131–132
  creep, 125–127
    contract breach, contrast, 126–127
    difficulty, 132
    revelation, 154–155
  examination, 126e
ExxonMobil, 156

F
Fair returns, initiation, 138
Faraday, Michael, 1
Fat tails, display, 57
Federal Energy Regulatory Commission (FERC), 119
Feedback effect, 137e, 186
  example, 164–165
Financial crisis (2008), 56

Financial distress
  costs, 79
  occurrence, 84
Financial equity holders, 92–93
Financial innovation, 72
Financial Times Stock Exchange (FTSE)
  All-World Developed Index, correlation, 64
  Global Equity Index Series, 54
    weighting, 55
  MGII introduction, 51
Financing, governance mode, 81
Fines, imposition, 123
Fixed dollar-denominated coupons, payment, 206
Fixed-income products, pension fund holdings, 23
Fixed-line telecommunications
  fixed location connection, 100
  technology, impact, 3
Fixed-price contracts, 158
Fixed telecom lines, analysis, 18
Floating-exchange-rate regimes, 129
Force majeure (Act of God), 116, 130
Foreign asset beta, 185–186
Foreign currency
  store of value asset, example, 28
  value, 117
Foreign risk-free rate, 186
Foreign trade policy, import/export allowance, 123
Forward integration, 108
Franklin, Benjamin, 1
Free capital flows, 155
  discount, 178
Free cash flow (FCF)
  attention, 134
  equation, 179
  method, CCF method (equivalence), 183
  net effect, 6
  surplus, 42–43
  theory, 76–78
    infrastructure, relationship, 77–78
    suggestions, 77–78
  valuation method, 181
Front-load cash flows, 139
Fuel transmission assets, 108
Fundamental transformation, 97–98
Funds, availability, 19–25
Future cash flow, precommitment, 154

G

Gas Authority of India Ltd. (GAIL), 228
Gas extraction, example, 22
Gas pipelines, holdup susceptibility, 100
Gas supplier payments, reduction, 98
Gas transportation, 39
General Electric, arbitration, 128
Geographical distribution, 12–13
Global capital flows, conditions, 123
Global Equity Index Series (FTSE), 54
  weighting, 55
Global lending banks, 154
GMR Infrastructure, 91
Goldman Sachs Commodity Index (GSCI),
  52–53
  commodity representation, 63, 206
Governance
  capital structure, relationship, 81–82
  private equity form, 93
  structure, improvement, 84
Government
  bonds (cash flows), projected pension
    payments (contrast), 25e
  capital, contribution, 172–173
  commercial acts, 133
  interaction cost, delay reduction,
    174–175
  objectives, alignment, 135–136
  role, 172–175
  sovereignty, 123
Government-led renegotiation, 173
Gross Domestic Product (GDP), 138
  growth, energy infrastructure factor, 8
  per capital growth, road/rail demand
    (relationship), 11–12
Gross National Income (GNI)
  methodology, 6
  usage, 13–18
  per capita, 14e
    range, 14
  usage, 5
Growth opportunities, value, 74–75
Growth options, 39–44
  future NPV investment opportunities,
    relationship, 41–42
  importance, 42–43
  NPV, in-the-money call options
    (comparison), 42–43
  present value, 42
Grupo Solari, 219

H

Hamada equation, 181–182
Hedging strategies, 118e
Hell-or-high-water contract, 167
High leverage, 154–155
High-risk assets, 79
High-technology assets, government
  expropriation, 43
High volatility, implication, 108
High-yield debt market, closure, 88
Historical investment patterns, usage, 5
Holdup
  contrast, 100
  incomplete contract characteristic, 104e
  mitigation, 151
  prevention, debt usage, 111
  probability, 112
Holdup cost, 96–97
  representation, 98
  threat, 99e
  transaction, relationship, 95
Holdup problems, 100
  identification/measurement, difficulty,
    100–101
  resolution, 153
  solutions, 102–113
Holdup tax
  demand, 106
  impact, 105
Hopewell Partners Guangzhou Highway,
  147
Host country
  public relations problem, 126
  violence, 116
Host currency, devaluation, 129–130
Host government, contract breaches,
  125–126
Household size data (*United Nations
  Demographic Yearbook*), 17
Hyper-inflation, impact, 116

I

ICE Ingenieros, 121
Iceland, pension fund assets (GDP
  comparison), 20
Income stocks, 15e
Incomplete, term (usage), 99
Incomplete contracts, 99–101
  holdup characteristic, 104e
  problem, 153

Incontrovertibility, 129–130
Incorporation, separation, 148–151
Independent power producer (IPP)
    contracts, 165
India, cumulative investments, 17e
Indonesia
    Asian financial crisis, impact, 46
    cumulative investments, 17e
Industrial Bank of Japan Trust Co., 160
Industry
    cash flow mean, 37e
    CV measure, 37e
    debt to capital ratios, 73e
    EBITDA, example, 34e
    valuations, PE ratio (example), 41e
Inflation
    hedge, 64–65
    rates, 138
Information asymmetry, 152–153
Information costs, relationship, 96
Information symmetry, 74–75
    exploitation, 79
    vestiges, elimination, 75–76
Information technology infrastructure, 2
    investment attractiveness, 27
Infrastructure
    definition, CSFB EMII usage, 60–61
    equity indexes, correlations, 63–65
    exposure options, 50e
    feedback effect, 186
    financing, public expenditure (reliance),
        19
    firms, bond issuance (investor purchase),
        51
    free cash flow theory, relationship, 77–78
    funds, investor investment, 51
    holdup threat, relationship, 95
    impact, 80
    indexes
        addition, 66
        returns, 56–57
    indirect investor investment, 50–51
    industries, PE ratios, 40–41
        example, 41e
    lending, Basel II (relationship), 187–199
    life cycle, 85
    long-duration investment, 174
    monopolistic nature, 173–174
    monthly bond return distribution, 205e
    pecking order theory, relationship, 75–76

PF debt, default characteristics, 190, 198
project finance, relationship, 145
projects
    equity investor involvement, 85–86
    total transaction costs, 148
providers, cash flow generation, 36
returns
    historical analysis, 31
    increase, probability, 84–85
sector
    governments, importance, 120
    stocks investment, 50–51
sovereign holdup, impact, 122–123
term, usage, 1
valuation theory, overview, 178–187
Infrastructure assets
    average life, 38e
    cash flow generation, 38
    characteristics, 27
    direct investor investment, 49–50
    equity stakes, 89
    growth options, 39–44
    holdup problems, 100
    implications, 88–89
    investor exposure, 119
    life cycle, 85–86
    location specificity, 39
    managers, skill, 43–44
    monopolistic characteristic, 35
    nature, 125
    output/revenue generation, 44–45
    political risk
        relationship, 115
        vulnerability, 93
    returns, 84–85, 120
    risk, 90
    store of value assets, contrast, 28, 29
    tangible stable assets, relationship, 75–76
    valuation, bond returns (relationship),
        177
    value, 80
    variable costs, level, 35
    wasting assets, 184
Infrastructure bonds
    description, 200e–203e
    efficient frontier, usage, 206, 208
    monthly return correlations, 207e
    portfolio correlations, 206
    portfolio returns, 204
    pricing information, 204

returns, 199–208
  syndicated debt, contrast, 198–199
Infrastructure demand, 1
  drivers/interactions, 4e
  forecasts, 5–6
  geographical distribution, 12–13
  inelasticity, 35
  overview, 2–18
  term, usage, 2
Infrastructure investments
  case studies, 211
  horizons, 93–94
  illiquidity, 39
  irreversibility, 38–39
  options, 49–51
  paradox, 137
  recovery, inability, 39
  requirement, 33–34
  sequencing, 112–113
  space, pension fund participation, 23
  unit costs, 16e
Infrastructure-related activities, revenues
    (firm collection), 55
Infrastructure services
  consumption, 13–14
  demand, increase, 35
  monopolistic characteristic, 6
Infrastructure stocks
  comparison, 14e, 15e
  composition, historical change, 3e
  contrast, 16
  demand, 5
  replacement, consideration, 5–6
Initial public offerings (IPOs), 86–87
Input/output prices, 152
Input shocks, probability analysis, 109
Institutional development, S&P subcategory,
    168–169
Inter-American Development Bank (IDB),
    216
Interest, debt holder receipt, 82
Intergen, leverage usage, 91
Internal Rating-Based (IRB) approach,
    187
International Centre for the Settlement of
    Investment Disputes (ICSID) (World
    Bank), 154–155, 211–212
  arbitration, 219
  establishment, 127
  lawsuit, 122

International Energy Agency (IEA)
  electricity demand estimate, 7–8
  methodology, usage, 8, 10
International Finance Corporation (IFC),
    216
International infrastructure valuation,
    184–187
International investment, CCF method, 186
International law, breach, 132
International Project Risk Assessment
    (IPRA) model, 152–153
  risk breakdown structure, 162e
International Treaty Arbitration (ITA)
  inclusion, 153
  mechanism, 169
    existence, 127
  system, 128
International Water, consortium, 120–121
Inter RAO UES, 135–136
In-the-money call options, growth option
    NPV (comparison), 42–43
In-the-money growth options, exercise plan,
    42–43
In-the-money options, creation/
    identification/funding, 43
Inverse cumulative distribution function,
    188
Investable market capitalization,
    comparison, 56
Investing, private equity model, 86–94
Investments
  absence, social undesirability, 98–99
  debt mode, equity mode (contrast), 71
  fundamental transformation, 97
  funds, 1
  incentives, 106
  needs, interpretation, 6
  objectives, alignment, 135–136
  opportunities, reduction, 41–42
  payoff, occurrence, 81
  single ownership, 106–107
  sunk characteristic, 97
  targeting, 18
Investment treaty arbitration (ITA), 118
  mechanism, 124
Investor-controlled technology, 145
Investors
  bargaining position, 110
  incentives, 153
  loss, 130–131

Irreversible investments, 38–39
  capital outlay, combination, 39
Itochu Corporation, 156

J
Japan Australia LNG (MiMi), 32
Japan Bank for International Cooperation
    (JBIC), 131, 168
Joint incorporation, separate incorporation
    (contrast), 149
Joint ownership, 151
  structure, 108

K
Knowledge assets, growth options, 42
Knowledge growth option, present value, 42
Knowledge-intensive assets, usage, 43–44
KOGAS
  inclusion, 156
  responsibility, 157
Korea Gas
  gas payment, 159
  marketers, 156

L
Large up-front investments, 32–34
Larson, Alan, 226
Law/order, breakdown, 116
Lending syndicate, reputation mechanism
    (activation), 156
Leptokurtosis, display, 57
Leverage
  activation, 156
  impact, 153–154
  increase, 79
  project default, relationship, 168
  strategic use, 145
  usage, 91
Leveraged buyout (LBO)
  candidates, profitability, 87
  capital structure form, 77
  financings, leveraged recapitalizations,
    112
  public equity purchase, 86–87
Leveraged recapitalizations, 112
LG&E, Argentina claim, 128–129
Limited cognitive capabilities, 99–100
Limited-growth-option assets, tangibility, 43
Limited rationality, 99
Lingap Barangay, 140–141

Lingap Kabuhayan, 140
Lingap Kalikasan, 141
Liquidation
  preference, 81
  proceeds, 79
Liquified natural gas (LNG)
  processing, example, 33
  sale, 223
LNG marketers, 156
Loan life coverage ratio (LLCR), 158–159
Local community support, 136
Local currency
  devaluation, 164–165
  foreign currency value, 117
Local currency-denominated revenues,
    value, 117
Local partners, alignment, 137
Location specificity, 39
Locus standi, 156
Lominadze, Niko (murder), 136
London Interbank Offered Rate (LIBOR),
    152–153
  loans, 152e
Long-duration investment, 174
Long-duration liabilities, pension fund
    matching requirement, 24
Long-lived capital investments, necessity, 110
Long-term contracts, 153–154
  economic value, 103
  holdup solution, 103–104
  issues, 105–106
  third-party enforcement reliance, 102
  usage, 103–106
Long-term infrastructure exposure, 130
Long-term power purchase agreements, 147
Loss, probability (impact), 170–172
Loss given default (LGD), 44, 187
Low-risk assets, 79, 165, 167
Low-volatility returns, providing, 49

M
Macquarie Global Infrastructure Index
    (MGII), 51, 206
  addition, 66
  annual returns, correlation, 64
  efficient frontier, example, 67e
  fat tails, display, 57
  investment value, example, 52e, 53e
  leptokurtosis, display, 57
  monthly total return, distribution, 57e

returns
    distribution, 57
    increase, 53–54
    interpretation, 56
    sectors, 55e
    Sharpe ratio, comparison, 61
    S&P500, performance comparison, 56
    standard deviation, comparison, 59
    usage, 54–58
Macroeconomic factors, 3
Maharashtra government
    one-sided deal, 225–226
    purchase power, 130
Maharashtra State Electricity Board
    (MSEB), 224
    investment, 228
Management
    fees, 139
    internal costs, incorporation, 109–110
Managerial skills, analysis, 43
Managers
    above-market salaries, 78
    investment risk, 79
    problems, concealment, 80
    self-aggrandizement, opportunity, 78
Manila Water Company, 139–141
Market capitalization
    comparison, 56
    sensitivity, 56
Market capitalization-based index (S&P GII
    example), 58
Market portfolio, return, 180
Market risk, 169–170
    default probability, 171–172
Markowitz portfolio theory, 29
Marubeni Corporation, 155
McDermott, J. Ray (joint venture), 158
Me-first rules, 72
Menem, Carlos, 212
Metropolitan Waterworks and Sewerage
    System (MWSS), 139
Mezzanine debt
    placement, 87–88
    providers, coupon demand, 88
    usage, 88
Mezzanine private equity funds, debt
    provision, 87–88
Middle-market firms, 88
Miller Modigliani theorem, 71–72
Mineral transportation, 39

Mitigation strategies, 118e
Monte Carlo simulation, 138
Monthly asset class return characteristics,
    55e
Monthly returns, CSFB EMII distribution,
    63
Monthly total return
    MGII distribution, 57e
    S&P GII distribution, 60e
Morgan Stanley Infrastructure Partners,
    concession period, 93–94
Multilateral Investment Guarantee Agency
    (MIGA), 131
    coverage, 132–133
    insurance provision, 155
    policy, 133
Multilateral lending institutions, 154–155
Multinational Enterprises (MNEs), 93

N
Nationalization, 125
National Thermal Power Corporation
    (NTPC), 228
Netherlands
    AUM comparison, 23
    pension fund assets, GDP comparison, 20
Net present value (NPV), 177
    growth options, 77–78
    investment opportunities, consideration,
        41–42
    projects, 79
        avoidance, 80
New York Convention, 129
Next-ranked firms, negotiation, 174
Nissho Iwai Corporation, 156
Nongovernmental organizations (NGOs),
    pressure, 122
Nonhonoring on guarantee insurance, 133
Nonpolitical objectives, 134
Nonrecourse debt, 151, 158–159
    impact, 151
Nortel, bankruptcy, 56
North Fields, development/exploitation
    rights, 157–158
North Sea oilfields, development, 147
North West Shelf (NWS) project, 32–33

O
Oil pipelines, holdup susceptibility, 100
Oil transportation, 39

Ontario Teachers Pension Plan of Canada
  (OTPP)
  investment expertise, 49–50
  purchase, 91
Operating margin, measure, 34
Operating profits, net effect, 6
Operational restrictions, 125–126
Operations, interference, 116
Operations and Maintenance (O&M)
  expenses, 159
  lender contracting, 44–45
Opportunistic behavior
  possibility, elimination, 103
  proclivity, 116
  propensity, 110, 134–135
Options
  buyers, asymmetric payoff, 83–84
  value, 83e
    determination, 82
  volatility, 83e
Options, approach, 82–86
Organization for Economic Cooperation
  and Development (OECD)
  infrastructure demand methodology, 5
  pension fund asset allocation guidelines,
    24
  surface transportation infrastructure
    estimates, 11–12
Output, infrastructure asset generation,
  44–45
Output price shocks, 108
Output shocks, probability analysis, 109
Overseas Private Investment Corporation
  (OPIC), 131, 155
  political insurance, 227
  product, 132–133
  reimbursement, 132–133

P
Paetrozuata heavy oil project (Venezuela),
  147
Paiton Power Project (Indonesia),
  45–46
Pari passu rights, 159
Partial risk guarantees, 133
Passive plan members, 24–25
Payoff profile, 82
Pecking order theory, 74–76
  assumption, 76
  infrastructure, relationship, 75–76

Pension fund asset allocation, 20–23
  challenges, 23–25
  comparison, 22e
  OECD guidelines, 24
Pension fund assets, GDP percentage, 20e
Pension funds
  analysis, 19–20, 124
  capital allocation process, 21
  infrastructure investment space
    participation, 23
  long-duration liabilities matching
    requirement, 24
Per capita income growth rates, 138
Percentage of Gross Domestic Product
  (GDP) methodology, 5–6
  explanation, 7–12
Per-vehicle driving distance, elasticity, 12
Pipeline networks, estimates (OECD
  avoidance), 13
Policy risk, 125
Political capital, sufficiency, 124
Political force majeure, 130, 134
Political risk, 90
  categories, 115–116
  characterization, 115
  definition, 115
  determination, elections (impact), 117
  incontrovertibility, 129–130
  infrastructure assets, relationship, 115
  mitigation, 92–93
  typology, 115–120
  usage, 116
  vulnerability, 93
Political risk insurance (PRI)
  contracts, 127
  insurance purchase, 118
  risk coverage, 131
Population growth, energy infrastructure
  factor, 8
Portfolio construction, 199, 204
Portfolio risk, 65
Positive feedback effect, 137
Post-construction infrastructure assets, 165,
  167
Post-construction phases, 162
Post-default recovery, 168
Powell, Colin, 226
Pre-IPO firms, 88
Preston Resources, 170
Price/Earnings (PE) ratios, example, 41e

Price fluctuations, impact, 117–118
Principal payments, debt holder receipt, 82
Private capital, source, 19–20
Private equity
  model, 86–94
  political risk mitigation, 92–93
  structure, debt (usage), 91–92
  usage, 88
Private placement, 88
Probabilities, vector (example), 30
Probability of default (PD), 44, 187
  estimates, risk categories, 188–190
Processed gas, domestic consumption, 33
Productivity
  increase, 108
  threshold, 111
Profits
  reallocation, incentive, 108–109
  repatriation, 125–126
Project breakdown structure (PBS), 161
  analysis, 161–162
  chart, 163e
  RBS, combination, 164e
Project default, leverage (relationship), 168
Projected pension payments, government bond cash flows (contrast), 25e
Project-financed investments, comparison, 150
Project finance (PF)
  corporate finance, corporate, 147–156
  debt, default characteristics, 190, 196
  features, 172
  infrastructure
    bonds, investment value, 205e
    relationship, 145
  loans
    risk category slotting criteria, 191e–197e
  loans, contrast, 152e
  nonrecourse debt, 158–159
  projects, 148
  structure, 146–147
    usage, 169–172, 171e
  transaction, 159–160
Project financing, cost, 148
Project risk analysis, 161–165
Project variables, hierarchy, 162, 164
PSEG, 155

PT Perusahaan Listrik Negara (PLN), 45–46
Public agency insurers, 131
Public equity purchase, 86–87
Public expenditure, reliance, 19
Pure S&P500 portfolio, negative returns, 65–66
Put options, loss, 84

Q
Qatar
  development/exploitation rights, 158
  law changes, 158–159
Qatar General Petroleum Corporation (QGPC), 156

R
Rail construction forecast, 13e
Rail investment, estimate, 11e
Ras Laffan Liquified Natural Gas
  bankruptcy-remote SPV, organization, 157
  company project, 145
  contracts, web, 157e
  EPC contracts, 158
  examination, 156–161
  flowchart, 145e
  investments, 157
  lender rights, 160e
Rationality, limitation, 99
Ratnagiri Gas and Power Private Ltd. (RGPPL), 227–228
Real estate investment trust (REIT) index, correlation, 50–51
Regulatory risk, 125
Renegotiations
  occurrence, 117, 173–174
  production cessation, 150–151
Repatriation rules, changes, 116
Replacement investments, 6
Reputation effect, 51
  implication, 155–156
Reputation mechanism, activation, 156
Request for proposals (RFPs), 173
Research and development (R&D)
  cost reduction, 111
  expenditure, 73
  intensity, 110
  investment, 41
Residual rights, 108
  transfer, 108

Return
  asset characteristic, 29
  historical measure, 30
  risk, contrast, 54e
Return on investment, 138
Returns correlation, asset characteristic, 29
Revenue
  infrastructure asset generation, 44–45
  volatility, 108
Risk
  asset characteristic, 29
  capital, increase, 169
  categories
    EL risk weights, relationship, 189e
    impact, 188–189
    UL risk weights, relationship, 189e
  coverage, 131
  hierarchy, 162, 164
    chart, 166e
  importance, 116
  measurement, 30–31
  mitigation
    debt, role, 86
    strategies, 134–142
  return, contrast, 54e
  shifting, 79
  types, 124–130
  weights, 188, 189
Risk breakdown structure (RBS), 161
  analysis, 161–162
  chart, 162e
  PBS, combination, 164e
Risk-free rate
  calculation, 186
  excess, 180
  yield spread difference, 184
Risk/return profile, 86
Risk-weighted assets (RWA)
  calculation, 187–188
  multiplication, 188–189
Road construction forecast, 13e
Road infrastructure inputs, usage, 12
Road investment, estimate, 11e
Rocca, Christina B., 226
Rockefeller, John D., 101
Royalties
  fees, 139
  increase, 123
Russian Federation
  cumulative investments, 17e
  infrastructure stocks, 16–17

S
Sectoral structure factors, 3
Self-aggrandizement, induction, 135
Separate incorporation, 148–151
  allowance, 150
  joint incorporation, contrast, 149e
Servicio Municipal de Agua Potable y
    Alcantarillado (SEMAPA), 121–122,
    136
Shareholders
  contracts, writing, 77
  interests, safeguarding, 76–77
  revenues, usage, 80
Sharpe ratio, negativity, 204
Shell, NWS domestic phase shareholder,
    32
Short-listed firms, 174
Short put option, debt, 83e
Short-sellers, loss (occurrence), 84
Single-purpose asset, 152–153
Small-numbers bargaining, problem, 100
Social infrastructure, grouping, 2
Social unrest, 116
Sovereign entities, joint ownership, 151
Sovereign holdup, 115
  counterparty holdup, contrast, 100
  forms, evolution, 125
  hedging, 130–134
  impact, 122–123
  investor exposure, 119
  investor management, 117–118
  prevention, 138
  reference, 116
  risk, 130, 134
  usage, 120–124
Sovereign risk, coverage, 131
Sovereigns/investors, long-term contracts,
    123
Special-purpose vehicles (SPVs), 148
  problems, 165, 167
  requirement, 152
  structuring, 151
Specific performance remedy, 104
Sponsors, 147–148
  bargaining position, improvement, 150
  risk management, 224–227
Standard deviation
  reduction, 87
  usage, 53
Standard Oil, transaction cost economics,
    101–102

Standard & Poor's
  contractual foundation subcategory, 167
  credit rating framework, 165
Standard & Poor's 500 (S&P500)
  bonds, investment value, 205e
  efficient frontier, examples, 66e, 67e, 68e
  equity REIT index, correlation, 50–51
  index, investment value (example), 52e,
    53e
  MGII performance, comparison, 56
  negative correlation, 31
  negative mean return, 53
  pure portfolio, negative returns, 65–66
  Sharpe ratio, comparison, 61
  standard deviation, comparison, 59
Standard & Poor's Global Infrastructure
    Index (S&P GII), 51, 206
  addition, 67
  efficient frontier, example, 68e
  emerging market stocks selection, 59
  investment value, example, 52e, 53e
  limitation, 56
  market capitalization minimum, 58
  market capitalized-based index, 48
  monthly total returns, distribution, 60e
  returns
    distribution, examination, 59
    increase, 53–54
  sectors, 58e
  standard deviation, comparison, 59
  stocks, average daily trading value, 58
  usage, 58–59
Stocks
  correlations, 64e
  CSFB EMII geographic distribution, 61
Store of value assets, 28–29
  infrastructure assets, contrast, 29, 38
Suez Canal, project-financed transaction,
    147
Sunk costs
  commitment, 102
  impact, 115, 150
  occurrence, 97–98
Supervisory slotting criteria approach,
    188–189
Surcharges, imposition, 123
Surface transportation infrastructure, OECD
    estimates, 11–12
Switzerland
  AUM comparison, 23
  pension fund assets, GDP comparison, 20

Syndicated debt, infrastructure bonds
    (contrast), 198–199
Syndicated lending, 155–156
Systematic risk, 180

T
Tamil Nadu Electricity Board, 155
Tangible assets, cash flow stability, 82
Tangible stable assets, infrastructure assets
    (contrast), 75–76
Tanqueros water, advantages, 136
Taxation
  absence, 72
  increase, 116
  policy, 123
Tax shields, value, 181–182
Technology
  assets, growth options, 42
  energy infrastructure factor, 8, 10
  growth option, present value, 42
  industries, PE ratios, 40–41
    example, 41e
  risk, 170
Telasi, AES sale, 135–136
Telecommunications
  concessions, data set, 117
  term, usage, 1–2
Tesla, Nikola, 1
Thomson SDC project finance database,
    154
Total fixed costs, reduction, 98
Total portfolio, weights/proportion
    (variation), 65
Trade-off theory, 80
Transaction cost economics (TCE),
    95–102
  example, 101–102
  transaction costs, contrast, 148
Transaction costs, 96
  excess, 96–97
Transactions
  cultural/institutional context, 135
  internal/external usage, 96
  replacement, 102
Transaction-specific investments, durability,
    103
Transformable assets, 28
Transportation
  concessions, data set, 117
  fixed location connection, 100
  term, usage, 1

Treasuries
  correlations, 64e
  efficient frontier, examples, 67e, 68e, 69e
Turnkey contracts, 158

U
Uncertainty, conditions, 99
Underinvestment, debt (impact), 112
Underlying asset, volatility, 149
Unexpected Loss (UL)
  risk category, 188–189
  risk weights, 189e
UNIREN, creation, 217
United Kingdom, pension fund assets (GDP
    comparison), 20
United Nations Demographic Yearbook,
    household size data, 17
United States
  AUM, comparison, 21, 23
  pension fund assets
    allocation, 22e
    GDP, comparison, 20
Up-front investments, 32–34
U.S. asset beta, 185
U.S. dollar-denominated debt, investment,
    129–130
U.S. dollar-denominated sovereign bonds,
    184
U.S. dollar revenues, devaluation, 219
U.S. Export-Import Bank (EXIM), 156–157
U.S. inflation rate, CPI representation, 206
U.S. risk-free rate, 186
U.S. Treasury bonds, 184
Utilities, nonprovision, 116

V
Vajpayee, A.B., 227
Valuation, FCD method, 181
Valuation theory, 178
Value assets, store, 28–29
  infrastructure assets, contrast, 29
Value-destroying negative NPV investments,
    prevention, 43
Value under default, 44–45
Venture capital (VC), 86–87
  funds, standard deviation, 87
  risk/return profile, 86

Vertical integration, 103
  costs, 107–108
  effectiveness, 107
  empirical evidence, 109
  holdup solution, 106
  impact, 108–109
  solution, 124
  test, 109–110
  usage, 106–110
Voice Over Internet Protocol (VoiP)
    telephony service, 18
Volatility, implication, 108

W
Wasting assets, 184
Water, concessions (data set), 117
Water/sanitation infrastructures,
    comparison, 14, 16
Water supply networks, fixed location
    connection, 100
Weighted average cost of capital (WACC),
    178
  method, 183
WiMax, usage, 18
Wireless wide area network (WWAN),
    development, 18
Woodside Petroleum, NWS domestic phase
    shareholder, 32
World Bank
  breach of contract, 133
  country classification, 13–14
  infrastructure demand methodology,
    5
  International Centre for the Settlement of
    Investment Disputes (ICSID),
    154–155, 211–212
    arbitration, 219
    lawsuit, 122
  International Finance Corporation (IFC),
    216
  political risk insurance, 131
World energy demand, fuel estimates,
    10e

Y
Yield bonds, EMBI representation, 63
Yield spread difference, 184

Printed in the United States
By Bookmasters